Refugee
Communities

To Jeanne
and Larry,

Best wishes
Steve Gold
Jan 1995

SAGE SERIES ON
RACE AND ETHNIC RELATIONS

Series Editor:
JOHN H. STANFIELD II
College of William and Mary

This series is designed for scholars working in creative theoretical areas related to race and ethnic relations. The series will publish books and collections of original articles that critically assess and expand upon race and ethnic relations issues from American and comparative points of view.

Volumes in this series include
1. Roger Waldinger, Howard Aldrich, Robin Ward, and Associates, ETHNIC ENTREPRENEURS: Immigrant Business in Industrial Societies
2. Philomena Essed, UNDERSTANDING EVERYDAY RACISM: An Interdisciplinary Theory
3. Samuel V. Duh, BLACKS AND AIDS: Causes and Origins
4. Steven J. Gold, REFUGEE COMMUNITIES: A Comparative Field Study
5. Mary E. Andereck, ETHNIC AWARENESS AND THE SCHOOLS: Irish Travelers in the American South (title tentative)

Refugee Communities

A Comparative Field Study

Steven J. Gold

**Sage Series on Race
and Ethnic Relations**
v o l u m e   4

SAGE PUBLICATIONS
The International Professional Publishers
Newbury Park   London   New Delhi

For information address:

 SAGE Publications, Inc.
2455 Teller Road
Newbury Park, California 91320

SAGE Publications Ltd.
6 Bonhill Street
London EC2A 4PU
United Kingdom

SAGE Publications India Pvt. Ltd.
M-32 Market
Greater Kailash I
New Delhi 110 048 India

Printed in the United States of America

Library of Congress Cataloging-in-Publication Data

Gold, Steven J.
    Refugee communities: a comparative field study / Steven J. Gold.
        p.   cm.—(Sage series on race and ethnic relations; v. 4)
    Includes bibliographical references and index.
    ISBN 0-8039-3796-2. —ISBN 0-8039-3797-0 (pbk.)
        1. Refugees—United States—Cross-cultural studies. 2. Refugees,
Political—United States—Cross-cultural studies. 3. Refugees,
Jewish—United States—Cross-cultural studies. 4. Refugees, Jewish—
Soviet Union—Cross-cultural studies. 5. Refugees, Political—
Vietnam—Cross-cultural studies. 6. Vietnamese—United States—
Cross-cultural studies. 7. Vietnamese conflict, 1961-1975—
Refugees—Cross-cultural studies. I. Title. II. Series.
HV640.4.U54G65   1992
325′.21—dc20   91-14695
                                                                                    CIP

FIRST PRINTING, 1992

Sage Production Editor: Michelle R. Starika

Contents

Foreword
John H. Stanfield II   vii

Preface   ix

Acknowledgments   xiii

1. Perspectives on Refugee Adaptation   1

2. Soviet Jews: Background and Migration Experience   25

3. Vietnamese Refugees: Background and Characteristics   47

4. The Soviet Jewish Enclave   67

   Photographic Essay: Soviet Jewish Refugees   90

5. Recently Arrived Vietnamese   102

   Photographic Essay: Vietnamese Refugees   129

6. Resettlement Agencies and Refugee Communities   142

7. Self-Employment and Refugee Communities   167

8. Patterns of Community Organization   198

9. Refugee Adaptation: Concluding Comments   229

   References   237

   Index   252

   About the Author   257

Foreword

Professor Steven Gold's comparative ethnographic study of Vietnamese and Soviet Jewish refugee communities in California contributes significantly to the growing new refugees-in-America literature.

His critical reviews of immigrant and refugee studies and his interviews with refugees, along with his participant-observation analyses, suggest a host of research questions the standing literature has yet to address adequately. Perhaps the major question is, How do refugees develop communities that encourage and facilitate selective assimilation and preservation of valued social organizations and cultural traditions?

Professor Gold's *Refugee Communities* is the first of several studies in this series that will encourage new research questions and designs in the immigration and refugee field.

—John H. Stanfield II
Series Editor

Preface

"Those poor Haitians suffering with the Tontons-Macoutes [secret police] and coming to Florida in inner tubes are not refugees and we are? It doesn't make sense."

Felix Shulman, a 20-year-old Soviet refugee and engineering student,
San Francisco, 1983.

Between 1975 and 1989, over 1,214,500 refugees settled in the United States, constituting approximately 20% of all arrivals during that period (ORR 1989:113-117; Statistical Abstract of the U.S. 1989). Costly and extensive efforts have been made to resettle these recent arrivals. However, relatively little sociological research has considered their broader experience of adaptation to the United States.

Social science literature and U.S. government policy have generally regarded refugees and immigrants as fundamentally different social groups. Persons who cross borders for economic reasons are regarded as immigrants, while those who exit due to a "well founded fear of persecution" for religious, ethnic, political, or family reasons are defined as refugees (Reimers 1985). However, the difference between immigrants and refugees is a matter of continuum rather than simple categorization (Bernard 1977). Migrants' reasons for leaving one country and settling in another generally include a complex of interrelated personal, economic, political, and religious factors (Bozorgmehr and Sabagh 1991).

While the actual difference between immigrants and refugees is a question of degree rather than type, political and legal distinctions clearly separate the two categories. Refugees receive permanent residency status and the right to work in the United States; they are eligible for public assistance and a variety of resettlement services.

Immigrants, including those with impressive credentials, may have to wait years to enter the United States and, even then, are not entitled to receive government services.

Moreover, persons from countries with which the United States is at odds have been much more likely to receive refugee status than those who come from "friendly" nations (Zucker and Zucker 1987). For example, in 1975, the United States gave 80,000 Vietnamese the security clearance required for refugee status in only 3 months. In contrast, 2 years after 12,000 persons fled Chile's rightist coup, only 26 had been cleared to live in the States. The State Department cited delays in processing security clearances as the reason for the tiny number of admissions (Reimers 1985:185).

The arbitrary distinction between immigrants and refugees is an obstacle to serious research. While a massive literature addresses the long-term adjustment of immigrants and considers such factors as their community formation, ethnic identity, and economic development, refugees are frequently regarded simply as persons in need. De Voe (1981) describes how refugee status becomes a master status, causing both helpers and scholars to ignore refugees' own history, goals, and cultural orientations, as well as their gradual transformation from stateless exiles into members of self-defined ethnic communities.

Further, the definitions and concerns of agencies are imposed on the experience of recent refugees in such areas as mental health, self-sufficiency, and community organization, while the refugees' own views and the context that shapes them is ignored. Even when matters of refugee adjustment are considered, they are generally treated as a phenomenon separate from that of immigrants (Chan and Indra 1987; Liu et al. 1978; Simon 1985).

Viewing recent arrivals simply as refugees is, at best, a limited outlook. Especially since many populations have now been in the United States for over a decade, much of their experience can be understood in terms of another sociological category, that of "the new immigration" (Bryce-Laporte 1980; Hutchinson 1966). A product of the Immigration Act of 1965 and refugee admissions, the new immigration is characterized by Third World origins and higher levels of education, skill, urban experience, and female representation than has previously been the case for immigrants to the United States (Reimers 1985).

While the examination of recent refugees as new immigrants would appear to be the best way to understand their adaptation to the United

States, little research has utilized this approach. As a consequence, perspectives on recent refugees have been distorted in two important ways. First, by focusing exclusively on their status as refugees, researchers often ignore important realms of refugees' lives—those concerned with self-determination, internal diversity, and establishing themselves as an ethnic group in the new nation. Second, by assuming that refugees and immigrants are mutually exclusive social categories, the similarities and differences between these two kinds of migrants cannot be accurately specified. Insights gained in the studies of one group are not applied to the other.

The classification of migrants into one or another policy-based category is indicative of a larger problem that plagues the sociological study of immigration and ethnicity. Nearly abandoned is the long-standing tradition of the immigrant ethnography that seeks to understand the full richness, complexity, and diversity of ethnic communities. Instead, many of today's scholars are compelled to study migrants in a manner that disregards diversity and phenomenology in order to follow the dictates of policy-makers or add fuel to ideological debates (Stinchcombe 1984).

This book addresses the problem of refugee adaptation differently than most contemporary studies. First, while accepting that Soviet Jews and Vietnamese are refugees, I consider their actions in light of the literature on immigrant populations as well as that specific to refugees. Second, rather than focus on narrowly defined "policy relevant" aspects of their experience, I examine adaptation with an enthographically based, historically informed, and holistic approach. Finally, I pay special attention to the diversity and complexity present within these groups.

In this manner, I am able to offer a detailed portrait of recent refugee communities, one that bridges the generally unquestioned and often artificial distinction between refugees and new immigrants. Further, I provide a vision of contemporary ethnic populations that is explicitly concerned with internal diversity. Too often, popular and scholarly writings depict ethnic groups through one-dimensional stereotypes. Jews, Asians, and Cubans are classified as overachieving "model minorities"; blacks, Puerto Ricans, and Mexicans are portrayed as a hapless underclass; and between these extremes, Poles, Italians, and the Irish constitute a faceless mass of middle American white ethnics. By applying face-to-face research methods in ethnic settings, scholars confront diversity and context in a manner that

challenges ethnic pigeonholing. I endorse this goal. By using partici-
pant observation and in-depth interviewing, I am able to record the
complexity and diversity of Soviet Jewish and Vietnamese communities in a manner inaccessible to scholars relying on secondhand or statistical data alone. In so doing, I seek to remedy the approach that
would view such populations simply as stateless persons in search of
refuge.

—Steven J. Gold

Acknowledgments

Support for the completion of this study was provided by the John Randolph Haynes and Dora Haynes Foundation; the University of California at Berkeley Regents Fellowship and Chancellors Patent Fund; the U.S. Department of Labor, International Division; and Whittier College. Interview tapes were carefully transcribed by Shiela Jones and Sharon Reina. Tui Mai, Hoang Diem Hau, and Hsiao-Min Wang helped with translation. Kathy Buchoz, Ethel Taft, and Bruce Phillips provided many research contacts. Harold Wilensky offered suggestions for the revision of the dissertation upon which this book is based.

Frank Fratoe, Allen Martin, Paula Gillett, Mehdi Bozorgmehr, Pyong-Gap Min, Edna Bonacich, Ruben Rumbaut, and Robin Ward provided valuable comments and materials. Les Howard of the Whittier College Department of Sociology made sure that I would have time to work on the project. The series editor, John Stanfield, contributed valuable references and numerous insightful suggestions for revision. Mitch Allen of Sage Publications answered many questions regarding the book's preparation.

Arlie Hochschild and Ivan Light helped to shape the study and supplied continuing encouragement. Nazli Kibria and Doug Harper gave careful readings of several chapters and generously shared their sociological and editorial expertise. My parents, themselves the children of immigrants, instilled in me a perspective on the subject. My wife, Lisa Gold, read the entire manuscript and contributed her unflagging support. She also gave me the time to complete the book. To her and our children, William and Elizabeth, this book is dedicated.

Finally, I wish to thank all the respondents who cooperated with the research. Although they remain anonymous, the study would not have been possible without them. All of those mentioned above have generously contributed to the study. Any errors within it, however, are my responsibility alone.

—S.J.G.

1

Perspectives on Refugee Adaptation

This book is based upon fieldwork conducted over an eight-year period (1982-1990) with Soviet Jewish and Vietnamese refugees in Northern and Southern California. Collecting ethnographic data on recent refugees offered many methodological challenges. Classic sociological studies of immigrant populations refer to clearly established communities and neighborhoods—based on decades of settlement, widely accepted leaders, clear geographical boundaries, common bases of employment, ethnic churches, and other considerations (Reider 1985; Whyte 1955; Drake and Cayton 1945; Padilla 1987). While similar institutions do exist among Soviet Jews and Vietnamese, few were well established, and many were difficult to identify. Because Soviet Jews and Vietnamese are diverse populations, geographically mobile, and still in the process of developing their communities and ways of life in the United States, I had to use a variety of techniques and visit various settings to learn about these two groups.

STUDYING RECENTLY ARRIVED REFUGEES

To contact recently arrived refugees, I worked as an English teacher. Obtaining referrals from volunteer agencies, I visited Soviet Jewish and Vietnamese households on a weekly basis for 18 months in San Francisco and Oakland. To learn about the resettlement system and its clients, I served for two years as a resettlement worker, first as a volunteer and later for pay, in two Vietnamese-oriented resettlement agencies in San Francisco. I also taught a job-finding class for Soviet émigrés at the Oakland Jewish Community Center and became a member of the Los Angeles Jewish Federation's Immigrant Integration task force. Finally, as a college professor, I was invited by the Asian students at my institution (many of whom were Vietnamese) to be the faculty advisor of their association.

Although these settings provided long-term, stable opportunities to interact with refugees and service providers, they were limited in terms of the number and type of persons I was able to contact. To broaden my access to these communities, I conducted 112 in-depth interviews with refugees and others who were knowledgeable about these groups. For example, to increase my understanding of the resettlement system, I interviewed 55 persons involved in refugee resettlement; to learn about community formation activities, I interviewed a broad variety of community activists, religious leaders, and ethnic media figures. To gain information about refugee self-employment, I interviewed 67 refugee entrepreneurs and others who had special knowledge about refugee businesses. I attended numerous refugee community events, spent time in refugee neighborhoods, and reviewed popular and ethnic media reports and academic literature regarding Soviet Jewish and Vietnamese refugees. Finally, in the course of fieldwork, I regularly took photographs to document what I saw, and as a means of establishing rapport with the refugees I met. To protect respondents' identities, all names used in the book are pseudonyms.

During the eight years that I was involved in this study, many changes have occurred in Soviet Jewish and Vietnamese communities. Some developments took place gradually. For example, in the early 1980s, the center of Northern California's Vietnamese community was in San Francisco's Tenderloin district. By the late 1980s, thousands of refugees and their support agencies had left this skid-row neighborhood for the suburbs. In contrast, other transformations have been rapid. Due to political squabbles, influential leaders representing each ethnic population have been ousted from their associations, thereby drastically altering factional relations within their communities. These examples indicate that the element of process is a key factor in the study of refugee adaptation.

Through this patchwork methodology, based upon a variety of research techniques that concern populations in constant change, I bring together a picture of two refugee populations. If this image is not all-inclusive, at least it acknowledges the diversity and process that constitute a central theme of recent immigrant life.

Use of Comparison

Soviet Jews and Vietnamese, the most numerous refugee groups to enter the United States from the 1970s to 1990, feature a combination of similarities and differences that facilitate comparative study. Basic similarities between these populations include their common time and place of arrival (from the late 1970s to the early 1980s, with sizable groups settling in urban California), relatively high levels of skill and urban experience, origins in communist nations, entrance as refugees, and common involvement with roughly similar resettlement systems that shape adaptation and offered me a setting in which to perform fieldwork.

Contrasts between the two groups include levels of ethnic consciousness (Soviet Jews are well acquainted with minority group status, while the Vietnamese, except for the ethnic Chinese, are not); racial position in the United States (as Caucasians, Soviets are members of the dominant category, while Vietnamese, as Asians, are a minority group); presence of co-ethnics in the United States (Jews are a long-established U.S. ethnic group, while the Vietnamese are a new one); and internal diversity (Soviet Jews share similar class and religious origins; in contrast, the Vietnamese population incorporates a broad social spectrum). Finally, while the Vietnamese have experience in small business and other self-directed community endeavors, such as churches, Soviet Jews grew up in a society where economic and communal life were strictly regulated by the state.

This array of similarities and differences between Soviet Jews and Vietnamese allows me to address several issues of theoretical importance to immigrant adaptation, including their reaction to minority group status, the effect of previous collective experience on ethnic community development, the role of established co-ethnics on resettlement, and the impact of prior business experience on self-employment in the United States. Methodologically, the comparisons between these two populations allow me to make generalizations and conclusions about the broader social categories of "refugees" and "new immigrants" rather than group-specific findings that would be generated by studying a single population.

Plan of the Book

The remainder of this chapter outlines theoretical perspectives through which sociologists have viewed ethnic communities. Chapters 2 and 3 summarize the premigration history, traditional culture, immigration experience and social characteristics of either group. Chapters 4 and 5 describe life for grass-roots Soviet Jews and Vietnamese in the United States, as well as institutions of refugee life. The relationship between refugees and their resettlement systems are explored in Chapter 6, and Chapter 7 considers the effects of ethnic small businesses on Soviet Jewish and Vietnamese communities. Chapter 8 discusses the nature of activism and community formation within these two populations. The final chapter offers some conclusions about recently arrived refugee communities.

PERSPECTIVES ON IMMIGRANT COMMUNITIES

While immigrant communities are in flux, so are the theoretical prisms through which social scientists view them. Over the course of this century, sociologists have radically transformed their interpretation of immigrant collectivism. Until the 1960s, most studies depicted ethnic communities as unsavory settings that had a harmful effect upon their members. Since that time, however, immigrant communities have been appreciated as the source of many benefits for their participants and for the larger society as well.

Typical of early studies of immigrant communities is Thomas and Znaniecki's *Polish Peasant in Europe and America* (1920). While acknowledging the importance of immigrant self-help, it offered a dismal view of Chicago's Polish enclave, asserting that the community was marked by vice and marginality. Immigrant affiliation, it held, kept new arrivals isolated from the "superior" social form of American society.

> Until methods of completely incorporating the immigrant into the intimate of American society and making him take part in all lines of American culture—political, economic, moral, intellectual, religious, hedonistic— his life-organization will depend on the efficiency of the Polish-American structure, and any weakness of the latter must inevitably manifest itself in a personal decadence of its members. (Thomas and Znaniecki 1920:xvii)

Articles in the 1932 edition of the *Encyclopedia of the Social Sciences* (Ware 1931) reflect similar views, stating, "in the United States, these 'little Italies' and 'little Polands' have been denounced as evidences of the failure of the process of assimilation called for by national policies." Acknowledging that immigrant communities suffered from prejudice (natives, "branding the members of these communities as 'wops,' 'hunkies,' or 'kikes,' exerted social pressure to force them back into their ghettos"), the *Encyclopedia* associated several pathologies with immigrant enclaves. It noted, for example, that immigrant communities are ripe for exploitation by natives and co-ethnics and "may play as center for propaganda by enemy or radical groups." While "their colorful, teeming life lends a picturesqueness to otherwise drab cities; they have in the United States no status as quarters—they are part of the slums, which their leaders leave as soon as they achieve a measure of individual success" (Ware 1931, 5:607-613; 7:587-595).

Early sociologists' views concerning immigrant communities were not limited to the realm of academic speculation. In the years following World War I, scholars contributed to ethnocentrism and xenophobia through the eugenics movement and in the "campaign to assert Nordic superiority." These ideologies contributed to the passage of immigration laws that virtually excluded all but Northern Europeans (Lane 1987; Reimers 1985). Later, fears about immigrants' susceptibility to "enemy or radical groups" resulted in the internment of thousands of Japanese Americans.

Ethnic Community Redeemed

Influenced by the ethnic revivals of the 1960s and 1970s, the views of American sociologists regarding immigrant communities have changed dramatically. Rather than seeing immigrant communities as a hindrance to their members, many recent studies attest to the numerous benefits (social support, clearly defined roles and values, cultural preservation, economic and informational resources) that ethnic enclaves offer:

Within these "ghettos," merchant guild associations, burial societies, caravansary clubs, hostelries for students, itinerant merchants, and visitors and clubs for special purposes fulfilled the functions necessary for proper city life. . . . Through these associations in the city he [an immigrant] could obtain the recognition and response that make the difference between being a lonely and friendless alien and a newly arrived stranger (Lyman 1974:18,20).

We newly see "ethnic community" as good after all, something to preserve and extend. It gives life and charm to cities; it can be a focus for progressive organizing; it keeps the crime rate down. We can have our cake and eat it too: we can keep the country in the city. (di Leonardo 1984:133).

Several studies suggest that ethnic communities are, in various ways, superior to established U.S. social forms. For example, a recent article on the mental health of Mexican-Americans in Los Angeles revealed that the more highly Americanized an immigrant is, the worse his/her mental health is likely to be. Consequently, insofar as ethnic communities limit assimilation, they protect mental health (Burnam et al. 1987). Similar conclusions about the value of ethnic community are offered in *Habits of the Heart,* an influential study of community and commitment in American life. Its authors assert that in contrast to the narcissistic, consumption-oriented forms of association that have come to dominate mainstream America, ethnic communities maintain support, mutual responsibility, and a genuinely collective outlook. They constitute "an inclusive whole, celebrating the interdependence of public and private life and the different callings of all" (Bellah et al. 1985:72-73).

Finally, a large body of literature details the economic benefits immigrants receive by virtue of their attachment to ethnic communities. Several studies have shown how immigrant communities have helped groups overcome harsh discrimination to become prosperous in American society (Glazer and Moynihan 1963; Light 1972; Sowell 1981). Most recently, scholars have argued that immigrant groups that create economic enclaves are able to provide themselves with better paying jobs than those available in the larger U.S. economy (Min 1988; Portes and Bach 1985).

Along with the positive re-evaluation of immigrant communities has come a new understanding of the nature of ethnicity and ethnic solidarity. Prior to the 1960s, ethnicity was generally regarded as a fixed and externally defined social characteristic, determined at birth. In contrast, recent reports interpret ethnicity as situational in character (Lyman 1977; Nagel 1986; Nielsen 1985; Patterson 1975). This means that immigrants and their communities are able to shape and deploy their group membership in order to develop alliances and identities that are most rewarding in a given setting. For example, Vietnamese activist Ky Loi Le demonstrated the flexibility of ethnic identification as he referred to himself in terms of many ethnic, national, and status groups, including "veteran," "Oriental," "minority," "businessman," "social worker," "refugee," "recent immigrant," "product of French culture," "Vietnamese nationalist," "member of a disadvantaged immigrant group," and "devotee of Chinese customs," in order to establish connections on behalf of the resettlement center that employed him.

The situational character of ethnic identification is important for understanding the positive effects of ethnic community because it demonstrates how ethnicity functions as a flexible and ongoing basis for community organization that may retain its utility generations after ethnic groups have left their country of origin. "The ethnic group in American society became not a survival from the age of mass immigration but a new social form" (Glazer and Moynihan 1963:16).

While political and cultural movements favoring minority rights and ethnic pluralism have certainly contributed to the reevaluation of ethnic communities, so too has the experience of recently arrived immigrants themselves (Greeley 1974; Kim 1981; Light and Bonacich 1988; Mangiafico 1988; Novak 1971; Portes and Bach 1985; Sowell 1981). Under the general category of "the new immigration" (Bryce-Laporte 1980; Hutchinson 1966), a large body of popular and scholarly work has focused on the accomplishments and rapid mobility achieved by immigrants who have entered the United States since World War II. Many journalistic reports have overemphasized the success of recent immigrants and tended to focus upon the cultural and psychological basis of their accomplishments rather than the world events and immigration policies that have resulted in numbers of remarkably skilled and educated immigrants arriving on U.S. soil (Kitano and Daniels 1988; Rose 1985). Nevertheless, many members of the new immigration—Korean greengrocers, Cuban bankers, Indian professors, and Asian students, to name a few—have made remarkable strides in a relatively short time (Mangiafico 1988; Reimers 1985). Consequently, the image of the ethnic community has certainly been enhanced by the visibility of affluent and successful immigrants in American society.

This new positive evaluation of ethnic collectivism has broadened sociological views of immigrant communities and provided a useful antidote to the nativism and bigotry with which ethnic communities are too often regarded. However, in some cases, it also results in a simplistic evaluation of ethnic collectivism. Serious fieldwork within ethnic communities often reveals problems underneath the glittering success stories. For example, co-ethnic exploitation, labor paternalism, child and wife abuse, intra-group conflict, political intimidation, welfare dependency, youth gangs, isolation of the elderly, and over-work are documented in recent studies (Arax 1987; Gold 1989; Leba 1985; Light and Bonacich 1988; North 1988; Vigil and Yun 1990; Wilson 1987).

Further, although immigrant entrepreneurship and ethnic self-help have benefited many recent immigrants, it is unrealistic to believe that these ethnic institutions can solve the problems of all migrant groups. Studies of ethnic cooperation-based success among Jews, Japanese, Cubans, and Koreans demonstrate what immigrant groups *can* accomplish if a combination of cultural, historical, economic, human capital, and situational factors come together.

But while these groups have been able to achieve upward mobility in a manner enhanced by their communities, this does not mean that all immigrants can or will encounter similar success. Research informed by an understanding of the broader social structure shows how government and corporate policy, discrimination, and large-scale economic developments can have overarching power in determining the fate of American ethnic populations in ways that immigrant collectivism cannot overcome (Massey 1989; Wilson 1987).

Applying this perspective on the local level, recent studies have tempered the assumption that by creating an ethnic economy, immigrant groups can provide themselves with better paying jobs than would be available in the larger economy. "The ethnic solidarity school emphasizes the positive influences of ethnic solidarity on the socioeconomic attainment-minority groups, while it ignores many of the negative consequences of ethnic solidarity" (Sanders and Nee 1987: 764; Zhou and Logan 1989).

Structural Approaches to Immigration

While a large body of recent scholarship has argued that immigrant and ethnic groups are often able to shape their fate, another body of contemporary work has sought to explore the macrosociological processes that foster migration and channel migrating groups into specific social and economic positions in countries of settlement. This scholarship understands immigration not simply as the result of the sum of individual choices, or even of national policies. Rather, it sees migration as determined by the greater historical processes of the world system.

> Immigration, like other international processes, does not so much take place between compartmentalized national units as within an overarching system, itself a product of past historical development. Nation-states play an important, but not exclusive role within this system which also includes the activities of a multiplicity of private actors from large corporations to working class households. (Portes and Borocz 1989:626)

According to this perspective, economically developed capitalist nations require a continual flow of labor (an industrial reserve army) to maintain economic growth. Because native-born workers may be scarce, expensive to educate, or unwilling to accept low-paying, rigidly controlled, or undesirable work, needed labor is acquired through migration, usually from less-developed nations. In other words, rich nations obtain cheap, motivated workers from poor ones. This offers industrialized nations many benefits.

Since immigrant workers come from less-developed economies, even low wages in industrial nations seem generous. Because migrants have been raised and educated abroad, the cost of labor reproduction is externalized; it is incurred by the country of origin, not the country of acceptance. As immigrants and minority group members, foreign workers are disadvantaged (do not know English, lack U.S. degrees and legal resident status) and subject to employment discrimination. Accordingly, they are forced to accept low-level jobs and have few options for advancement. Finally, as newcomers, they have not learned to expect the benefits that natives anticipate (Castells 1989).

The presence of job-hungry foreign workers can be used by employers as a tool for controlling domestic labor. If native workers demand higher wages or improved conditions, they will be fired, with migrants willingly accepting their jobs (Burawoy 1976; Castles and Kosack 1973; Portes and Borocz 1989). This attribute of migrant labor is especially important during the present era of economic restructuring, wherein thousands of unionized jobs with high wages and ample benefits (in manufacturing, steel, the automotive sector, and shipbuilding) are being phased out and replaced with non-unionized, low-wage service jobs (Castells 1989). Finally, in the event of an economic downturn, immigrant workers (who, as noncitizens, are unlikely to make strong demands for social change) are likely to return home until they are again needed.

While many of the benefits associated with immigrant workers are in the economic realm, it is important to note that the social structure of immigration is not simply an economic process controlled only by the laws of supply and demand. Many social and political motives are also involved in labor migration. The state does much to precipitate and control migrant labor flows—establishing political or economic relations with countries to foster immigration and then creating a legal environment to regulate foreign workers (Light and Bonacich 1988; Burawoy 1976).

For example, U.S. investment in Mexico, the establishment of the Bracero guest worker program, and a variety of immigration laws fostered a pattern of Mexican worker migration to the United States that is now augmented by complex migrant networks (Burawoy 1976; Massey et al. 1987; Samora 1971). In the case of Soviet Jewish and Vietnamese refugees, U.S. involvement in the Vietnam conflict and the Cold War initiated the flow of refugees from Vietnam and the Soviet Union to the United States. Moreover, once in the States, these groups were granted refugee status by the government, including legal residency, welfare eligibility, and access to job training and placement.

Another noneconomic factor basic to the experience of migrant workers (but one that yields economic benefits) involves patterns of disadvantage and discrimination. While neoclassic economic theory assumes that all workers compete equally for all available jobs in a given economy, sociologists emphasize the importance of social factors in allocating jobs through institutions, such as the dual labor market (Bonacich 1972; Portes and Bach 1985). In American society, well-paid, prestigious, and stable jobs that offer opportunities for promotion—the "primary sector" of the labor market—are generally "reserved" (by traditions, networks, credentialing, and institutional discrimination) for native-born, middle-class, white males. Poorly paid, dead-end, and undesirable jobs—the secondary sector—are filled by disadvantaged groups: women, immigrants, and minorities. By maintaining a dual labor market, wages for certain jobs are kept low, allowing more profits for corporations and less competition and higher wages for primary sector workers.

In sum, political and social factors like government involvement and the dual labor market, as well as economic factors like wage differentials between rich and poor countries, specify job options available to immigrant workers. While the structural perspective accepts that immigrants possess the ability to organize their communities so as to facilitate smooth adaptation, it also asserts that many aspects of their experience (including the nations from which immigrants originate, their legal rights, the degree of disadvantage and discrimination they encounter, and the jobs for which they are eligible) are the result of the world system and out of immigrants' direct control:

> The individual cannot be conceived of as a rational actor maximizing interests under market forces. Instead, the flow of labor is directed by supramarket institutions beyond the control of an individual or even a group of migrants. (Burawoy 1976:1051)

The structural perspective has been most commonly applied to the experience of unskilled immigrants. As such, it imperfectly corresponds to skilled Soviet Jews and Vietnamese. However, this approach offers some interesting insights into the migration and settlement of these groups.

The world system perspective emphasizes the benefits accrued by industrialized nations as they acquire skilled workers from other countries. For example, the cost of training a skilled engineer who will take a job in an American corporation is many thousands of dollars. However, if such a worker is educated in the USSR and then moves to the States, the U.S. economy benefits from his or her skills, but at little cost. Further, while skilled immigrants are relatively well paid, nevertheless, due to disadvantage and discrimination, they often accept less desirable jobs and earn lower wages than their native-born peers (Castells 1989:80; ORR 1990; Parlin 1976). Since Soviet Jewish and Vietnamese refugees are skilled, their migration represents a huge net gain in human capital for the U.S. economy.

Much world system theorizing focuses on the developed nations' inducements for gaining skilled workers: the high wages, cultural amenities, good working conditions, and access to advanced equipment that may lure professionals from Taiwan, Jamaica, or India to the United States, Britain, or Canada. However, revolutionary and totalitarian nations, which are often engaged in political and economic struggles with advanced industrial nations such as the United States, also maintain a policy of marginalizing skilled and professional workers in such a way as to encourage their emigration. Skilled refugees from numerous revolutionary and repressive nations (the USSR, Vietnam, Iran, Haiti, Nazi Germany, Ethiopia, China) were generally reluctant to leave their home countries and did so only because they were systematically compelled to do so (Anderson 1975; Brym 1985; Gold 1985; Long and Kendall 1981).

Just as the government and corporate sector of the advanced industrialized nations benefit from the arrival of migrant workers, revolutionary and repressive societies reap advantages by ejecting middle- and upper-class members. Revolutionary regimes evict intellectuals and technocrats who could use their access to productive capacity and media for counterrevolutionary purposes; the jobs and belongings of the former middle to upper classes are often expropriated and then used to reward loyal cadres; and out groups' assets may be incorporated into the national treasury to solve financial problems (Teitelbaum 1985). Finally, scapegoating is routinely directed against former power holders to achieve social unity and defuse potential criticism directed at revolutionary elites. Minority groups, such as Jews in the USSR or Chinese in Vietnam, are the prime targets of scapegoating campaigns because they have few allies and can be attacked with impunity (Chen 1987; Chesler 1974; Long and Kendall 1981; Orleck 1987; Ngan 1982; *Vietnam Courier* 1979). "In brief, what the (Soviet policy of) elite integration means for the Jews is that they must be got rid of in order to make room for members of other national groups" (Brym 1985:29).

State policies that dislodge skilled workers in revolutionary and repressive societies have been pervasive since World War II, accounting for a huge flow of manpower to industrialized nations. Their movement cannot be accounted for by brain-drain theories that see the movement of skilled workers as induced by wage differentials. Rather, they have been systematically forced out of their homelands by harassment, firing, threat of imprisonment and, worse, in campaigns of state-organized terror (Reimers 1985; Teitelbaum 1985). In a strangely symbiotic relationship, revolutionary and repressive societies systemically enjoy benefits through the ejection of skilled classes, while capitalist nations take advantage of the stateless status of such workers to fill their own social and economic needs.

While certain aspects of the flow of skilled refugees can be understood in terms of structural perspectives on immigration, the applicability of this model is limited. Two ways in which the experience of refugees contradicts the structural model are in their demographic characteristics and the legal rights to which they are entitled in the United States.

Various scholars have noted that the demographic characteristics of migrant labor—often young workers without families—are economically advantageous to host societies since they consist of a self-selected population of workers who will place little burden on welfare services (health, education, pensions, housing) in the accepting nation (Burawoy 1976; Castles and Kosack 1973; Portes and Borocz 1989; Simon 1986).

In contrast, refugee populations have much lower rates of labor-force participation than most immigrants (ORR 1990). As a group, they are traumatized and may be ill prepared for employment. Further, their age makeup means that they include many persons who are not productive workers. For example, the Vietnamese population contains many children, and the Soviet Jewish community features a large number of retirees—individuals who do not work, but consume welfare services such as education, health care, housing, and old-age support (ORR 1990).

Another way that refugees are more expensive than immigrant workers (thus violating the economic emphasis of the structural model) is in the privileges given to them by the host society. Immigrants generally occupy a precarious legal position designed to benefit the U.S. employers. They must demonstrate the ability to be self-supporting and are ineligible for most government welfare benefits. Undocumented immigrants are further disadvantaged and ripe for exploitation since they must avoid being detected. Both of these groups incur fewer maintenance and reproduction costs than native-born citizens while working hard and paying taxes (Simon 1984). Refugees, on the other hand, are entitled to cash assistance for their first 18 months in the United States and are eligible for the same benefits and services as citizens.

Consequently, the demographic and legal status of refugees violates the structural theory of immigration's postulate that immigrants constitute "low-cost labor." According to this model, if the U.S. government really sought to obtain more low-cost, skilled workers, it would do better by increasing the admission of highly educated immigrants

(Taiwanese, Filipinos, or some similar group) than by granting refugee status to Soviet Jews and Vietnamese (Mangiafico 1988).

However, the structural theory of immigration stresses that international movements of manpower are not determined solely by economic concerns. Perhaps the political and ideological value (in
domestic and international spheres) of giving refugee status to almost
a million Soviet Jewish and Vietnamese refugees is valuable to the
U.S. government and economy to the point of compensating for these
groups' extra costs versus non-refugee immigrant labor.

In summary, while world-system-based structural models of immigration do not perfectly fit the experience of Soviet Jewish and
Vietnamese refugees, such a formulation reminds us of the larger factors that account for the presence of these groups in the United States.
It also highlights the fact that immigrant and refugee community development and adaptation occur within a structure of opportunity that
is shaped by larger social, economic, and political factors external to
the refugee community itself.

Refugee Adaptation in Context

Structural theories of immigration describe the context in which
immigrants travel abroad, resettle, and build communities. That does
not mean, however, that social structures inevitably define
immigrants' and refugees' efforts at self-determination. Rather, these
spheres of behavior are interrelated; each must be understood in terms
of the other (Light and Bonacich 1988; Portes and Borocz 1989). In
fact, several scholars have revealed that the social structure of urban
America matches with the abilities and aspirations of collectivized
immigrant groups to complement the needs of both. Studies by Light
and Bonacich (1988), Min (1988), Sassan (1988), Waldinger (1986),
and Waldinger et al. (1990) show how middle class migrants have
been able to experience entrepreneurial success by filling the economic niche in U.S. cities left as native-born whites have migrated to
the suburbs.

Due to structural factors, understanding the current effects of ethnic collectivism on immigrant mobility is especially complex. During
the same time (and due to some of the same reasons) that sociologists
were reevaluating the viability of ethnic communities as a means of
advancement for immigrants and minority groups, American society
was offering expanded opportunities to highly skilled and educated

immigrants, minorities, and women (Hutchinson 1966; Wilson 1978). In fact, a specific goal of the Immigration Act of 1965, which created the new immigration, was to permit the entrance of skilled and educated Third World workers into the U.S. labor market (Reimers 1985).

During the late 1960s, de jure residential segregation and blocks to minority political participation were also eroding. American society was marked by discrimination and prejudice, and still is, but to a lesser degree—especially for middle-class immigrant-minorities—than it had been prior to the 1960s (Fernandez 1972; Kanter 1977; Kitano and Daniels 1988; Mangiafico 1988; Parlin 1976; Wilson 1978, 1987). So, ironically, just as the value of ethnic self-help was being appreciated, the need for certain skilled and educated immigrants and minorities to create ethnic niches for themselves outside the institutions of mainstream American society was being reduced (Portes and Manning 1986).

Accordingly, the form of adaptation and the nature of ethnic community created by recently arrived groups continues to be a key question in the study of immigration. Because such groups are skilled and educated and are entering American society during a time of increasing tolerance of ethnic pluralism, they have the potential to merge with the dominant culture, to create their own ethnic communities, or to engage in some combination of both activities.

The section that follows considers styles of adaptation that are likely for Soviet Jews and Vietnamese. Since they are refugees and "new immigrants," the effects of both of these statuses upon their adaptation will be evaluated.

Bases for Ethnic Solidarity

Several models suggest that the structural conditions of modern industrial societies may facilitate immigrant community building. One such perspective is ethnic mobilization: "the process by which groups organize around some feature of ethnic identity (for example, skin color, language, customs) in pursuit of collective ends" (Olzak 1983:335). In contrast to classical theories that predicted that ascriptive ties would be of decreasing importance with increasing modernization, ethnic mobilization sees ethnic ties to be of increasing value in modern societies. Ethnicity functions as a viable interest group as the correlates of modernism (urbanism, the increased scale of organizations, the breaking down of discrimination in the labor market, and the extension of political participation to minorities) make ethnicity an especially viable base through which groups can compete for scarce resources (Nagel and Olzak 1982:127; Portes 1984). It is precisely in a historical period defined by universalism that ascriptive ties become both salient and a useful means of mobilization. Since recent immigrants and refugees have access to ethnic ties, this theory suggests that Soviet Jews and Vietnamese are likely to use ethnic solidarity as a means of expressing group interests as they adjust to life in the United States.

Recent changes in the acceptance of ethnicity within American society might also foster ethnic collectivism. Unlike earlier migrants who were encouraged or even coerced to abandon ethnic identification, today's immigrants and refugees are entering a society more open to ethnic pluralism (Rischin 1962; Gorelick 1982; Greeley 1974). Not only are their own efforts to create ethnic solidarity tolerated, but in addition, such activities may be encouraged by the host society. Soviet Jewish and Vietnamese refugees are resettled by public and privately funded agencies and ethnic Mutual Assistance Associations (MAAs) that encourage participation in and maintenance of ethnic culture. Resettlement workers frequently refer to organized immigrant groups (Chinese, Japanese, Jews) rather than Anglo-Americans as role models for adjustment. Finally, today's multicultural and multilingual public school curricula facilitate the maintenance of ethnic traditions in ways previously unknown. This toleration of ethnic pluralism would appear to encourage ethnic solidarity among recent immigrant and refugee groups.

Disadvantage and Collectivism

The literature is rich with examples of groups whose organization is facilitated by disadvantage and discrimination. Such reactive solidarity unifies groups whose members experience shared liabilities and common outside threats (Cohen 1969; Light 1972, Light and Bonacich 1988; Wirth 1928). For example, Durkheim's *Suicide* advanced this line of reasoning: "Indeed the reproach to which Jews have so long been exposed by Christianity has created feelings of unusual solidarity among them" (Durkheim 1951:160). Since Soviet Jews and Vietnamese are refugees, they experience several kinds of disadvantages that may foster reactive solidarity.

A major distinction between refugees and immigrants is in their ability to prepare for and accept the difficulties involved in living in a new culture (Boswell and Curtis 1984; Fagen et al. 1968; Portes 1984; Rumbaut 1986). Immigrants often make extensive plans before their foray into a new nation. In contrast, refugees have much less of a chance to plan for their new life, learn English, or collect capital. For example, 61% of the members of the first wave of Vietnamese refugees to arrive in the United States in 1975 had less than 24 hours to prepare for their exit, and 83% had less than one week (Liu et al. 1979:15). While later-arriving Vietnamese and Soviet Jews had more time to prepare their exit, such plans were limited in scope because they were made under conditions of extreme duress (Long and Kendall 1981; Teitelbaum 1985). Voluntary immigrants may carry substantial amounts of capital and return home to arrange business deals, recruit countrymen, borrow money, or re-immerse themselves in native culture. Refugees generally arrive without assets. Soviet Jews, for example, are permitted to take only 90 rubles (valued at approximately $145 when this book went to press), and even the number of valuable articles that can be brought out for resale (cameras, jewelry, artworks) is limited (Chesler 1974).

While immigrants are able to plan their sojourn to the United States in order to participate in the nation's economy, many refugees fled their homeland in order to survive (Bonacich 1973; Ngan 1982; Reimers 1985; Teitelbaum 1985). Consequently, refugee populations include many persons who would be unlikely to leave home on a voluntary basis. They are far from being a self-selected labor force. Instead, their numbers include many unemployables: young children, elderly individuals, religious and political leaders, and people in poor mental and physical condition. Further, because of the sizable differences between the economies of the country of origin and the United States, even educated members of recent immigrant and refugee populations are unable to find appropriate jobs in the States. I interviewed teachers who became shop owners; engineers who worked in construction or drove cabs; concert pianists who were retrained as technicians; professors who took jobs as gardeners; and colonels, bureaucrats, and judges who staffed resettlement agencies (Liu et al. 1979; Kelly 1986:142; ORR 1990). Because they have lost status, skilled refugees and immigrants may be attracted to co-ethnics to rebuild self-esteem. Finally, various forms of host hostility, ranging from paternalistic resettlement systems and stereotyping in the media to violent confrontations with natives, may stimulate solidarity.

In addition to the solidarity-fostering social and economic disadvantages experienced by refugees, these groups also maintain cultural and political outlooks that may yield collectivism. For example, while voluntary immigrants have frequently made a conscious decision to accept the indignities of dealing with an alien culture, refugees often cling to their traditional roles and values and may resist adaptation (de Voe 1981, 1987; Kim 1987; Piore 1979; RIIES 1976; Woldemikael 1987). Aware of the transformation that has occurred in their home countries, some refugees believe that they are the sole repository of their traditional culture (Farber 1987). Hence, refugees may be united by a commonly held culture in a way that economically motivated immigrants are not.

The shared political concerns of refugees may provide a basis for collective action. Cuban refugees in Miami, for example, built social and economic endeavors on the footing of the anti-communist bodies they created upon arrival in the United States (Portes 1987). Soviet Jewish and Vietnamese refugees, who share similar political sentiments, sometimes unite within their respective communities to express common beliefs.

Although blocked mobility can spur reactive solidarity, the opposite phenomenon, rapid adjustment, can also foster the maintenance of ethnic ties and outlooks. Because of their high levels of skill, certain new immigrants and refugees achieve middle-class status in the host nation with relative ease. Hence, they are less likely to associate the learning of American customs with upward mobility, as is often the case among migrants with peasant or proletarian origins. Instead, they may be committed to the assertion of native traditions, which they seek to retain and pass on to their children (Gold 1989; Underwood 1986; Woldemikael 1987). In summary, resettlement systems, social and economic disadvantages, cultural concerns, and an ethnicity-tolerating host society may foster the creation of ethnic solidarity among recent, skilled migrants. Further, because they are refugees, Soviet Jews and Vietnamese may have even greater incentives for organization.

Factors That Discourage Large-Scale Community Formation

Many factors surrounding the experience of recent immigrants and refugees may encourage the development or maintenance of ethnic solidarity. However, the situation of these groups is also marked by certain tendencies that may propel their rapid adaptation to mainstream American society and, consequently, discourage the creation of stable ethnic communities.

Current migrations are shaped by legislation that selects individuals on the basis of skills, family relationship, or experience of persecution (Fuchs 1985; Reimers 1985; Schuck 1985). As such, the ability of recent refugees and immigrants to engage in chain migrations and immigrant networks that import structures intact, maintain or reinforce links, and include traditional authority figures is limited (Light and Bhachu 1990; Massey et al. 1987). Instead, new immigrants and contemporary refugees come from locations throughout the geography and social structure of the home country and arrive in the host society with few social ties (Almirol 1978; Gitelman 1978; Min 1985; Okamura 1983). These factors make the creation and maintenance of mutual assistance networks difficult (Finnan and Cooperstein 1983; Gitelman 1978; Orleck 1987; Rose 1985).

In fact, many researchers have noted a high level of mutual suspicion and divisiveness, based on background factors like ideology, religion, ethnicity, region of origin, class, experience of settlement, and past occupation, among recently arrived populations (Gold 1985; Nguyen and Henkin 1984; Skinner 1980). For example, the Soviet Jewish community is marked by regional, class, religious, and generational diversity (Gitelman 1978). Similarly, the Vietnamese population reveals three distinct subgroups and two eras of migration. These include the South Vietnamese elite who entered the United States in 1975, and two more recently arrived populations: the largely working class "boat people" and the ethnic Chinese (Rumbaut 1989b; Skinner 1980).

Although recent refugees and documented immigrants encounter some forms of discrimination in the United States, these are relatively minor when compared to those that restricted earlier immigrants, who were highly exploited, segregated, had few legal rights, and were sometimes subjected to exclusion acts and pogroms (Lyman 1974; Wirth 1928). While this is a positive trend for American society, it probably serves to limit the development of mutual assistance associations among today's arrivals. For example, many immigrant and ethnic groups who are noted as examples of ethnic collectivism developed cooperative activities because of the harsh discrimination they experienced at the hands of native populations. Groups including Jews, Japanese, and Chinese in the United States; Hausa in Ibidan, Nigeria; and Surinamese in Amsterdam were forced to develop ethnic economies because jobs were almost impossible to obtain in the larger society (Bonacich and Modell 1980; Bossevain and Grotenbreg 1986; Cohen 1969; Light 1972; Parlin 1976).

In contrast, competent in English, well educated, and little restricted by the severe discrimination and economic exclusion that created the ethnic ghettos of turn-of-the-century America, many new immigrants and recent refugees find jobs in the primary sector of the economy and settle throughout the United States, often physically distant from co-ethnics (Kim 1981; Lyman 1974; Min 1988; Portes and Manning 1986; Underwood 1986). While discrimination persists, when compared to the era prior to the 1960s, it is now easier for skilled and educated immigrant and minority workers to find good jobs and otherwise enter mainstream American society (Kanter 1977; Kitano and Daniels 1988; Takaki 1989; Wilson 1978).

Further, while certain disadvantages, such as a shared experience of discrimination, may encourage reactive solidarity among immigrants and refugees, other liabilities are less likely to provoke collectivism. For example, high levels of disadvantage may make ethnic institutions weak to the extent that community members may view them with contempt or be forced to deal with dominant institutions in order to fill basic needs (Drake and Cayton 1945; Gold 1988; Whyte 1955). Further, as refugees, Soviet Jews and Vietnamese are affected by physical and psychological problems that are much more severe than those of immigrants (Bernard 1977:270; Boswell and Curtis 1984; Chan and Indra 1987; Cohon 1981; Portes and Rumbaut 1990; Rose 1985). A prevalence of health problems in a given population would likely sap the resources that population could muster for various purposes, including collectivism.

Many studies of ethnic collectivism—notably those associated with "ethnic mobilization" theory—suggest that in the modern era, major benefits are reaped by those populations that organize on a broad, group-wide, or international scale. Consequently, rewards are not likely to be realized for ethnic mobilization on the local level. "Modernization . . . first eliminates collective action on the basis of small-scale and local cleavages" (Nielsen 1985:147).

However, new immigrant and refugee populations are marked by diversity in terms of background, interests, and experiences. For them, ethnic identification and community formation tend to take place within subgroups that share commonalties rather than at the level of the entire population (Breton 1964; Buchanan 1979; Finnan and Cooperstein 1983; Gitelman 1978; Gold 1986; Herbstein 1983; Kim 1981; Nguyen and Henkin 1984). For example, Ilsoo Kim describes Koreans in New York:

> No centralized organization or leadership has emerged to integrate, coordinate and direct the various community activities. Community activities and leaders are segregated mainly along occupational lines or among different walks of life. One of the main functions of each organizational leader is to link his or her group's activities to the corresponding set of institutions of the larger society. . . . Decentralization thus characterizes the Korean community structure. (Kim 1981: 185)

Consequently, the small, local-level organizations of contemporary immigrant and refugee groups may be insufficient bases for meaningful, resource-oriented mobilization. Unrewarded, these subgroups might soon dissipate. In fact, a "too many leaders, too few followers syndrome" is typical of many Soviet Jewish, Vietnamese, and other new immigrant communities (Finnan and Cooperstein 1983; Gold 1988; Kim 1981).

Eligibility for refugee cash assistance and other resettlement benefits is an additional factor, one specific to the experience of today's refugees, that may limit their creation of organized communities. While immigrants must enter the labor market upon arrival, refugees have the option of living on cash assistance for at least 18 months. Refugees can and do make use of language, job training, and placement services that allow them to avoid ethnic labor markets that would foster co-ethnic dependence and further community formation. Further, for some Vietnamese and most Soviet Jews, resettlement is intended to facilitate their assimilation to American society and/or establishment of links with American co-ethnics. These resettlement benefits may hinder the maintenance of connections between individual immigrants and their communities. Consequently, while helpful to refugees in many ways, the availability of benefits and services may ultimately hinder their formation of ethnic communities.

As noted above, refugee status may encourage groups to be especially concerned with preservation of traditional culture. On the other hand, because refugees (unlike immigrants) know they cannot return home, they are often aggressive about connecting themselves to the host society. Skilled refugee groups, such as Cubans and Vietnamese, have the highest rates of naturalization of all immigrant populations in the United States (ORR 1989; Portes and Bach 1985; Portes and Rumbaut 1990). Interestingly, Cubans are both highly mobilized as an ethnic group *and* heavily naturalized, suggesting that ethnic mobilization and assimilation are not always mutually exclusive categories.

For these reasons, many elements of skilled immigrants' and refugees' situation may not be greatly conducive to the creation of inclusive forms of ethnic organization. As Portes and Manning suggest: "Acculturation of primary sector immigrants is of a more cosmopolitan sort . . . immigrant professionals . . . tend to disappear in a cultural sense soon after their arrival" (Portes and Manning 1986:64-66). For such groups, common language and nationality may be the only characteristics shared by the entire population. If and when organizations are created, they are often based upon activities and experiences in the accepting nation.

Ethnic Solidarity and Adaptation

While ethnic mobilization and assimilation are often treated as polar opposites, in fact such developments may occur simultaneously (Gusfield 1967; Mayhew 1968; Wilensky and Lawrence 1979). For example, ethnic groups may organize in order to gain power in the U.S. political system to influence federal government policies toward their home nations (Ahrari 1987). Similarly, immigrants often apply assimilation-based knowledge and skills in order to function as brokers between native and immigrant communities (Goebetz 1980). Finally, ethnic entrepreneurs commonly utilize ethnic-based resources to run businesses so that they can compete with those of the mainstream society (Kim 1981; Waldinger 1986). Such examples show how assimilation and ethnic solidarity can function simultaneously, with each further developing the other. This position offers the most accurate description of the experience of most Soviet Jewish and Vietnamese refugees. It will be discussed throughout the book.

Modes of Immigrant Incorporation

According to this brief literature review, research and theories on immigration and ethnicity suggest possible modes of immigrant incorporation, but no one model appears conclusive. Instead, various patterns are possible. Even single characteristics associated with recent refugees suggest opposing patterns of adaptation. For example, the relatively high level of ethnic tolerance now institutionalized in the United States permits both the development of ethnic interest groups and the entrance of skilled minority immigrants into high status occupations in ways previously impossible. Similarly, while resettlement systems provided by the American welfare state facilitate refugees' acculturation, allow them to avoid ethnic labor markets, and may undercut the need for ethnic self-help organizations, the same programs deliver cultural maintenance activities and may be run by ethnic associations.

Refugees' economic and social disadvantages might yield reactive solidarity, but they could also limit the viability of ethnic associations, thereby directing recent arrivals toward the larger society. Likewise, the stateless condition of refugees can motivate cultural preservation and simultaneously encourage rapid and near unanimous naturalization. Finally, the theory of ethnic mobilization indicates that immigrant collectivism offers a basis for interest group formation, but at the same time suggests that small-scale, local-level forms of ethnic solidarity—the type often associated with new immigrants and recent refugees—are unlikely to wield much power.

The Predominance of Localism in Refugee Adaptation

The perspective followed within this book is based upon a synthesis of the models reviewed above. While appreciating the value of collectivism to immigrant adaptation, I also realize that historical and contextual factors surrounding Soviet Jewish and Vietnamese refugees discourage their formation of highly organized and mobilized communities. Further, drawing from structural models of immigrant incorporation, I understand that in many cases, the broader context of refugees' settlement, including economic opportunities, state-imposed privileges and restrictions, and social factors such as discrimination and disadvantage, often determine the nature of refugee adaptation and community development.

Finally, throughout this book I argue that segmented communities predominate. While the image of a highly organized, unified ethnic community is frequently advanced in popular and social science literature, I found little evidence of this kind of association during my research. Both Soviet Jewish and Vietnamese populations are marked by diversity in terms of region, immigration experience, religious outlook, ideology, and background. I observed no institutions capable of unifying either of these diverse populations in a meaningful way.

Consequently, refugees tended to associate within small, intimate networks of family and friends. These groups reinforced social and economic ties among their members and built shared, situational interpretations of ethnic identification that reflected common experiences and concerns. These segmented communities may be united eventually. At present, however, localized communities, forms of cooperation, and patterns of identification are the modal social units of these refugee populations.

2

Soviet Jews:
Background and Migration Experience

Soviet Jews share a common ethnic identity and class position prior to their migration to the United States. This makes them "twice minorities" who, according to several scholars, are especially likely to create mobilized communities in the country of settlement (Bhachu 1985; Bonacich 1973; Espiritu 1989; Portes and Bach 1985). However, Soviet Jews form few ethnic organizations in the United States (Gitelman 1978; Gold 1988; Orleck 1987). This chapter examines the background, ethnic identification, and immigration experience of Soviet Jewish refugees in order to understand their adaptation to the United States.

A BRIEF HISTORY OF SOVIET JEWS

Jews have resided in regions of Eastern Europe and the Soviet Union for hundreds of years. From the time of the czars, through the pogroms in the 1880s, Stalin's purges, Nazi invasion, and until the present era of coerced assimilation without full acceptance, they have been persecuted, massacred, marginalized, and driven out of those regions. Nevertheless, Russian Jews have survived. By the 1960s, they were perhaps the most highly educated and urbanized of all nationalities in the USSR. Their membership in the Communist party exceeds their representation in the Soviet population (Andreski 1979). Consequently, Soviet Jews have a long and complex history in the USSR and hold mixed feelings toward the country that has provided them with both suffering and opportunity.

The migration of Russian Jews to the United States can be traced to the mid-nineteenth century, when they were restricted to particular geographical regions known as "the pale of settlement" and excluded from all but a few fields of economic endeavor (Bonacich 1973; Kuznets 1975; Zenner 1983).

Under the May Laws of 1892, the congestion of the Jewish population, the denial of free movement, and the exclusion from the general rights of citizens were rendered more oppressive than ever before.

The congestion within the pale is the cause of terrible deprivation and misery. Fierce massacres occurred in Nizhniy-Novgorod in 1882 and in Kishinev in 1903. Many other pogroms have occurred, and the condition of the Jews has been reduced to one of abject poverty and despair. (Abrams 1911:409)

From 1881 to 1924, 2,338,941 Jews entered the United States mostly from Russia (Wirth 1928:150). Many who remained became ardent revolutionaries. "Jewish workers and intellectuals looked to the general revolt of the masses as the surest means that would bring political and social equality to them" (Wirth 1928:106). "Jews played a crucial role in the victory of the Bolsheviks, and it seems likely that without the Jewish brain power their revolution would have failed. . . . At the end of Lenin's life most members of the Politburo were Jewish by origin though not, of course, by faith." (Andreski 1979:153). While the Soviet system seldom gives credit to the role played by Jews in its inception, anti-communist ethnic nationalists in the Soviet Union who have gained strength under glasnost remember and overstate the Jews' role in the revolution to fan the fires of anti-Semitism (Chesler 1974).

Following the Russian revolution, the communists banned Jewish religious activities, as well as those of other denominations. However, Yiddish (the German-based, Hebrew-scripted language of Eastern European Jews) and additional secular-cultural activities were encouraged until the 1930s. In interviews, elderly Soviet Jews remembered this time of "building communism" with idealism and fondness, and younger émigrés described the upward mobility that their families experienced between the wars. A doctor in Los Angeles details how her family took advantage of the educational opportunities offered prior to World War II:

My grandparents were poor people. They lived in a small Ukrainian village called Schkarfkray. But they had five children and all of these children left this small village and came to Kiev and all got high education. My father was the highest because he got all the degrees—doctor and Ph.D.—but the other brothers and sisters were also successful.

While opportunities for educational advancement were open to Soviet Jews from the 1920s until the 1960s, other Stalin-era developments limited their prospects for equal treatment. It was during this time that the Soviet Union established a policy for dealing with ethnic and national diversity by creating a series of Soviet republics, such as Armenia, the Ukraine, and Georgia. While these regions were subject to Soviet hegemony and Russification, they did provide their residents with a measure of autonomy. Jews—whose passports were marked "Jew" as nationality even though most live in the Russian or Ukrainian republics—were assigned a homeland in Birobidzhan on the Manchurian boarder, thousands of miles from the European cities where they mainly resided. Few Jews migrated to this republic. Its existence is seen as an early example of the Soviets' long-standing efforts to isolate Jews from co-ethnics outside the USSR (Jacobs 1981:4).

Along with attempts to isolate Jews within the USSR was a similar policy of limiting their power in the nation's government and bureaucracy. From the 1920s to the "Doctor's Plot" and Crimean Affair of the post-World War II era, Stalin's purges included disproportionate numbers of Jewish victims (Chesler 1974). "Without a gross distortion, Stalin's defeat of Trotsky, Zinoviev and Kamenev can be summarily described as the victory of the party's sergeant majors and managers over its doctrinaire intellectuals, who were predominantly Jewish" (Andreski 1979:153). Jewish influence was cut back in all areas of Soviet life. Between 1937 and 1974, the number of Jewish deputies in the Supreme Soviet was reduced from 47 to 6 (Simon 1985:8). "After World War II, Stalin climaxed his anti-Jewish campaigns by arresting and executing the nation's twenty-four leading Yiddish writers" (Orleck 1987:283).

Post-World War II activism by Soviet Jews was linked with the formation of Israel. The USSR initially had a positive regard for this nation, which upheld many socialist values. However, following the 1967 Arab-Israeli War, the Soviets took an increasingly dim view of the Jewish state. This was partly due to Soviet efforts to curry favor

with Arab nations. Soviet opposition to Zionism was also based upon
its long-standing program of limiting Jews' relations with co-ethnics
outside the USSR.

Scholars and informants alike suggest that the anti-Zionist articles
that appeared with increasing frequency in the Soviet media after
1967 fostered anti-Semitic attacks in the USSR (Goodman 1984; Jacobs 1981). In interviews, Soviet émigrés claimed that because newspaper articles were approved by the government, anti-Zionist
polemics were interpreted as veiled instructions. "Getting the hint,"
ambitious officials would carry out personal projects of harassing, de-
moting, or refusing to hire Jews as a means of currying favor with su-
periors.

The "lack of nationalism and patriotism" attributed to Jews from
the czarist era continued to be a justification for keeping them
from positions of power and influence. Since Jews have been permitted to emigrate in the 1970s, it has also rationalized their exclusion from higher education—allowing the Soviets to claim that
they cannot invest in the education of persons likely to leave. Such
accusations of disloyalty became a self-fulfilling prophecy when
Jews, who were denied opportunities within the USSR, were forced
to seek them abroad.

Prior to the 1960s, Soviets offered Jews access to higher education
because technical experts were required for the nation's military and
industrial development. More recently, this path has been restricted
(Brym 1985). "As Khrushchev pointedly indicated, 'we' no longer
need the Jews because we have 'our own' experts" (Jacobs 1981:5).
After 1967, the number of Jews able to receive a university education
was reduced by 50 percent, and few, if any, were admitted to Moscow
University, the "Harvard" of the USSR (Simon et al. 1982). In my
many interviews, I talked to only one Jew under the age of 35 who
was able to obtain a higher education in the Ukraine, generally regarded as the most anti-Semitic Soviet republic and also the home to
almost 800,000 Jews (Simon 1985:8). I did interview young Ukrainian Jews with university degrees, but their degrees were obtained
outside their home republic. In sum, the Soviet system provided Jews
with opportunities and rights that were unavailable under czars. Nevertheless, anti-Semitic policies continued. At the same time, however,
the atheistic communist state hindered the ability of Jews to maintain
traditions of religious and ethnic collectivism.

Migration Becomes Possible

Few Soviet citizens were allowed to exit the USSR during the Stalin era, but by the early 1960s, a small number of Jews were permitted to emigrate. Some who were Polish nationals found their way to the United States. The 1967 Arab-Israeli War increased media anti-Semitism and inspired Russian Jews, motivating a religious resurgence and prompting contacts with co-ethnics outside the USSR (Pinkus 1985). Concurrently, the Soviets began to pursue a policy of détente and trade with the West. In the United States, sympathizers of Soviet Jews raised the issue of emigration at this time, using it as a bargaining chip. They wished to make the Soviets' access to American technology conditional upon the right of Jews to exit the USSR. This policy was institutionalized by the Jackson-Vanik Bill in 1974, which offered Moscow "most favored nation" trade status if it relaxed emigration policy (Ungar 1989). The bill and the policy were effective. The number of Jews leaving the USSR increased. During the entire decade of the 1960s, only 7,000 Jews were permitted to exit the USSR. In 1971 alone, over 13,000 exited, and in 1979, the peak year of migration, 51,000 left (Jacobs 1981:6-7).

Following the Soviet invasion of Afghanistan in 1979, relations between the United States and the USSR decayed, drastically reducing the exit of Soviet Jews. Through the early 1980s, fewer than 1,000 were permitted to leave annually. However, with the dawning of the glasnost period, immigration once again increased. By 1989, the number of Soviet Jews allowed to exit far exceeded the number during the previous peak year of 1979 (ORR 1990).

Leaving the Soviet Union is only half the story of migration. Once they exit, Soviet Jews must decide on a place to settle. The two major choices are the United States and Israel. There has long been a debate over who should be able to choose Soviet Jews' country of refuge. Officially, the Soviets permitted Jews to exit for either of two reasons. The first was family unification, allowing Soviet citizens to join relatives in other nations. This affected relatively few. The second reason for exit was the law of return. Since the passports of Jews were stamped with "Jew" instead of the Soviet republic in which they were born, they were allowed to go to Israel. Initially, the majority of Soviet Jews granted exit visas settled in Israel. However, between 1976 and 1989, at least half opted instead to dwell in the

United States. By the late 1980s, less than 10% each year chose the Jewish State.[1]

Many members of the international Jewish community believed that Soviet Jews should be required to settle in Israel. They pointed to Israel's need for settlers and the fact that émigrés have been invited to reside there. Soviet Jews who opted for other destinations were slapped with the stigmatizing label *neshrim* (dropouts) and were subject to inferior treatment. For example, it was the standard practice of Jewish immigrant aid agencies to provide émigrés who chose Israel with rapid resettlement, while those who migrated to the United States had to wait weeks or months before placement (Panish 1981; Woo 1989).

On the other hand, the émigrés themselves and their supporters felt that Soviet Jews should be permitted to decide where to settle. The debate between those favoring Israeli versus U.S. settlement became fierce during the late 1980s because so many Jews were leaving the USSR and so few opted for Israel. Israel's supporters successfully demanded that the United States deny Soviet Jews group-level refugee status, making the Jewish state their sole destination. While Soviet Jews continued to enter the United States in record numbers, the U.S. government announced that after October 1, 1989, it would no longer accept Soviets who sought to enter the United States with Israeli visas (Woo 1989:B12).

DAILY LIFE FOR SOVIET JEWS

The historical factors summarized above provide the context of Jews' lives in the USSR. But what were these lives like? The paragraphs that follow describe the existence of Soviet émigrés prior to emigration, including their experience of anti-Semitism, their religious identification, and factors contributing to their decision to exit.

Despite the fact that they left the USSR as refugees, most Soviet Jews described their former home with a degree of fondness. In the words of an engineer now living in San Francisco:

> I had to leave my country—and I think it's my country. I don't think those sons of bitches who rule that country have more rights than I. This is something I can't forgive, ever. You lose your friends, you lose your language, you lose all your ties. You lose the countryside that you love.

There are some places, we go to sleep and we close our eyes—every minute we dream we see these places and there is nothing in the world that will substitute for that.

A former concert pianist, now an x-ray technician, recounts her immersion in Russian culture:

Spiritually, you grow in Russian culture. You see we are Jews but we related a lot to all of the Russian music, Russian culture, Russian theater, literature. You listen to the music and the choir, you could emotionally relate to that because that was your childhood experience, not with the church but with that part of the culture.

In addition to their positive valuation of the Russian landscape and culture, Soviet Jews were also proud of their ability to "make do" and enjoy a high standard of living in the USSR despite the anti-Semitism, war, shortages, and purges they have encountered. As the following quote from my study suggests, Soviet Jews often become skillful manipulators of the system (di Franceisco and Gitelman 1984; Gold 1987).

I had a lot of connections and I had the *blat* [influence], because of my work. I could make favors to people and they, of course, returned. There are a lot of ways to do something. It was usual thing in Russia, it was way for survivors. Because if not, if you would be just straight, you wouldn't be successful. If not, you live like most of the Russian people, ordinary people. Too much trouble and their life is very hard.

Especially Jewish people, they are flexible and they can find place to get something and to get some privileges. It's Jewish nature. I would say it's because of Jewish history. Jewish, you know, tens of generations okay, they always have to do something.

As Erving Goffman pointed out in *Asylums,* his classic study of total institutions, the sense of accomplishment a person derives by obtaining scarce privileges or goods through unconventional means is often more valuable to the recipient than the physical possession of the good or privilege in itself (Goffman 1961). In maintaining a decent standard of living, Soviet Jews are able to prove the strength of their character and their ability to triumph over adversity. This "culture of savvy" is retained by many Soviet Jews in the United States. It provides motivation in times of difficulty and, as the quote above from my study indicates, contributes to positive feelings about secular Jewish identity. However, this outlook also has detrimental effects on the communal life of émigrés. Because Soviet Jews are so invested in individualistic and conniving solutions to problems, they often avoid formal, collective approaches to adaptation and community formation.[2]

A strong basis of Soviet Jews' ability to cope with their environment is found in the family. Due to the shortage of housing endemic in the USSR, it is common for extended families of three or four generations to reside together in very close quarters (Orleck 1987). In addition, because the birthrate among Soviet Jews is low, a small family size makes for a great deal of parent-child interaction (Simon 1983).

In contrast to American children, who are socialized by peer groups, Soviet youth—Jewish and gentile alike—are more involved with kin (Hulewatt 1981). Relatives provide young Soviet Jews with political/ bureaucratic influence as well as emotional support. For example, one Ukrainian Jew who, due to anti-Semitism, was unable to secure admission to higher learning in his hometown, described how an uncle living in Moscow utilized connections so that he could gain admission to college.

The Experience of Anti-Semitism

Because they are denied the ability to participate in religious activities, many Soviet Jews most directly realized their ethnic identity through anti-Semitism. As a negative experience, this does not immediately lend itself to the development of organized communities, either in the USSR or in countries of settlement. Further, Soviet Jews confront different kinds of anti-Semitism depending upon their age, occupation, and geographical origins. Accordingly, the experience of anti-Semitism does not always provide a viable basis for community unification.

Every émigré I interviewed acknowledged the existence of Soviet anti-Semitism. However, they disagreed about its nature and effects. The most common experience was in the realm of career advancement. Soviet Jews who sought high-status positions confronted institutional anti-Semitism (Goodman 1984). That is, even if they never experienced personal hostility, they knew that opportunities for themselves and their children were limited (Wellman 1977).[3]

The role of institutional anti-Semitism is verified by data on the enrollment of Soviet Jews in higher education. While the Jewish population of the USSR remained relatively stable between 1960 and 1970, the percentage of Jews in institutions of higher learning dropped from 3.2% in 1960 to 1.9% in 1970 (Simon 1985:8). Young émigrés told me that they had to go to great lengths to mobilize all kinds of connections in order to be admitted to a university or other institute of higher learning. Many had been repudiated despite their achievement of outstanding high school grades and gold medals on graduation exams. When rejected students demanded an explanation, officials offered fabricated excuses. For example, one young man who commuted 30 kilometers daily by bicycle was denied admission to Moscow Railway Institute because of "poor health." A Soviet Jew now living in Los Angeles describes his difficult but ultimately successful efforts to enter Kiev's language institute:

> It was sad because many talented Jewish applicants such as myself were not admitted because of their background—because they were Jewish. This was initially my experience as well. Even though we hired some tutors and my parents had some connections, I could not get in. I was not admitted although I got very fine grades and passed all the tests. In fact, I can see they made a mistake even by letting me have the grades because we started complaining to the Ministry of Education.

> I had all "A's" and according to their own rules, there was no way that they couldn't let me in. To keep us quiet and also because we had such a legitimate case, I was admitted by a special order from the Minister of Education. But I was just lucky.

> And by the time I graduated, I had to transfer to the correspondence school, because otherwise they would have sent me to a small village in the Ukraine where the population is extremely hostile to Jews. I was also harassed by the KGB.

Anti-Semitic blocks to advancement did not end once Jews gained access to professional training. They continued to encounter obstacles when they sought jobs or promotions. Such was the case for an electronics engineer:

> I wanted to continue my education and get a promotion in my field but I could not go above a certain level. It's not so much anti-Semitism among the people I worked with—I had good relations. But my bosses were lim-

ited with what they could do. It was Brezhnev time—it was state anti-Semitism. It wasn't much from the people. This is what is so outrageous—is that it's a state anti-Semitism, they just impose it.

They never said it out loud. Or they would say that the state is spending so much money on the education of Jews and then they leave for Israel or the U.S. Why should they waste all that money? They deliberately confuse the cause and effect.

This kind of blocked mobility was described by educated and ambitious Soviet Jews with origins throughout the USSR. However, the experience of personal discrimination varied by region. Émigrés from Moscow, Leningrad, and Odessa claimed they confronted little direct hostility. However, both personal and institutional anti-Semitism was the fate of Ukrainian Jews, especially those from the republic's capital of Kiev. Ukrainian Jews endured daily insult and harassment. Because Soviet apartment buildings have cooperative kitchens and bathrooms, Jews confronted anti-Semitic neighbors even in their homes. An émigré from the Ukrainian port city of Odessa recalled rampant anti-Semitism during his visits to Kiev:

Kiev is the worst city, I mean the worst anti-Semitism because it's terrible, it's bandits you know. They are like Nazis. They would put Jews in camps. They hate Jews, they hate them.

I had a lot of business trips to Kiev. It was a kind of experience for me. When I came to Kiev, I took a bus usually from railway station or from airport. And I told myself, "How long will it take before I hear something about Jews?" And usually, it took 15 or 20 minutes and I would hear something already. These anti-Semitic feelings and thoughts, it's first place for them. Their anti-Semitic feelings and anti-Semitic conversations and everything, for them it's problem number one.

In contrast, Jews from other regions described their encounters with anti-Semitism as being more subtle. A former coach from Odessa says:

Anti-Semitism, even if you never feel it, you know it exists. Anti-Semitism does exist in USSR. But some people, they try to put everything on it. They use it like an excuse.

But it's wrong because a lot of the Russians in Russia have the same problems that Jews have—maybe worse—because they have low income, poor education. My Russian friends had the same problems that I had—but anti-Semitism—I had their problems plus. So it's a problem. It's too complicated. You can't always point it out but you can feel it.

In summary, most émigrés acknowledged feeling institutional anti-Semitism in the USSR through blocked opportunities for education and promotion. Those from the Ukraine, especially Kiev, experienced direct personal prejudice. Others perceived discrimination as subtle, but there all the same.

Generational Variation in Religious Experience

As a consequence of state policy and historical factors, Soviet Jews of different generations have diverse religious outlooks and orientations (Kochan 1978; Orbach 1980; Orleck 1987). This places Soviet Jews in an ironic position: They are a religiously defined refugee population whose community lacks broad-based religious ties.

Elderly émigrés were often familiar with traditional Eastern European Judaism that they learned from their parents or before the Stalinist restrictions of the 1930s. Upon resettlement, they were more religiously involved than younger émigrés, especially in Russian language congregations (see Chapter 8). A more youthful group of religious Soviet Jews were those from republics that have only been communist since World War II. A Latvian husband and wife residing in San Francisco described their feelings of religious estrangement from émigrés hailing from Russian and Ukrainian republics that have been communist since 1917:

[Wife:] I'm from a very religious background. I did know everything. From my earliest age, I knew I am Jewish. I am proud because of that. My native language is Yiddish. You wouldn't find it in Russia, but you can find it very often in Latvia or Lithuania.

[Husband:] My family wasn't so religious—but despite that, I know my father spent 6 years of his life in Israel when it was Palestine around 1926.

[Wife:] In Russia, a lot of people mixed up (intermarried). A lot of Jewish people want their kids to be married out, so their grandkids won't have this problem. But I would hate this for me.

Most middle-aged Soviet Jews, however, come from the Russian and Ukrainian republics that have been communist since the revolution. They grew up in an atheistic environment that encouraged their assimilation. Consequently, their experience of Judaism is secular. An engineer in his forties describes his loss of Jewish knowledge:

No Jewish culture at all . . . you know our family lost it completely. It was a shame. When we went to Vienna (after leaving the USSR), the resettlement staff was sorting people who the agencies would be taking care of. And they looked at our family—we didn't look like Jews to them. And they started to ask questions what we know about Jewish life. Do we know any holidays? And we were so ashamed—we didn't know any.

Then I remembered. When I was a little kid, my grandfather gave us Hanukkah gold—*Gelt*. I recalled getting presents. And I told them about the Hanukkah *Gelt*—they started to laugh like crazy.

Like this man, many young and middle-aged Soviet Jews have little religious knowledge or sentiment. Many Soviet Jews actively sought to escape anti-Semitism by assimilating to Russian culture and identity (Karklins 1987; Pinkus 1985). "Tens of thousands of Soviet Jews have simply stopped being Jews" (Jacobs 1981:7). I interviewed a number of émigrés with Russian or Ukrainian last names who told of a Jewish name in their families' past. Intermarriage with non-Jews was another vehicle for assimilation. Through this means, one could change the nationality on a passport from "Jewish" to "Russian." An additional form of assimilation was to avoid circumcising male children.[4]

Despite this movement toward assimilation, several émigrés described their continued interest in religious activities in the USSR. A man from Kiev described how his frustration with the Soviet system motivated his religious involvement:

You reach a point in your life and you just say "enough is enough." And I started being rather outspoken and we had a group of Jewish people gathering in my apartment. We would listen to the Voice of America.

They used to have programs for Soviet Jews. We would record them and we would have celebrations of Jewish holidays and Hanukkah and we would learn some of the songs. Of course by American standards, we were not quite following the instructions because they were not quite explicit. But the feeling was there.

In sum, the meaning and experience of Jewish identity for each generation of Soviet Jews is distinct. These differences are often maintained when émigrés arrive in the United States, limiting their amalgamation into a single religious assembly.

Motives for Emigration

While the image of the pious refusenik who wishes to leave the USSR to live a religious life is common in the media, most Soviet Jews are not religious. More often, Jews leave the USSR as the result of a combination of *push* factors that encourage their exit and the *pull* extended by desirable Western locations. Push factors include personal and institutional anti-Semitism, blocked mobility, a low standard of living, and a repressive political environment. Pulls that motivate emigration involve advantages of life outside the USSR, such as political and religious freedom, the presence of friends or relatives overseas, a higher standard of living, the availability of resettlement services, and a stimulating social and cultural environment. Finally, aware of ever-changing Soviet policies toward their group, Soviet Jews realize that the "window of opportunity" to migrate may slam shut at any time, making the possibility of migration in itself a motive for exit.

Soviet Jews almost universally claimed that their children's future, and not religious freedom, was their main reason for leaving the USSR (Levkov 1984; Simon 1985). Soviet Jewish parents stated that their desire to improve the lives of their children caused them to sacrifice their own relatively secure status and the easy retirement of their own parents. In the words of a former doctor:

I probably decided to leave for my kids. Their future was not really obvious for me. Anti-Semitism is one point. And the second point is that I want my kids to be normal members of society, to be educated. And [in the Soviet Union] I don't think for them it's gonna be possible for them to get an education.

Another comments,

> I have one kid—he is a very good guy—and as any normal parent, I am trying to make him an honest and good person. That's why we have kids. And in the Soviet Union, you can't make him completely honest because there is a double standard, double life, double talk, double meaning. . . .

> So me, like most of the people [from the Soviet Union] you are talking to, will give you as the main reason for immigration that they wanted to save their kids from that system.

This explanation for exit, while commonly expressed by Soviet Jews, is not universal. In the words of one émigré: "I don't believe and I don't trust people who say 'I left Russia only for the kids. . . .' It is first of all for *yourself* and only then for your kids."

In addition to their desire to benefit children, a large number of Soviet Jews also offered ideological reasons for their exit from the USSR:

> I had a good life over there for someone of my nationality. There was no special reason for me to hate the communists for what they have done to me except this one particular case, okay. Put it this way. A person that was raped and had a deep emotional reaction on it will never forgive the rapist.

> The rape was not that they have done something to me—but that they made me a part of their system. If you live long enough in that system and you are at a certain level, then this is a normal way for a person to be. You don't want to be dishonest or whatever. But after a while, you understand that you really become a part of that system and that they pass whatever they do through you and there is no way that you can escape it. And that is what I name a rape.

> I'll give you an example. I was working as a deputy division engineer and partly I was responsible for hiring people—we needed people really badly. So people start to come in. Who comes in first? Jews.

> You are talking to this [Jewish] guy and you know that there is no way that you can take one more Jew in your division. You have to tell him that you cannot hire him. It's because he is a Jew, but you cannot tell him that straight. So you got to lie.

> I was myself in that kind of situation. It makes you part of that incredible vicious circle and you can't break it. So the feeling of being raped is there all of the time. . . .

At my latest years in Russia, I had a feeling of physical impossibility to be there. Like you are going to vomit. Along the street there is the Lenin memorial and I can see the young kids standing and saluting this idol and I feel like I am going to vomit right away.

Despite the impassioned and ideological reasons that some émigrés suggest for exit, others offer less dramatic motives. For example, in the words of . . .

A doctor from Leningrad:

Maybe because of anti-Semitism, maybe for better life. We knew we had the opportunity now, we didn't know what would happen the next day, so we took it.

A couple from Latvia:

All our friends, relatives were in U.S. We had no reason not to leave.

A woman from Odessa:

In Russia, everything is bad, nothing is good. Everything now is very expensive. Food—you can't find nothing in the stores. To buy something is terrible trouble. It's a good country but lots of problems. They spoiled all the country—environment, everything is spoiled. It's the wrong system, the basis is wrong. No idealism now, the kids 5-6 years old are pragmatic, they don't believe anything.

A taxi driver in Los Angeles:

In Soviet Union, I always listened to BBC, Voice of America. So language problem was not bad—I could understand a lot. My hobby was jazz, so through that I learned a lot about America. Russian people know about America and we know about the good life here. So we want to come.

In summary, Soviet Jews offered a variety of reasons for leaving the USSR, many of which were related to negative aspects of Soviet life that "pushed" them out. Nearly all referred to various forms of anti-Semitism as having shaped their decision. Others mentioned political or ideological opposition to the Soviet regime. Finally, "pull" factors attracted Jews to the United States, including a high standard of living, family members abroad, and familiarity with the United States. For a group that entered the States as refugees, Soviet Jews have complex feeling about their exit. Although they opted to leave, few did so without regrets.

The basis refugees have for leaving the USSR has important effects on their style of adaptation and co-ethnic interaction in the United States. Those who exited on the basis of ideological factors tended to retain this orientation. They were interested in political and religious activities in the United States and often became involved in ethnic organizations. In contrast, the pragmatically motivated were attracted to other émigrés with whom they pursued common financial, rather than ideological, goals in the United States. Finally, those who emigrated solely to accompany relatives, especially the young and the old, often felt alienated in the States and questioned the soundness of their decision to exit.

The Process of Immigration

When Soviet Jews apply for their exit visas—an act that is seen as traitorous in the USSR—they become *persona non grata* and must live on the margins of society for months or even years before they are permitted to leave. Ironically, it is not until they apply for the exit visa that most Soviet Jews truly become persons in need of refuge (Levkov 1984). During this waiting period, émigrés are frequently fired from their jobs. If they get into trouble with authorities, their migration will be further delayed, yet once they apply to leave, they are generally deprived of the resources needed to lead a normal life. As a result, they are forced to survive in any way they can, relying on savings, support from friends, or picking up work in the informal sector (Goodman 1984). Doctors become night watchmen, electrical engineers repair small appliances, and students who have been expelled from the university work as tutors. An émigré with a Ph.D. in electronic engineering described life following his application to leave:

> I expected to be a refusenik for 2, 3, 4 years and that is why I didn't apply earlier—I was afraid they wouldn't let me go. I quit my job, because my mentor, a brilliant, decent person, asked me "If you can quit, please do." I didn't want to make trouble for him.

So I hid my diplomas because it's against the law in Russia to work un-derskilled, and I got a night shift job as an electrician in an emergency service with some Russian alcoholics. I worked like this for a few months, and then they let me emigrate.

To obtain the exit visa, émigrés must get statements of non-indebtedness and permission from their parents and former spouses (as in the United States, divorce is common in the USSR). Since having relatives who have gone abroad can harm a Soviet citizen's repu-tation, the interactions required to gain consent are often awkward and difficult. And a relative's refusal to grant permission can delay or prevent exit.

Soviet Jews make extensive plans before applying to leave. Many sell their possessions and hire an English tutor. The application for an exit visa is in itself a complex process. An engineer who was em-ployed in a low-security position within the Soviet defense industry described how he carefully timed his application in order to expedite its approval:

My application was calculated. At the end of 1977, they were supposed to have a meeting in Belgrade on the Helsinki Human Rights Agreement. It was to be in October, so I applied just a month before this, counting that, with the bureaucracy, the left hand doesn't know what the right hand is doing. It just worked. They let a whole lot of people out without checking thoroughly. In Rome, after we got out, I met several others who also had a security clearance.

Soviet Jews who left the USSR prior to late 1989 took a train to Vi-enna, where they stayed for about a week while initial processing took place. From there, a small percentage flew directly to Israel. A much larger group traveled to the outskirts of Rome, where they re-mained for two or three months while their settlement to the United States was arranged. Because the Soviet government limits the amount of money and goods that émigrés can take out of the country (only about $100 in rubles is permitted), the period in Italy was en-dured on a minimal budget. Finally, when plans for resettlement to the United States were complete, Soviet Jews flew to a preselected destination, where they either joined relatives or were sponsored by the local Jewish community. Since the fall of 1989, émigrés have traveled directly from the USSR to the United States.

Because they were officially granted visas for emigration to Israel, Soviet Jews usually had well-developed reasons for moving to the United States; consistent with their motives for exiting the USSR, a primary factor was their childrens' future (Orleck 1987; Simon 1985). Many claimed that they personally were not afraid of military service in Israel but nevertheless wanted to protect the younger generation from involvement in war.

Others mentioned the high standard of living in the United States or the presence of relatives here.

Émigrés also offered ideological reasons for their choice of the United States, claiming that Israel was "too socialist" and maintained excessive control over citizens' private lives.

A Los Angeles émigré activist described his choice of the United States over Israel:

Financially I'm better off than I would have been in Israel. But there is another level as well. A lot of people who went to Israel—they were very idealistic about it, and considered themselves to be Zionists—they were disappointed. The resettlement doesn't do a good job. Many people who were idealistic and went to Israel wound up in Los Angeles.

And this is very sad and something has to be done because you just can't impose a way of life on people. There are plenty of things which you have to take into consideration when dealing with Soviet émigrés. To a great extent, Israel is perceived as a socialist country. It's very, very socialist. Israeli bureaucracy is world famous. Obviously, being a Soviet Jew, I had enough of bureaucracy.

Others were opposed to living in a society that was not pluralistic:

I didn't go to Israel because I am not an Orthodox Jew. I am not religious. And I know that Israel is Orthodox country. Their religion and their civil life is very close in Israel. Like in Russia, the civil life and the ideology. Oh, I don't need it anymore! I am mad about this for my 50 years. This is why I cannot live in Israel. This is my position and I can tell it to anybody. I know I am Jew. I like Jewish people, but this is my headache. This is why I don't go to Israel.

For many émigrés, the decision not to go to Israel continued to occupy their thoughts for years after settlement in the United States, and Israel was the frequent destination of choice for a first trip outside the

United States. A Latvian woman living in San Francisco reflects on her ambivalence about settling in the States:

> It was my main driving point to move to Israel so that my kids would not have to solve these identity problems ever. What you have to do, what you don't have to do, are you Jewish and what do you have to do to be Jewish. Living in Israel, you don't have to worry about this. But we did decide to come here, and we haven't left yet.

CHARACTERISTICS OF SOVIET JEWISH REFUGEES

Soviet Jews are well equipped for the task of adjusting to life in the United States. They are skilled and educated, and they are familiar with urban life. Further, they enjoy refugee status and are therefore eligible for a variety of resettlement services, training programs, cash assistance, and permanent resident status in the United States. Finally, due to Soviet policy, the unit of immigration for Soviet Jewish refugees is frequently an intact family (Jacobs and Frankel Paul 1981; Panish 1981; Simon 1985).

The Soviet Jews are an elderly immigrant group. Their average age is 40.5 years, with 48% being over 45 years of age (Eckles et al. 1982; ORR 1986).[5] Family size for this population is very small; a recent study found that the average Soviet Jewish household consists of three persons (Simon 1983:503).

Soviet Jews are highly educated, having attended school for an average of 13.5 years, a period that is greater by one year than the average educational level of the U.S. population (Simon and Brooks 1983; Statistical Abstract of the U.S. 1984).[6] These high levels of education, coupled with the fact that Soviet Jewish women are accustomed to being employed outside the home (often in lucrative professional and technical occupations[7]), makes their family income ($20,000 by 1980; and $34,000 in 1989 for those in the United States at least 8 years) substantial for a recently arrived immigrant group (Kosmin 1990; ORR 1984; Simon 1985).[8]

The high quality of Soviet education also benefits school-age émigrés. Their knowledge of science and math is generally years ahead of that of Americans of the same age (Orleck 1987). Because Russian culture values literacy, Soviet Jewish students are frequently well read and have been exposed to Russian, European, and American classics (in Russian translation) upon arrival in the United States. Among both students and professionals, Soviets are well prepared in theoretical areas.

On the other hand, the lack of technology in the USSR limits émigrés' training and skill in many practical areas. Even personal computers and desk-top calculators are relatively rare. Advanced electronic and laboratory equipment are even scarcer. Consequently, Soviet Jews' preparation in these areas is limited, especially for older professionals who received their training prior to the 1970s détente period when the USSR acquired advanced Western equipment.

The agency that resettles Soviet Jewish refugees, the HIAS (the Hebrew Immigrant Aid Society), is long established and well funded, and works in conjunction with other Jewish and public agencies, such as Jewish family and vocational services and Jewish community centers, to offer a variety of services. These range from initial settlement to job training and placement, social activities, religious socialization, and mental health programs. Due to the efforts of these agencies, Soviet Jewish immigrants were generally resettled in middle-class neighborhoods rather than the inner-city enclaves that are the usual location of recently arrived immigrants (Eckles et al. 1982; Gorelick 1982; Orleck 1987; ORR 1987; Rischin 1962). Furthermore, because Soviet Jews are resettled by American Jewish agencies, they are distributed among cities that already have sizable Jewish populations. These include New York, Los Angeles, Chicago, Boston, and San Francisco.

CONCLUSIONS

Soviet Jewish immigrants are highly skilled and generally enter the United States in intact, cooperative families. Further, they enjoy a very high quality of resettlement services. Consequently, their adaptation to the United States is often rapid (Simon 1985). As a group, they share commonalities of education, language, and ethnicity. In addition, their Soviet experience has taught them to be skillful at manipulating bureaucracies.

However, Soviet Jews are also marked by diversity in several areas, including class, occupational background, region of origin, religious and ideological outlook, and experiences with anti-Semitism.

Generational factors are important in shaping the outlooks of Soviet Jews. Elderly émigrés tend to be religious and may retain an element of idealism in their views of the Soviet system. Further, they are likely to speak Yiddish, the language of Eastern European Jews. In contrast, younger émigrés have little knowledge of the Jewish religion and tend to be less idealistic. Because their occupational training was acquired relatively recently, their skills are likely to be more compatible with those required by the U.S. economy.

The religious, ideological, regional and generational diversity of the Soviet Jewish population sets the context of these refugees' adaptation and community formation in the United States. Their experience with Soviet anti-Semitism leaves them with a sense of minority group identification. However, their lack of religious training, limited ability to form associations, and high level of assimilation to Russian society have largely deprived them of their heritage in such a way as to inhibit their creation of the ethnic self-help bodies that are customary among non-Soviet Jewish immigrant communities (Wirth 1928; Gorelick 1981; Howe 1976; Kliger 1989).

NOTES

1. After October 1989, when the United States refused to grant refugee status to Soviet Jews en masse, the number of Jews migrating to Israel dramatically increased and exceeded the number entering the United States (Ungar 1989).

2. Ironically, émigrés who feel guilt or ambivalence about emigrating from the USSR sometimes call upon the culture of savvy to reject their group's refugee status. One young Soviet refugee told me that since Jews can always find a way to do well in the USSR, if they really wanted to, they could also lead a Jewish life there. This point is reinforced through mythology concerning underground Jewish life in the USSR. Tales describe a small group that, despite all odds, is able to live a fully Hasidic or Orthodox life, run Jewish schools, train rabbis, and even cross the border out of the Soviet Union undetected. *Exit Visa* by Paul Panish (1981) describes the underground Jewish life in the Soviet Union in a way that is corroborated by my interviews with Russian-trained Chabad rabbis.

3. In *Portraits of White Racism* (1977), Wellman describes how in the United States, via institutional racism, racial inequality can be maintained even though individuals do not make prejudiced comments. This model is useful for understanding the career experience of Jews in the Soviet Union. Its explanatory value is indicated by the fact that some interviewees spontaneously used a term with a similar meaning—*state anti-Semitism*—to describe the problems they faced in getting into universities or receiving promotions.

4. Adult émigrés sometimes undergo the *Briss* (religious circumcision) in the United States or Israel as they become more involved with their religious and ethnic identity.

5. Soviet Jews, whose average age is 40.5, are 15 years older than the average immigrant entering the United States between 1970 and 1980 (U.S. Bureau of the Census 1983:Table 196).

6. The education of Soviet Jews is exceeded by only one group of recent immigrants: Indians (Bureau of the Census 1983:Table 196).

7. While only 3% of U.S. women are engineers or technicians, 22% of Soviet Jewish women in the United States were employed in these occupations in the USSR. Further, a full 60% of these Soviet Jewish women were professionally employed in the Soviet Union. In contrast, 16.5% of U.S. women have professional occupations, according to 1980 data (Eckles et al. 1982:29; Statistical Abstract of the U.S. 1984:415).

8. As of 1981, the unemployment rate of Soviet Jews was 9.7%, only slightly higher than that of the U.S. population as a whole (Simon 1985, Statistical Abstract of the U.S., 1984). Further, 26% of time-eligible Soviet refugees are dependent upon cash or medical assistance. This is higher than the rate for Polish refugees (12%) and lower than the rate of 64% for Vietnamese refugees (ORR 1987:34-35).

3

Vietnamese Refugees:
Background and Characteristics

The background of Vietnamese refugees contrasts dramatically with that of the Soviet Jews. While Soviet Jews have a strong consciousness of kind, the Vietnamese—with the exception of the Chinese-Vietnamese—must develop the shared identity required for community mobilization in the United States. In addition, background, experience of flight, and ethnicity divide the Vietnamese into three distinct subgroups: the expatriate elite, the boat people, and the Chinese-Vietnamese. These factors shape their adaptation and contribute to their creation of segmented communities in the United States.

A HISTORY OF CONTACT
WITH POWERFUL OUTSIDERS

The United States and Vietnam were intensely involved with one another for only 21 years (from 1954 to 1975). However, neither this relationship, nor the experience of the Vietnamese in the United States, can be understood without considering the history and culture of the Vietnamese people. Vietnam's location as a relatively small, agriculturally rich country located between Asia's two largest societies, China and India, has shaped much of its history. Vietnam was occupied by the Chinese for 900 years. Achieving independence in 939 A.D., Vietnam later became a point of interest to European nations, most notably France, which set up a colonial administration

there in the nineteenth century. Finally, Vietnam's geographical setting made the United States choose it as the place to make a stand
against the spread of communism in the 1950s and 1960s. The
Vietnamese ultimately ejected the French and Americans, but not before their way of life was indelibly colored by foreign habits, ideas,
and tools and their identity forged through centuries of oppression,
collusion, and rebellion.

Relations With China

The Chinese, who governed Vietnam from 111 B.C. until 939, contributed many of their customs, traditions, and institutions to Vietnam. Until the 1600s, when French and Portuguese priests developed
Quoc Ngu, a system for writing the Vietnamese language in Latin letters, Vietnamese was written in Chinese characters. Further, it was
from the Chinese that Vietnam acquired its three major religious/phil-
osophical traditions: Buddhism, Taoism, and Confucianism. Much of
Vietnam's technology is of Chinese origin. Millions of the Chinese
who came to Vietnam initially served as colonial administrators and
mandarins, with later arrivals working in French industries. Some became powerful entrepreneurs in their own right. Chinese practices
have not only shaped the great traditions of Vietnam, but the daily
lives of its people as well.

All of these influences accepted, it is a mistake to consider Vietnam simply as a southern outpost of Chinese civilization. The
Vietnamese language is unrelated to Chinese, most Vietnamese are
ambivalent about Chinese culture, and the sizable overseas Chinese
population of Vietnam (including those who have migrated to the
United States) are often the subject of derision and scapegoating. Finally, much of Vietnamese tradition and many of its folk heroes are
derived from its two millennia of conflicts with the Chinese:

> In fact, it was during the many centuries of intensive efforts to make
> them Chinese that the Vietnamese completed their ethnological forma-
> tion as a separate people, with a beginning of political and cultural aspi-
> rations of their own. (Buttinger 1958:94)

Between 39 and 939 A.D., the Vietnamese engaged in a dozen up-
risings against the Chinese. In the process, they developed national
sentiments and a tradition of dealing with foreigners. After achieving

independence in 939, Vietnam quickly embarked upon its own colonial enterprise. The period from the eleventh to the nineteenth centuries was spent expanding Vietnam's borders to include the fertile regions that are now central and southern Vietnam at the expense of the Champa and Cambodians (Buttinger 1958:166). National consciousness was maintained through periodic conflicts with invaders, especially the Ming-dynasty Chinese, who captured and mercilessly exploited Vietnam from 1406 until 1428, when Le Loi led a successful campaign for independence.

Contacts With the West

In 1535, Vietnam experienced its first contacts with Western nations as Portuguese explorers arrived. During the next century, the Dutch and later the English also established trade offices. From Catholic countries came missionaries who, along with militarists and profiteers, spearheaded the European colonial enterprise. In 1857, a French flotilla sailed to annex Indochina. While the Vietnamese resisted, the French were ultimately successful, first capturing the southern region of what is now known as Vietnam in the 1860s and occupying the entire nation by 1883. They ruled with brutal force, planted large rubber plantations, and established a "divide and rule" program whereby the nation was split into three regions: Tongking in the north, Annam in the center, and Cochinchina in the south. The French also set up a puppet administration, directed through a series of Vietnamese emperors, the last of whom, Bao Dai, was installed in 1926 and remained until 1955.

During the 90 years of French occupation, many members of the Vietnamese upper class became westernized. In 1960, 2,500 Vietnamese were attending institutions of higher education outside the country, including over 2,000 who studied in France (Harris et al. 1962:119). These and many others learned French, the official language of government and education until independence, and were exposed to Western ideas and European ways of life.

As Vietnam's alliances with the West shifted from France to the United States, so did its flow of international students. Thousands of Vietnamese came to the United States in the 1960s and early 1970s for academic and military training. However, not all of those with exposure to Western life sided with Western interests. Many of Vietnam's nationalist and communist leaders put their Occidental learning to the task of winning Vietnamese independence.

After France's defeat at Dien Bien Phu by the Viet Minh in 1954, Vietnam was partitioned into a Communist North and a Nationalist South. At this time, close to a million Northerners, including many upper-class persons and thousands of Catholics, fled south. Many would take high positions in South Vietnam's government, only to flee to the United States in the 1970s.

The United States and the War

Following the partitioning of Vietnam, in 1955, Ngo Dinh Diem was elected president of South Vietnam. He instituted a series of policies intended to increase national security and unity. However, Diem, a Catholic, offended members of the nation's Buddhist majority, who sought a political solution to the conflict rather than a military one. When in 1963 a Buddhist monk named Thich Quang Duc set fire to himself in a highly publicized protest, an international controversy resulted. Diem was ousted and killed in 1964. As Buttinger asserts, Vietnam's U.S.-backed leaders from the Diem era until South Vietnam's defeat were deeply involved in dishonest activity:

> Rule by force was accompanied by widespread corruption in the administration and the army, from the top to the bottom. Corruption, it was reported by informed American observers, was taking no less than 40 per cent of U.S. aid to South Vietnam. The beneficiaries of this corruption were not only contractors, high administrators, landowners, generals and intermediary agents between business and government, but also lower officials in the administration who exacted bribes from any citizen for whatever service he may have needed and had a right to receive. (Buttinger 1972:102)

In contrast to this Western scholar's view, nearly all refugees have a very high regard for Diem. Several told me they believed that Diem was killed by the CIA because of his opposition to bringing large numbers of U.S. soldiers to Vietnam. By overruling Diem's wishes and engaging U.S. troops, the refugees hold, the United States allowed Ho Chi Minh and the communists to mobilize Vietnam's 2,000-year tradition of anti-colonialism, hence gaining wide popular support. According to the refugees, if Diem's dictates had been followed, the South Vietnamese would not have appeared as colonial collaborators, and the communists would have been deprived of a

major basis of power among the Vietnamese people, thereby prevent-
ing communist victory.

Regardless of how wartime events are interpreted, the face of
Vietnamese society was significantly altered during the Vietnam War
period, not only through the conflict itself, but also due to the social
upheavals brought on by the war. One major transformation that
would influence persons who would later migrate to the United States
was urbanization. While the U.S. and South Vietnamese forces were
able to control Vietnam's cities, the rural areas were often strong-
holds of the communist Viet Cong. Constant fighting caused millions
of Vietnamese to leave the villages and settle in Saigon.

By the 1970s, the nation had became rapidly urbanized, thus bringing millions of rural Vietnamese into contact with Western-tinged
urban culture and a money economy. European, American, and Japanese products were widely available, and a consumer economy flour-
ished. A generation of South Vietnamese kids listened to The Who
and Creedence Clearwater Revival on Sony tape recorders while their
parents traveled on Lambretta scooters and in Peugot automobiles. As
a consequence, thousands were exposed to a culture and way of life
that they would encounter once again upon fleeing from their homeland (Harris et al. 1962). Several refugees, including the man quoted
below, described their exposure to urban and Western life as a process that began in Vietnam and continued in the United States.

> I was born in a small village in the countryside. When I was about 14, I
> got a job on a truck that would go into the bigger towns. As time went
> by, I learned more about the way of life, the better food, the different
> things in the city. Once I got used to these, I decided I would never go
> back to living in the small village. Now here in America, I miss my
> homeland, but I still enjoy the many things here.

In retrospect, we can understand how years of experience with foreign invaders, colonists, missionaries, and allies shaped the consciousness and way of life of the Vietnamese, both those who would
remain and those who would leave for other nations. From the Chinese, French, Japanese, Americans, and others, their cultural and intellectual horizons were broadened. They were exposed to both the
wealth and the greed of the great nations, and their highest moral traditions, as well as their most inhuman acts of violence and exploitation. Some Vietnamese became the outsiders' administrators,

sharing in profits extracted from their countrymen, while others upheld the long tradition of anti-colonialism. Most Vietnamese, however, just tried to survive and maintain a normal life, wary of both the native-born and foreigners who would use them for their own purposes.

Despite these suspicions, many Vietnamese remained open to the possibilities offered by contacts with other social groups and ways of life. This interest in enjoying the fruits of many nations is expressed in a popular saying regarding the best of all possible worlds: "Chinese food, French house, Japanese wife."

VIETNAMESE CULTURE: RELIGION AND FAMILY

Upon arrival in the United States, Vietnamese refugees (with the exception of the ethnic Chinese) lack a clear concept of ethnic group membership (Espiritu 1989). However, they are party to a strong national tradition and culture forged by centuries of conflict with powerful nations. This cultural baggage, along with other aspects of the refugee experience, provides a basis for their group formation in the United States.

Two Vietnamese cultural forms that strongly affect refugees in the United States are religion and family.

Religion

Vietnam's religious outlook, called *Tam Giáo,* actually consists of three faiths: Buddhism, Confucianism, and Taoism. From China came Mahayana Buddhism (Henkin and Nguyen 1981), a religion that emphasizes the ethical principle of "good works" toward all living things. It argues for detachment from the material world and views wealth, power, and status as corrupting forces that cause suffering. For the Buddhist, true peace, or *Nirvana,* is achieved by the renunciation of worldliness. A process of reincarnation, whereby a person achieves his or her station in life as a result of good or bad deeds in previous lives, is also a major postulate. Buddhist priests *(Bonzes)* were figures of influence in Vietnam and retain some authority in the United States (Hickey 1964:64). By the early 1980s, the financially strapped refugee community had funded the creation of several Buddhist temples in the United States. Their monks are sources of guidance, healing, and emotional support to the refugee population (Farber 1987).

The second Vietnamese religious tradition is Taoism. Like Buddhism, it also emphasizes humility and renunciation of the material world.

Finally, Confucianism, a philosophy of life rather than a religion, is the third major Vietnamese faith. "While Buddhism and Taoism emphasized the unreality of the physical world and renunciation and eternal life in a supernatural world, Confucianism focused on life in the present and on social obligations by affirming that man is above all a social being" (Henken and Nguyen 1981:12). Confucianism is generally regarded as a conservative and sexist social tradition that posits the patriarchal family as the ideal human institution (Harris et al. 1962:130). It requires each man's and each woman's obedience to higher authorities: rulers, parents, husbands, and older siblings. Modeling politics after its view of the family, the Confucian image of a good society is one of loyal citizens following the dictates of the father-emperor (Harris et al. 1962:128).

Despite its conservative tendencies, Confucianism mandated a meritocratic social structure whereby mandarins (learned men who had great social influence) achieved their status by civil service examination rather than birth. However, because education was not provided by the state, it was generally those with financial assets and links to the elite who achieved these positions of prestige. There was, however, a tradition of allowing especially gifted, but lowly born, persons the opportunity to achieve this lofty rank (Buttinger 1972:54; Henkin and Nguyen 1981:15-16). As part of the colonial enterprise, Confucianism was vilified by the French colonists, who eliminated examinations for the mandarinate in 1918. Nonetheless, this philosophy, with its prescriptions for family patterns and value of education, remains influential among Vietnamese Americans today.

In contrast to monotheistic Westerners, most Vietnamese find no contradiction in combining multiple belief systems. Hence, Vietnamese adhere to each of the three faiths as well as folk religion, astrology, a pantheon of spirits, Catholicism, and sometimes Protestantism (Hickey 1964:74-76). In the words of a Methodist Vietnamese, "Our Christianity has a lot of Confucianism and Eastern beliefs in it. Even my father, who is a Protestant minister, kind of believes in the horoscope. Lots of people ask the astrologer when they get married or plan to hire a worker."

In discussing their ability to tolerate the suffering of wartime, the flight from Vietnam, and the difficulties of adjustment to the United States, Vietnamese refugees frequently made reference to their spiritual traditions. While Western intellectuals often lean toward atheism, I found that, among the Vietnamese, it was the more educated who describe religious convictions and prerogatives in the greatest detail. In the words of a former professor:

> When I came here, I heard of stress. I could not understand what people meant. I looked it up in the dictionary. To understand the Vietnamese people, you have to look at the cultural factors. Confucianism, Buddhism, Taoism, the three schools of philosophy act on Vietnamese life. Confucianism: you have to work, help the community. Buddhism: you have to live in harmony with other persons, not arguing. Resignation. You have to suffer—don't complain. Endure and accept fate. Taoism: if necessary, you have to withdraw and not do anything at all.
>
> I do not think that we have stress at all. With the three philosophies, Buddhism, Taoism and Confucianism, we have no stress.

The Vietnamese Family

Vietnamese religious cosmology, influential in itself, also shapes another institution of central importance: the traditional Vietnamese family. It is perhaps the most basic, enduring, and self-consciously acknowledged form of national culture among refugees.[1] The Vietnamese family is customarily a large, patriarchal, and extended unit that includes minor children, married sons, daughters-in-law, unmarried grown daughters, and grandchildren under the same roof. Individualism is discouraged, while collective obligations and decision-making are encouraged. Rights and duties, such as inheritance or care for the elderly, are prescribed according to age, gender, and birth order. A vocabulary far more extensive than that available in the English language describes a complexity of relationships among siblings, cousins, and other relatives on both sides of the family. Since deceased family members are also venerated, death constitutes no real departure from family life (Hickey 1964:85-88).

The eldest male has primary responsibility for the well-being and moral guidance of the entire family unit and supervises ancestor worship rituals (Henkin and Nguyen 1981:20). He is likely to make decisions for family members, choosing their occupations or marriage partners, for example. Further, family finances are generally collectivized, with the father determining how individual earnings should be spent for the aggregate good. The Vietnamese frequently emphasize blood ties over those of marriage. For example, a married Vietnamese may decide to exit Vietnam depending on the needs of parents or siblings rather than of husband or wife, claiming, "I can always get another husband, but I have only one set of parents" (Haines et al. 1981:318).

Although Confucianism stresses the obedience of females to males, Vietnamese culture also contains a strong tradition of female autonomy and independence. The first protagonists of Vietnamese anti-colonialism (the Vietnamese equivalents of George Washington) are the Trung sisters. Women have traditionally held a major role in controlling family finances. Their domestic activities include entrepreneurship, thereby allowing them to maintain a degree of authority over assets (Finnan and Cooperstein 1983; Harris et al. 1962; Hickey 1964; Kibria 1989; 1990; Nguyen 1949). "In Vietnam, the woman was always the money manager of the family, and was referred to as *Nôi Tuóng* or 'Chief of Domestic Affairs'" (Finnan and Cooperstein, 1983:31). Research by Kibria (1989, 1990) reveals that Vietnamese refugee women participate in informal networks that counteract male abuses while simultaneously supporting a traditional family structure.

Finally, Vietnamese culture is rich with references to romantic love and covert liaisons, forms of association that subvert the Confucian doctrine of male supremacy. Vietnamese refugees that I worked with enjoyed teasing one another about sexuality and manipulative relationships. For example, upon seeing a photograph of my wife, a female refugee joked, "Oh, she's good looking, she can find a better guy than you." Similarly, at a Vietnamese cultural festival, a singer performed a centuries-old, "Romeo and Juliet" folk song about a couple in love despite their parents' objections. In these ways, the official ideology of male dominance is moderated by women's ability to assert themselves and maintain some autonomy.

The traditional Vietnamese family has been altered as a consequence of Western influence, urbanization, and war-induced male absence, especially among the affluent (Henkin and Nguyen 1981). Regardless of movement away from the traditional ideal, many Vietnamese continue to uphold this social form as the preferable basis of social organization in the United States.

A former professor, now a San Jose-based refugee activist, described the importance of the Vietnamese family in shaping resettlement:

> To Vietnamese culture, family is everything. There are aspects which help us re-adjust to this society. It is easy for us because of tradition of helping in the family.

> We solve problems because the family institution is a bank. If I need money—and my brother and my two sisters are working—I tell them I need to buy a house. I need priority in this case. They say "okay," and they give money to me. And after only two years, I bought a house.

> Some Americans ask me, "how come you came here with empty hands and now you have a house?" I told them, it is easier for us because my brother and sister help with the down payment. Now I help them. They live with me and have no rent.

> The family is a hospital. If mom is sick, I, my children and my brother and sisters care for her. We don't need a nurse. She stays home, so we don't need to send her to nursing home.

Even disadvantaged and isolated refugees re-created "pseudofamilies" based on the traditional model in order to provide themselves with social support (Gold 1989; Kibria 1989; Owan 1985). In interviews, refugees' most frequent complaint that about American society involved its violation of a basic value of Confucian ethics: treating the elderly with deference and respect.

In sum, pre-immigration history, religion, and family forms underlie many basic relationships that exist within California's Vietnamese-American communities. The role of the ethnic middleman, played by resettlement workers and entrepreneurs who serve as brokers between Vietnamese refugees and American society, can be traced back to Vietnamese colonial administrators. Likewise, the notable accomplishments of Vietnamese students in California high schools and colleges can be seen as a continuation of the tradition established by meritocratic examinations for the mandarinate and civil service that were established in the eleventh century, as well as a product of class resources retained from Vietnam (Buttinger 1958; Henkin and Nguyen 1981). Finally, the propensity of Vietnamese to open small businesses in California is partly the result of the transplantation of Vietnam's entrepreneurial Chinese minority to the United States and

Vietnamese village women's practice of running small enterprises as an extension of their domestic duties (Finnan and Cooperstein 1983; Harris et al. 1962; Hickey 1964; Nguyen 1949).

The patterns of adaptation that Vietnamese reveal in the United States reflect their history, current situation, and the structure of opportunity that exists in this host nation. The movement of the Vietnamese to the United States was at least partly initiated by their wartime urbanization in the decades prior to the communist takeover. In the longer view, this development can be considered to be hundreds of years old and linked to Vietnam's role in the world system.

EXPERIENCE OF FLIGHT FOR THREE SUBGROUPS

Numbering only a few thousand individuals until the early 1970s, the Vietnamese immigrants, marked by a young median age and high birthrate, will be the third largest Asian-American ethnic group by this century's end (Gardner et al. 1985:37).[2] Most of the Vietnamese who live in the United States (more than 60%) arrived between 1975 and 1983 (ORR 1989:A-1). However, during this short time, three distinct subgroups established themselves in the United States: the 1975-era elite, the boat people, and the ethnic Chinese. While these groups frequently interact, they also retain many differences and have developed fairly distinct patterns of adaptation to the United States.

1975-Era Refugees

The first group of Vietnamese refugees, numbering about 175,000, avoided many of the most traumatic elements of the flight from Vietnam. Reaching the United States between 1975 and 1977, they were U.S. employees and members of the South Vietnamese military and government. As an elite, they feared punishment by the Northern communists, and their suspicions proved to be correct. While there was no bloodbath on par with that of neighboring Cambodia, many South Vietnamese were incarcerated in reeducation camps for up to 15 years. In the following quote, a woman from an entrepreneurial family that supplied U.S. forces in Vietnam describes her emigration:

My mother was very smart. She worry, she knows something will happen. She thinks she will have nothing to do when the Communists come in. She had a business and she is afraid. She left one week before the Communists came.

I didn't want to leave. And my husband is in the service—we can't leave. My husband stayed with the soldiers until the last minute. We hear the news on the radio. That's why he took me and my children. We run at once—we all so lucky. We all escaped at the last minute. We didn't know what to do, where to go.

I thought we would just go out in the boat to get off the land. But the older officers with us, they were experienced with the Communists. They say "no we cannot come back." So we have to go wherever—we run on the sea, by the navy ships for 18 days. At that time, the United States didn't accept us yet, so we decided to go to Australia. We decided to go anywhere they accept us. But then we hear that President Ford said he will accept all of the ship people. My mother had a relative who came to Michigan for college, so we all settled there.

I didn't want to leave. If my husband was not in the service, I would have stayed in Vietnam. A lot of people—like my cousin—stayed, but now they are leaving. The Communists, they took away from you everything.

Evacuated by U.S. forces, the first wave of Vietnamese avoided life under the new regime and spent only a short time in refugee camps before being resettled in the United States. Many early-arriving Vietnamese entered the United States with their families intact. Funds for their resettlement were relatively generous: They received 3 years of cash assistance. Their links to Western culture are indicated by the fact that almost half were Catholic, even though well over 80% of all Vietnamese are Buddhists (Hickey 1964; Kelly 1977:47). Drawing upon their skills, education, competence in English, familiarity with Western culture, and extended families, many adjusted rapidly. By the mid-1980s, the Office of Refugee Resettlement reported that their income matched that of the larger U.S. population (ORR 1989:148).

Despite their swift economic adjustment, the first cohort of Vietnamese refugees did encounter many difficulties. A major hardship was the rapidity of their exit. Sixty-one percent had less than 24 hours to prepare for their departure, and 83% had less than one week to do so (Liu et al. 1979). While this group has a greater proportion of unified families than later arrivals, many relatives were left behind.

Since there was no sizable Vietnamese community in the United States prior to 1975, the first wave of Vietnamese were resettled throughout the country, sponsored by churches and other voluntary organizations. Between April and December 1975, prior to permanent placement, refugees were housed in four resettlement camps: Camp Pendleton, near San Diego; Fort Chaffee, Arkansas; Eglin Air Force Base, near Pensacola; and Fort Indian Town Gap in Pennsylvania (Kelly 1977:61). While this system provided the Vietnamese with contacts valuable for finding work and learning about American culture and the English language, both refugees and sponsors experienced a great deal of culture shock as they encountered one another (Montero 1979).

The Boat People

The second group of Vietnamese began to enter the United States following the outbreak of the Vietnam-China conflict of 1978. Generally called "boat people," these refugees were often rural in origin. They lived for three years or longer under communism, sometimes laboring in re-education camps or remote "new economic zones" before leaving Vietnam. Their exit, involving open sea voyages in leaky, overcrowded boats or long journeys on foot across revolution-torn Cambodia to Thailand, was subject to attacks by pirates and military forces. Reportedly, up to 50% of the boat people perished in flight. Those lucky enough to survive spent several months in the overcrowded refugee camps of Thailand, Malaysia, Indonesia, the Philippines, or Hong Kong before entering the United States.

Many refugees who arrived in the United States as post-1978 boat people described making a conscious decision to stay in their homeland despite the communist takeover. They felt loyal to their families and country and thought they had nothing to fear from the communists (Long and Kendall 1981). For example, Xuan Chau, an enlisted man in the South Vietnamese navy, looked back at his decision to remain in Vietnam in 1975:

I was out in my boat and we heard on the radio that the Communists were taking over Saigon. We took several of the men to a big American ship. I could have gone too, but I love my country. We broke our guns, put up a white flag and sailed into port.

Doan Thanh described his life between the communist takeover in 1975 and his exit in 1980. The son of a bar owner, Doan was a cadet in Vietnam's air force academy before April 1975.

As a member of South Vietnam's military, he was remanded to a reeducation camp. Since he was only a cadet, his internment was relatively brief. While his "red camp" stay was only three months, his links to the defeated regime made him an outcast in a society already marked by oppression and scarcity. Lacking other options, he worked in his father's small store, where he was harassed by cadres for selling American cigarettes. Doan described how the cadres would take members of his family into different rooms and claim that friends or family members had confessed to various crimes in which Doan's family was implicated. Doan Thanh told how his family prepared answers in advance so that, when questioned, each would offer a consistent, safe reply to avoid incrimination.

Later, Doan Thanh's father-in-law gave the local communists sizable payments so that Doan would not be drafted to serve in Vietnam's occupation of Cambodia. Nevertheless, Doan was required to work on a canal project in a remote region. During this time, his wife, daughter, and several siblings escaped Vietnam by boat, eventually settling in Oakland, California. Doan managed to depart from the canal site by escorting an injured friend back to Saigon. He secured passage on a boat, and after a stay in a Malaysian refugee camp, was reunited with his wife in 1982.

In conversations, refugees described the insanity of their escape. Several recounted how they made numerous "false starts" toward the United States, only to be detected or detained. Luc and Vien Ung maintained a covert existence and had to pay off officials with large amounts of gold to exit. A former teacher told me how he had made nine unsuccessful attempts before finally leaving Vietnam. With embarrassed smiles and anxious giggles that reflected their discomfort, Nguyen Van Vien and Trung Ho Thien recounted how many on their boats had been harassed at gunpoint by pirates, suffered from dehydration, or drowned.

During a fieldwork visit, two former boat people described their very different experiences of escape. Xuan Chau, a navy veteran, had the skills that allowed him to secure free passage as the pilot of a sturdy, well-equipped boat. "I had all the food and gasoline I needed. Since I knew about the ocean, I could steer away from Thailand (where there were many pirates) to Indonesia. We spent only 3 nights and 2 days at sea." In contrast, Van Ngoc Nguyen went without food and water for three days. Then the Thai pirates came. They raped several of the women on the boat and threw their clothes overboard. Afterwards, the Vietnamese men gave their clothing to the women, and as a result, were left naked. In viewing a magazine illustrated with photographs of several refugee boats, Van pointed to the most overcrowded and primitive, stating, "That was me."

Having crossed the high seas, boat refugees then languished for months in Asian refugee camps, where they confronted an international bureaucracy of resettlement agencies under the supervision of the UNHCR (United Nations High Committee on Refugees). Several had been resettled in Pilau Bidong, a giant island-based camp off the coast of Malaysia. The Vietnamese were kept quarantined from the larger society because this Moslem nation feared that the heavily Chinese refugee population would upset the country's delicate ethnic balance between Chinese and Moslem (Rose 1982a; Wain 1981). In refugee camps, various ethnic and nationality groups were housed together, making them a microcosm of the nations that had been involved in the Indochina conflict and often reflected the ethnic and national antipathies long present in the region (Rose 1982a).

Although the largest number of Southeast Asian refugees (881,000) ultimately made it to the United States, the resettlement effort was truly international. Canada accepted 126,000; Australia, 122,000; France, 108,000; Germany, 24,000; and Britain, 18,000. In addition, about 260,000 Chinese-Vietnamese returned to China in 1978. As of December 1989, 117,000 refugees remained in Asian camps, waiting for resettlement (*Nguoi Viet,* 1989:E3).

Refugees selected for eventual resettlement in the United States received three months of training in English and American culture at one of two RPCs (Refugee Processing Centers) in Galang, Indonesia, or Bataan, the Philippines, to foster adaptation (Rose 1982b: 14). Following their term in the RPC, refugees boarded charter flights for the United States, where they were met by representatives of resettlement agencies or sponsors and set up with apartments in refugee neighborhoods.

Due to the dangers of escape, far more young men left Vietnam as boat people than did women, children, or the elderly. For example, in 1984 there were approximately 204,000 male Southeast Asian refugees in the United States between the ages of 12 and 44, but only 156,000 females in the same age group, making males outnumber females by 24% (Balvanz 1988:13). Accordingly, this group is marked by broken families. In addition, these boat people experienced financial troubles that were more severe than those of earlier arriving Vietnamese. While Vietnamese refugees coming to the United States in 1975 averaged 9.5 years of education, and two-thirds knew some English upon arrival, refugees arriving between 1980 and 1982 had an average of 7.05 years of education, and half had no competence in English (ORR 1983:25). Disadvantaged by lower levels of education and lower English language ability, and contending with the depressed economy of the early 1980s, boat refugees faced difficulty in finding their first jobs in the United States.[3] Further, while the 1975 cohort were sponsored by Americans who often provided job referrals, recent arrivals were resettled by Vietnamese who generally lacked connections to employers (Montero 1979:99). Recent arrivals also had to contend with shrinking benefits since refugee cash assistance (RCA) was cut from 36 to 18 months in 1982 and several other programs were eliminated altogether. Because of these many disadvantages, the post-1978 Vietnamese have had a more difficult time in adapting to the United States than their earlier-arriving counterparts.

The Ethnic Chinese

The third subpopulation of Vietnamese refugees, most of whom arrived after 1978 as boat people, are members of Vietnam's ethnic Chinese minority group. Constituting an entrepreneurial class, this group has a long history but a marginal status in Vietnam. Many Chinese-Vietnamese can trace their origins to China's Guandong province, directly north of Vietnam. Their communities were highly organized, most often on the basis of their dialect and region of origin. These regional/dialect groups include the Cantonese, Chao-Zhou, Hainanese, Fujianese, and Ha'kanese. Many Chinese-Vietnamese were self-employed, and occupational specialization often took place among various dialect groups.

Some Chinese-Vietnamese were highly assimilated to Vietnamese culture and intermarried with ethnic Vietnamese. Such a family, the Ungs, who settled in Oakland, were patriotic toward Vietnam and described their arguments with other ethnic Chinese over loyalty to their prior homeland:

Some Chinese-Vietnamese don't care about where they are, only about business and money. I say to them "What are you eating, man?"

They say "Rice."

I say "Where is it from?"

They say "Vietnam."

I say "So you are Vietnamese."

Other Chinese-Vietnamese maintained a strong Chinese identity in Vietnam and were little involved with Vietnamese language, culture, or politics. These refugees frequently created independent Chinese-Vietnamese organizations in the United States.

Following the 1978 outbreak of hostilities between Vietnam and China, the ethnic Chinese were permitted—for a sizable fee—to exit Vietnam. As a consequence, their exit experience was much the same as that of the boat people. Relying on past experience and sources of capital and goods from overseas Chinese communities, a fraction of the Chinese-Vietnamese have been able to reestablish their role as entrepreneurs in the United States. However, lacking a Western-style education and sometimes subject to discrimination from ethnic Vietnamese in the United States, as a group, their adjustment has been slower than that of the ethnic Vietnamese, and is marked by distinct patterns of education, residence, and occupational distribution.[4] The size of the Chinese-Vietnamese population in the United States, a population that is divided by political and linguistic differences and varying degrees of assimilation to Vietnamese culture, is difficult to determine. One estimate, based upon census data, suggests that approximately one-third of all Vietnamese in Southern California are of Chinese ethnicity (Tran 1986).

By the time the Vietnamese set foot on U.S. soil—only to begin their resettlement—they have been through an extensive and often traumatic series of events. However, they have only begun the work of building their lives in a new country. In the chapters that follow, I will describe how these three subgroups of Vietnamese (the elite, the boat people, and the ethnic Chinese) maintain generally distinct communities in the United States.

CHARACTERISTICS OF VIETNAMESE
IN THE UNITED STATES

Vietnamese refugees who arrived in the United States between 1975 and 1977 have made remarkable strides in adapting to life in the United States. The more recently arrived, however, have encountered greater difficulty in adjusting to the States[5] (ORR 1987). For example, a high proportion (30%) of Southeast Asians who have been in the United States at least 44 months are living below the poverty level.[6] A study of Vietnamese in San Diego found the poverty level to be twice as high, or 61% (Rumbaut 1986:Table 3).[7] Vietnamese refugees also display high rates (64%) of welfare dependency (ORR 1987:35). Only 31% of Southeast Asian refugee households in the United States are fully self-supporting (ORR 1988:140). According to one report, "Ten years after Southeast Asian refugees first entered the United States, 50% of California's 400,000 refugees, making up 43,000 families, are fully reliant on welfare" (Arax 1987:1). Because of the low level of payments provided by welfare, 64% of those Southeast Asians who rely on it live below the poverty level (Caplan et al. 1985:189).

As suggested by these high levels of poverty and welfare dependency, Vietnamese refugees have low rates of labor-force participation and high rates of unemployment (Bach and Carroll-Seguin 1987; Haines 1987). For example, in 1988, Southeast Asian labor-force participation was only 37% compared to 66% for the U.S. population as a whole; while the national unemployment rate was 7% in 1985, 17% of Southeast Asian refugees were unemployed (ORR 1988, 1989:131).[8] Downward mobility in terms of occupation is common among the Vietnamese, as it is for most immigrant groups (Lyman 1974): "Thirty percent of the employed adults sampled had held white collar jobs in their country of origin; 17.5 percent held similar jobs in the United States in 1988. Conversely, far more Southeast Asian refugees hold blue collar or service jobs in the U.S. than they did in their countries of origin" (ORR 1989:135).

These economic difficulties caused many problems for refugee families, one of which was overcrowded housing conditions. Vietnamese refugees had the largest number of occupants per housing unit of any ethnic group in San Francisco (Finnan and Cooperstein 1983:123).[9]

As a group, the Vietnamese are among the most youthful of all immigrant populations in the United States, with an average age of 26 years for all Southeast Asian refugees in the United States (ORR 1989:115). Since most of these people arrived prior to 1981 and have been in the United States for a period of 7 to 13 years, their age at arrival was extremely young. Vietnamese families are large in size (ORR 1987; Simon 1983), and many refugees that I interviewed came from families having between 9 and 12 children. The population includes a larger number of males (55%) than females (ORR 1989:114-115). The fertility of the Vietnamese in the United States is 1,785 children born per 1,000 women age 15 to 44, a figure substantially higher than that of the U.S. population, which is 1,429 children per 1,000 women age 15 to 44 (Gardner et al. 1985:17). Mean household size for Vietnamese Americans, according to a 1983 San Diego survey, was 5.5 persons (Rumbaut 1989a).

Vietnamese refugees reveal a very high level of geographical mobility and secondary migration within the United States. Only months or years after their arrival, thousands of Vietnamese left their initial locations of settlement in the South, East, and Midwest for the West Coast or Texas, where the climate was more moderate, and in the former, Asian culture was more prevalent, welfare more generous, and the economic downturns of the late 1970s and early 1980s less severely felt. For example, in fiscal 1982, 24,000 Southeast Asian refugees entered California from other states, constituting about 4% of all Southeast Asian refugees in the United States at that time. Similarly, in the same year, almost 5,000 Southeast Asian refugees left Texas, about 10% of the refugee population of that state (ORR 1982:20, A-16). By 1988, 40% of Southeast Asian refugees congregated in California. With the exception of Texas, where 7.5% of Southeast Asian refugees reside, no other state was home to more than 5% of the total Southeast Asian refugee population (ORR 1989:120).

Such statistics conceal many of the significant variations that exist within the refugee population as a result of such social factors as time of arrival, ethnicity, region of settlement, links to family or social networks, and mental and physical health. These variations will be discussed in the chapters that follow.

In conclusion, the Vietnamese refugee population is marked by social diversity in terms of class, ethnicity, background, ideological outlook, occupation, and experience of migration and resettlement. These factors, as well as their cultural orientation and the structure of opportunity they encounter in the States, shape their adaptation to the United States.

NOTES

1. However, it is interesting to note that the women refugees I interviewed were less enthusiastic about patriarchal Vietnamese family traditions than is the case among male refugees.

2. By the century's end, their numbers will be exceeded only by Filipinos and Chinese (Gardner et al. 1985:37).

3. For example, in 1980, 31% of the households of refugees who arrived in the United States in 1975 had an income of more than $21,000. In the same year, only 4.6% percent of refugees who arrived in the United States after 1978 had incomes of $21,000 or more (Nguyen and Henkin 1980:104-110).

4. Ethnic Chinese refugees experience "disadvantage . . . with respect to both acculturation and economic self sufficiency variables." (Desbarats 1986b:405; Rumbaut 1986).

5. In 1979, 41.4% of the Vietnamese refugee families in California were below the poverty line, versus 7.6% of the native born (U.S. Bureau of the Census, 1983:Table 196A).

6. Refugees who have been in the United States less than 44 months have much higher rates of poverty (Caplan et al. 1985:180-81).

7. Percentage below the poverty level by ethnic group, 1982: national average, 15%; white, 12%; black, 35.6%; Hispanic, 29.9%; Southeast Asian refugee, 30% (Caplan et al. 1985:180-181).

8. These figures may overestimate the unemployment of the Vietnamese because they are concerned with Southeast Asians, a group that includes Cambodians and Laotians. However, studies that have been specifically concerned with the Vietnamese show that they also lag significantly behind the rates for the general population.

9. The average number of occupants per housing unit is as follows: Vietnamese, 4.3; white, 1.8; black, 2.5; Hispanic, 2.8 (Finnan and Cooperstein 1983:123).

4

The Soviet Jewish Enclave

In the San Francisco Bay Area, the geographical and social center of the Soviet Jewish community is located in the Sunset and Richmond districts of San Francisco. In Los Angeles, a much larger concentration resides in Beverly-Fairfax and West Hollywood. I call these areas "Soviet Jewish enclaves,"[1] loose networks of émigrés representing a wide variety of occupations, regional origins, degrees of religious identification, and outlooks on adjustment to the United States.

Within the sizable Soviet Jewish enclave in Los Angeles, a fairly high level of "institutional completeness" exists, meaning that émigrés have established an encompassing network of businesses and other ethnic activities (Breton 1964). For example, in West Hollywood, Soviet Jews can socialize with neighbors; shop for food, clothes, real estate, securities, or appliances; see a doctor or dentist; attend religious services; take in a floor show, read a newspaper; watch cable TV; visit a local park to play dominoes; and interact with numerous acquaintances, all without speaking a word of English.

The Soviet Jewish enclave is marked by a paradoxical outlook on community. Émigrés reside near each other, share common values, and engage in frequent informal interaction. However, they also regard co-ethnics with a high level of suspicion and create very few formal organizations. Their lack of participation in formal activities is of special sociological interest because earlier-arriving Eastern European Jewish immigrants, as well as contemporary migrants with whom they share numerous similarities, are noted for high levels of ethnic organization (Collins et al. 1986; Glazer and Moynihan 1963; Gorelick 1981; Howe 1976; Kim 1981; Portes and Bach 1985; Rischin 1962; Wirth 1928).

The nature of the Soviet Jewish enclave is best understood in terms of the background and daily life of its members. The following case studies were selected from many Soviet Jewish family histories that I collected. They illustrate several of the basic social types, issues, and processes I observed within this émigré community.

CASE STUDIES

The Kushner Family

The Kushner family, consisting of a couple in their late 50s with two grown sons, arrived in the United States in the spring of 1982. They located in San Francisco because Mrs. Kushner's brother and his family had settled there in 1979. Yuzik Kushner, who worked as a sewing machine repairman in the Soviet Union, and his wife, Zenya, a former factory accountant, lived most of their lives in Kiev. Both speak Yiddish (it was Zenya's first language), as well as Ukrainian and Russian. Born soon after the revolution, they were among the last cohorts of Soviet Jews able to receive religious training. Yuzik had a bar mitzvah, and Zenya had attended a Yiddish-language Jewish school in her village before her family moved to Kiev when she was 9 years old.

As youths, both Yuzik and Zenya believed in communism and the Soviet system. Among the belongings they brought from Kiev are pre-World War II pictures of themselves with other idealistic young Jews who, in their words, were "building communism." Other souvenirs include Yuzik's military decorations earned during World War II. Yuzik saw action in the famous Battle of Stalingrad and continues to suffer from wartime injuries. Because the Ukraine was captured by the Germans, Zenya and her parents were evacuated east and spent the war in Uzbekistan. Yuzik's family, unable to escape, perished at the hands of the Nazis.

Like many older émigrés, Yuzik and Zenya complain about their ailments and make frequent visits to the doctor. Because of health problems and difficulties with English, neither works. Instead, they keep busy by shopping, attending English classes, visiting relatives and neighbors, and participating in religious activities.

While Zenya received post-secondary education, her husband did not. She is quicker than her husband to understand the details of

American life, has learned more English, and makes key family decisions. She also spends a great deal of time in the kitchen experimenting with American foods. Because Mrs. Kushner lost her job and many social contacts by coming to the United States, cooking is among the few activities that provide her with a sense of continuity with the past. One evening when the two younger Kushners and I were discussing cars (a Russian term for car is *machina*), Zenya Kushner patted her Soviet meat grinder and proclaimed, "*This* is my *machina.*"

Like many Soviet Jews, the Kushners emigrated to the United States with the hope of improving the lives of their children. Although their sons Mark (age 29) and Louis (22) were excellent students in the USSR, neither was granted admission to a university in their hometown of Kiev. Both, however, were able to attend the Institute of Railway Technology in Moscow, partially through the influence of Mrs. Kushner's brother.

Prior to their emigration, Mark and Louis studied English with the aid of a tutor and Polish-made language instruction records.

While Yuzik and Zenya Kushner hope for their sons' success, they also are aware of the loss of family togetherness that results from their children's assimilation. The accomplishments of their children immerse them ever more in a world to which the parents have little access (Rubin 1976). And while their readjustment has not been easy, the two young Kushners have made impressive accomplishments. Because Mark received training on IBM computers in the Soviet Union (acquired from the United States during the détente period of the 1970s), he found professional employment in the United States with relative ease. Nine months after his arrival, Mark was hired by the computer department of a small grocery chain. He was referred to the job by the Jewish Vocational Service of San Francisco. The grocery company was willing to give Mark a chance because his first 90 days of pay were subsidized with funds that the Mayor's Office of San Francisco had obtained from a Federal Targeted Assistance program intended to help counties burdened with large numbers of refugees.

Observing the grocery chain's poor financial condition and determining from community contacts that émigrés less skilled than himself had found positions with better pay and more responsibility, Mark continued to send out résumés. After eight months of searching, he was hired by a Bay Area municipality. Although this job was 30 miles from his family's apartment in San Francisco's Richmond District, he did not relocate. Rather, he made his workdays even longer by continuing to "moonlight" for the grocery chain in the evenings.

The reason Mark felt that he could not move closer to his new job was that his elderly parents, who knew little English and did not work, needed his care. At least in the Richmond district, they were near other émigrés. Mark's brother Louis, who was occupied with his studies at San Francisco State University and who had two part-time jobs, was unwilling to help their parents. Mark described his predicament:

> With my parents, it's not that they are just from a different country. They are from a different world. There are so many things they just don't understand. I have to take care of them. Father has problems with glaucoma, so he has to go to the hospital often. My younger brother, he won't do anything for them, so it's all on me. But I have my own life too.

Mark's work provided him with a middle-class income. He was soon able to acquire a new Toyota to make his 300-mile-a-week commute a little more tolerable. An acceptable social life, however, proved to be more elusive than financial security. Finding female companionship was especially difficult. Various dates arranged by other émigrés were disappointing and only made Mark pine for his former girlfriend, who remained in the Ukraine. He also missed the large group of friends he had left behind. While there were many young émigrés in San Francisco and Oakland, Mark considered most of them boorish and did not think they shared his interests. He occasionally complained that his occupational and economic achievements were without meaning since he had no friends with whom he could share them.

Finally, after two years in San Francisco, Mark met Marina Levy, a blonde émigré from Odessa who was eight years his junior. Within months they were married, with a child on the way. In keeping with the close family patterns that are common in the Soviet Union, the young couple moved into the apartment next to Marina's parents in a building nicknamed "The Moscow Hilton" by the émigrés who had been settled there by Jewish Family Service. Abandoning the Soviet pattern of the two-worker family, Marina remained at home with their son, while Mark provided the sole source of family income.

By the late 1980s, the entire extended family, including the young couple and both sets of in-laws, had moved to San Francisco's Sunset District, a neighborhood with a sizable Soviet émigré presence that was located on the opposite side of Golden Gate Park from where they had been initially settled. Years of saving permitted Mark's family and Marina's parents to buy homes in the city's hyperinflated housing market. The less affluent senior Kushners moved into nearby housing for the elderly.

Louis, the youngest Kushner, shared Mark's interest in electronics, but had not completed his education prior to emigration.[2] He spent his first year in the United States as a student at the Computer Training Institute, his tuition paid by refugee benefits. His aptitude impressed his instructors, and he was hired as a technician. Upon completing trade school, Louis continued his studies in electronic engineering at San Francisco State, and after graduation, found work in a Silicon Valley company.

Although both sons complained about the difficulty of getting along with and caring for their dependent parents, Mark was dutiful and cordial. Louis, still an adolescent and traumatized by their emigration, vacillated between behavioral extremes. One day, he would ridicule his family for their lack of Americanization, while the next, he would buy them gifts, brood over their problems, and search for a job for his father.

Mark's and Louis's experience was not unusual for Soviet émigrés with a technical education. Like other skilled new immigrants, they quickly adjusted to American life and enjoy a standard of living comparable to that of native-born Americans with similar credentials. Their careful preparations for exit and intact family played an important role in facilitating their smooth readjustment. However, heavy obligations to family and work, together with feelings of ambivalence toward co-ethnics and Americans alike, kept their involvement with others limited.

Mark, who has so quickly acquired commitments that are rewarding but also stifling, sometimes describes his success as almost too rapid.

In addition to the rapid adaptation of the Kushner sons, the Kushner family reveals another common pattern: the isolation and marginality of the elderly. Even within this single nuclear family, the generations have encountered dramatic differences in their adjustment to American society.

Vladimir Grossman

Whereas Mark Kushner's adjustment to the United States was quick and successful, Vladimir Grossman has a long way to go before he can equal the way of life he enjoyed in the USSR. Before entering the United States, 42-year-old Vladimir savored the privileges, travel, and responsibility commensurate with his prestigious rank of chief engineer in the oil industry. He was even able to maintain a semblance of a Jewish life—he and his wife, Eveta, met at a Moscow Synagogue.

In the United States, however, Vladimir and Eveta have been unable to find employment commensurate with their levels of skill. Mark Kushner was fortunate because his computer skills were directly applicable to the U.S. economy. However, there has been little demand for Vladimir's specialty—designing oil structures for the Siberian tundra. In addition, his 1960s-era Russian training was hopelessly outdated according to U.S. standards of the 1980s.

Status problems further complicated Vladimir's efforts to find work. In the Soviet Union, differences in wages between various occupations are much less than they are in the United States. For example, an engineer or medical doctor may make only a few more rubles each month than a factory worker. Hence prestige, rather than income, is the aspect of a job that is most significant to one's social rank. Raised under such a system, Vladimir Grossman was unwilling to abandon the occupational title with which he so strongly identified:

In Moscow, I was chief civil-structural engineer. I used to make huge monoliths—tanks for the oil industry. I was the one who signed the plans for many big projects, I was the one who gave final approval. Here, I will do the same. I will work volunteer, I will study English, but I will be chief engineer.

As a consequence of his views regarding status and prestige, he refused to consider the advice of job placement workers or the examples of émigrés who were more pragmatic about accepting available employment. Ashamed to be in such dire straits, Vladimir Grossman generally avoided other Soviet Jews.

Vladimir and his wife, Eveta, also an unemployed engineer, developed several strategies for coping with their inability to find the occupations they desired. Since coming to the United States, Eveta gave birth to a girl, who was 12 years younger than their first child.

The couple also immersed themselves in forms of Russian and Soviet culture that were prohibited in the Soviet Union; they passionately listened to records of Vysotski, the half-Jewish "Bob Dylan" of Russia. Although they were not involved with a religious congregation, they read Russian translations of various Jewish writings—mainstream texts as well as the ethnocentric tracts of Jewish separatists. Finding inspiration in Judaism but not in fellow Jews, they developed an elitist Jewish identity—one that correlated financial success with spiritual bankruptcy—in order to defend their wounded pride against the accomplishments of prosperous co-ethnics. Hence, rather than finding comfort and companionship in the Soviet Jewish community, they isolated themselves from fellow émigrés. Other Soviets, however, were not the sole targets of the Grossmans' scapegoating. Trying to feel superior, the couple often complained that "too many blacks and too many Chinese" were attending the Oakland community college where they took computer classes.

Most Soviet Jewish refugees go through a period of adjustment-related marginality like that experienced by the Grossman family. Usually, however, it lasts only a few months.

For example, Oleg Kipnis, a Soviet engineer in the same position as Grossman, also hoped to find a position equal to the one he held in Leningrad.

However, within weeks, his views changed. Confronting his situation, Oleg proclaimed, "The money, it doesn't smell," and accepted a lower status job.

Although not prestigious, this situation did allow him to support his family and get on with his life.

In contrast to Oleg's pragmatic outlook, Vladimir's resolve to find esteemed employment was only strengthened as the months passed. In the meanwhile, the couple charged their teenage son with the responsibility of being the intermediary between the entire family and the outside world. Despite their awareness that the boy had his own difficulties in adapting to the new country, both parents made clear their expectation that he would attend Stanford University.

In sum, although Vladimir Grossman possessed high levels of skill and motivation, he was unable to establish meaningful links to the culture and economy of the United States.

Instead, the two sources of identity that sustained him in the Soviet Union—profession and ethnicity—have led to his continued isolation in the United States. This pattern of nonadaptation was the experience of various middle-aged Soviet professionals. It reveals the unique challenges of immigration for those who occupied positions of skill and prestige in their native land.

Anna Gomberg

Anna Gomberg displayed a willfulness similar to that of Vladimir Grossman, but she expressed it in a more practical manner. In the United States for 10 years now, she has a rigorous daily routine.

Anna rises early six days a week in order to be at her bagel bakery by 5 in the morning. There, she minds the store and oversees the Chicano bakers who have worked under two successive owners: Anna and the Lebanese Armenian from whom she bought the business four years ago. After years of work, Gomberg looks forward to some easing of her demanding routine. Her younger daughter has just completed law school, thereby leaving Anna with a little more time and money for herself.

Anna Gomberg, her husband, and two daughters left the Soviet Union for Israel in 1975. Finding that country not to their liking, the family moved to Los Angeles after only eight months to join her brother, who had arrived earlier. While higher education and professional skill played a role in the rapid adjustment of Mark Kushner and contributed to the difficulties experienced by Vladimir Grossman, these issues were irrelevant to Anna and her husband, Arkady. Neither had attended college in the Soviet Union. The Gombergs, however, left the USSR with another resource that would ease their resettlement to the United States: money.

Unlike most Soviet émigrés who exit the Soviet Union with 90 rubles (the maximum permitted by Soviet law), the Gombergs arranged to take with them a considerable amount of capital (about $30,000). This nest egg was amassed through the sale of their possessions and from kickbacks acquired by Anna's husband, who diverted goods under his supervision to the Soviet black market.

Lacking inflated notions about the value of her skills, Anna accepted the first position offered by the Jewish Vocational Service: a job in a bakery. Initially taken as a way of making ends meet, the job provided her with experience that would later be valuable in running her own business. Anna claims that while the bagel store is not a big business, it does provide her family with a stable income and a feeling of independence. If she were younger, Anna explains, she would be more ambitious and expand her entrepreneurial activities. But since she is in her 50s, Anna feels satisfied with her current situation. The business has permitted Anna and her husband to acquire a small condo and put their daughters through UCLA and graduate school.

Although scholars have noted the importance of low-cost family labor in making immigrant businesses competitive, Soviet Jewish business owners, including the Gombergs, often eschew this potential advantage in order to shield their children from working in the store (Light 1972; Portes and Bach 1985). Soviet émigrés, entrepreneurs included, often retain the Marxist notion that private enterprise is indeed "dirty business." Consequently, they hope their children are employed in mainstream careers.

Business success did not come easily to the Gombergs. While the bakery is their third enterprise, it is the first to make a profit. Earlier, they had successively invested in two fast-food restaurants, each of which had to be sold at a loss, necessitating the couple's return to minimum-wage work. Even now, the bakery demands so much time that the couple have little leisure time. Like Vladimir Grossman, their social circle is limited to family. They participate in neither religious activities nor the informal business-owners' networks that provide social links for other Soviet immigrant entrepreneurs in Los Angeles. Anna's major concern now is that her daughters will get married. She hopes for Soviet Jews as sons-in-law because she believes they are more likely than Americans to see marriage as a serious commitment. Her daughters, she fears, do not understand this distinction.

Anna Gomberg, along with her husband, has turned persistence, savings, and business know-how into an acceptable standard of living in the United States. Running the business consumes most of their energies, leaving little time for religious, community, or leisure activities. While Anna and her husband have lived an isolated and arduous life, the couple's adult daughters, who are the recipients of their parents' efforts, have been able to grow up as middle-class Americans, a relatively rare status among migrant youth.

Discussion

Despite the broad differences in the adaptation experience of the individuals included in these case studies, certain commonalties are apparent. As middle-class immigrants, much of their fate in the

United States can be traced to resources brought from the Soviet
Union—most notably, cultural or financial capital. Further, each of
these émigrés is involved in and aware of their ethnic community.
Yet, none have formal connections to ethnic associations, religious
congregations, or other community institutions. Instead, family ties
are paramount. Finally, while the family is the basic unit of social interaction and support, generational differences in adaptation and outlook strain these families.

INTERACTION IN THE
SOVIET JEWISH ENCLAVE

As suggested in these case studies, members of the Soviet Jewish
enclave have frequent informal interactions, but they create few formal organizations. In the section that follows, general factors that account for this paradoxical approach to community are discussed.

Sources of Social Connection

Ties to family and friends were an important source of social attachment in the Soviet Jewish enclave. Established émigrés sponsored
friends and relatives who had recently arrived from the Soviet Union
or other parts of the United States. Enclave members exchanged a
great deal of information during frequent social visits. Services such
as child care and auto repair were provided by one émigré to others.
Because the recently arrived were baffled by the complexities of U.S.
economic life, refugees relied on their community to obtain information before making major decisions, such as looking for work, purchasing something expensive, or enrolling in trade school. Social
activities and the selection of mates and friends were often focused
within this collectivity. While American Jewish agencies offered resettlement services, many émigrés preferred to use informal community connections to avoid the cultural and linguistic problems inherent
in interactions with American service providers (Dorf and Katlin
1983; Gold 1987; Goldberg 1981; Merton 1949: 49; Thomas and
Znaniecki 1920).

Following the Soviet pattern, employed adult children frequently
lived with their parents. This arrangement provided parents with
translation and other essential services. However, grown children,

married or single, desired more privacy. Like Mark Kushner, they sometimes rented an apartment near that of their parents so they could pursue an independent life and still fulfill family responsibilities. Other Soviet Jewish youth coped with generational friction through patterns that émigré adolescents share with their U.S.-born peers: ignoring parents, spending little time at home, or immersing themselves in youth cultures of fashion, rock music, TV, personal computers, or homework.

An important source of social links in the Soviet Jewish enclave was the large number of aged émigrés; 48% of those who entered in 1981 were over the age of 45 (Eckles et al. 1982). Because aged émigrés do not generally become fluent in English and are much less likely than younger Soviet Jews to find employment in the United States (Simon 1985), they are dependent upon one another for a social life and upon their families for transportation, translation, and other necessities. Elderly émigrés with time on their hands met in parks, resettlement agencies, shops, apartment hallways, and synagogues. For example, Plummer Park, located in West Hollywood, was a center of communal life for Soviet Jews in Southern California. On any but the most inclement days, hundreds of elderly émigrés congregated there to visit, play cards and dominoes, or participate in English classes.

Because many aged émigrés could speak Yiddish and were knowledgeable about the Jewish religion, they socialized easily with Yiddish-speaking American Jews and were interested in attending religious services.[3] Younger émigrés, on the other hand, lacked the linguistic and religious skills that bonded their parents or grandparents with some American Jews (Orleck 1987). Because of the need of elderly émigrés to be near other Russian speakers, many families remained in the Soviet Jewish enclave rather than move to suburban areas where housing was less expensive. Hence, the presence of a large number of elderly émigrés contributed to the geographical concentration and frequency of social interaction that existed within the Soviet Jewish enclave.

Within the Soviet Jewish enclave, there was a great deal of social comparison. The successes and failures of various individuals were enumerated so that any given émigré might know where he or she stood relative to others. Because of a lack of established hierarchy within the community, those who felt they were at a disadvantage in social ranking would frequently bring into play discrediting information about apparently successful refugees in order to make their situation appear more equal. This was illustrated by the reaction of the Kushner brothers to their cousin, Sasha Waldman.

Sasha was economically successful. He had a high-paying job as a mechanical engineer, had gone on several business trips, and owned a new car and many other consumer goods. Also, Sasha spoke English almost perfectly, affecting a Western "twang" to mask his slight accent. While occasionally commenting on Sasha's accomplishments, his cousins and friends more frequently worked to neutralize these achievements by mentioning his crazy driving; how much weight he had gained; his garish taste in clothes, music, and entertainment; and his phone bill, which was bloated by calls to his girlfriend in Kiev.

This "bring him down to our level" process was common within the Soviet Jewish enclave. Comfort and reassurance were found in mentioning the faults of otherwise successful peers. For example, when émigrés experienced difficulty in finding work, they would produce a bit of solace by exchanging stories of less-educated émigrés who had found good jobs ("If that guy could do it, so can I"). Similarly, homesick young refugees would sometimes tell stories about their fellows who, despite possessing the outward characteristics of assimilation, disliked American life. In the words of Louis Kushner:

> They have been here 3 or 4 years, they have good cars, jobs, they have stereos, but they don't speak English as good as I can. They only know other Russians, they smoke pot all the time and wish they were back in Kiev.[4]

In using this "bring him down to our level" process, the Soviet Jewish enclave functioned like a family, which, in spite of wide variations in the external achievements of its members, works to maintain internal equality. Soviet Jews were interested in each other, but not always in ways conducive to the establishment of organizations.

An additional factor that served to unite the members of the Soviet Jewish enclave involved difficulties in establishing links with the native born. Initially hopeful about developing close ties with American Jews, many émigrés discovered that the cultural, linguistic, and moral gulf between themselves and the host community was difficult to cross. A survey of San Francisco's émigré community revealed that the average number of visits made by Soviet Jews to the homes of persons born in the United States was only 5.7 per year. This figure was lower than that obtained in New York, Chicago, or Boston, where Soviet Jews visited American homes twice as often: 11.6 times a year (Simon and Brooks 1983:62). A Soviet Jew who had lived in the Bay Area for 10 years commented on the difficulty of developing friendships with Americans:

> From the beginning, everybody wants to be assimilated, to get out of this ghetto and nobody wants to accept it that they are in a ghetto in the Richmond District, Sunset District. But after that, people get out and a lot of them probably didn't fill up their expectation and they had a problem socializing with American [Jews] and this is not their language. And after a while, they get back together and about 25% of the community still wanted to get out and 75% completely satisfied with what they have.

Soviet Jews' shared dislike of American values and cultural patterns provided them with a motive to turn toward co-ethnics. Conservative and authoritarian, émigrés complained about homosexuals, minority groups, graffiti, the crime rate, drug use, pornography, and the lack of discipline in schools. While retaining a fear of anti-Semitism, they nevertheless had a strong identity as whites and sometimes made disparaging comments regarding blacks and Asians. As refugees from communism, they were especially incensed by liberals (heavily represented in the American Jewish community) who opposed nuclear power, distrusted the military, and demanded lenient treatment for criminals.

Reacting to his new environment, an émigré doctor asserted that the United States has "too much freedom and too little order." Ironic perhaps for a Jewish refugee, he asserted the cultural superiority of West Germany over the United States:

> I think America must be strong. Many people at anti-nuclear demonstration. It's bad. American people not help his government, not help. I think it's too much freedom here, too much. West Germany, it's better. Not so much freedom, but order. They can go out at night on the street.

Ambivalence About Social Membership

While the Soviet Jewish enclave was united by common language, propinquity, immigration experience, networks of sponsorship, bonds among the elderly, interest in comparison, and antipathy toward

American values, it was also segmented by several factors. Feelings of distrust, individualism, and loss of status caused many émigrés to distance themselves from co-ethnics. Members of the Soviet Jewish enclave frequently described one another with indignation and questioned the moral integrity of their peers. Further, lacking ties based in the country of origin and experience in voluntary associations, émigrés found it difficult to build organizations based upon the shared factors mentioned above.

Émigrés frequently claimed that their fellows came to the United States not as religious refugees or even anti-communists, but, rather, as financially motivated immigrants. A mathematician from Leningrad commented:

> If they tell you about religion, don't believe them. Russian Jews don't know anything about religion. They just came over here because they heard that it is easy to get a car. None of them attend synagogue.

Reflecting their ambivalence toward co-ethnics, feelings of embarrassment and revulsion were common in émigrés' descriptions of community events. One man went so far as to claim that he avoided speaking Russian in public, lest he be associated with other émigrés. An unemployed engineer cast dispersions on his co-ethnics as he described the behavior of Soviet Jews at the showing of a sold-out Russian movie in San Francisco:

> The movie was sold out, so some people try to crash the door, pushing and shoving. I was disgusted. I went to a parade on Market Street, 300,000 Americans, the people get along fine, everyone happy and smiling. But only a few hundred of Russians get together at a movie and everyone is fighting already.

Sometimes the Soviet Jews' resistance to organization was so strong that it split even a single family. For example, while Alex Jugasvilli and his father were outside protesting a Soviet muscian's concert, Alex's mother sat inside and listened to the performance.

Unlike earlier immigrants to the United States who were forced to band together for reasons of survival (Bonacich and Modell 1980; Cohen 1969; Howe 1976; Light 1972; Okely 1979; Wirth 1928), Soviet Jews have access to an efficient battery of resettlement services (Eckles et al. 1982; Gold 1987; ORR 1984). Many such services were specifically intended to establish links between Soviet Jewish individuals and established American Jewish institutions and communities. Consequently, they may hinder the development of émigré self-help activities (Goldberg 1981; Schiff 1980; Schwartz 1980).

As noted by Gitelman (1978), despite their common language and religion, Soviet Jews come from diverse occupational, regional, and cultural origins in the USSR. As a result, many had little interest in or attachment to the mass of Soviet Jews in the United States. Further, because Soviet Jews frequently lost prestigious social ranks in coming to the United States, like Vladimir Grossman, many felt ashamed when confronting their countrymen. Several complained that being associated with a mass of uncouth émigrés with whom they had no connection in the USSR was unnatural and humiliating. An insurance salesman described his ambivalence toward other Soviet Jews:

> Here in America, there are too many levels and they mix up. You know in Russia, I was highly educated. I had highly educated friends. I never used to be in the company of haircutters . . . It wasn't because I didn't like them. They just weren't to my level. Now we are all together. You see it different times at this table: who drives the taxi and who makes manicure, a lot of different people. The life mix[es] all kind of people, so you can't stay alone. You can't stay from them.

Regionalism was another source of disunity among Soviet Jews in the United States. Generally, émigrés from the Russian Republic (Moscow and Leningrad) considered themselves superior to those from the Ukraine. Further, among immigrants with Ukrainian origins, those from Kiev often denigrated Odessans. In interviews, Soviet Jews from Moscow, Leningrad, and Latvia asserted that Ukrainian Jews were boorish, uncouth, and nouveau riche. Even those who held high academic degrees were denied distinction as "real intellectuals" by Russian Republic émigrés, who insinuated that the Ukrainians' Ph.D.s were obtained through political connections rather than scholarship.

In the following quote, an accomplished chemical engineer described the irony of losing his prestige as a Muscovite among the "common" Odessan émigrés of San Francisco: "The problem in my daughter too. Everyday she meet her friends from Odessa. And she begins to speak like Odessa with accent. I am mad about it. It's Odessa language, Odessa language. It's wrong Russian," he said and then laughed. Another Muscovite described Ukrainian Jews as "enfants terribles" who achieved success in the United States because of their simple and aggressive nature:

> By the way, for Odessa [man] to live here is easier than for Moscow. Because they are more aggressive. All business people here is Odessa people. He is aggressive, not so shy, so sensitive, like Muscovite.

One result of the ambivalence that Soviet Jews held for one another was the relatively small number of self-help organizations in Soviet Jewish communities. Oleg Kipnis exemplified the individualistic approach toward the ethnic community: "I am not too interested in other Russian Jews. I decided to come here myself, I came here myself and now I must adjust by myself, as must each of us."

In response to my queries about the lack of organizations within their community, Soviet émigrés offered a paradoxical answer. They were both sick of imposed cooperative activities and, at the same time, unfamiliar with freely organized voluntary associations. Émigrés described their resistance to formal organizations as a reaction against the compulsory collectivism that was an ubiquitous aspect of Soviet life. An X-ray therapist explained the resistance of Soviet Jews to cooperative activities:

> Russian Jewish for generations were under the pressure of communism and they are tired of the different organizations. Because organization is an obligation. To be in this organization, you should be in it and do something. And they [Soviet Jews] don't wanna, because from generation to generation they were under pressure. Here, Russian Jewish, they want to be free from actual everything. Free from all organization, because there is no freedom in Russia this way.

Despite the pervasive collectivism of Soviet life, these ever-present consortia were sanctioned, controlled, and monitored by the Communist party. As a result, Soviet Jews had no experience in creating their own associations. An émigré activist who was frustrated by her community's inability to create a viable association reflected on this problem:

> We got together and decided to form an organization. But then, very soon, it kind of split up. Everyone had their own opinion. I feel that a separate group for immigrants would be productive, but right now we don't have so many

interested people who would like to form [one]. Because, you know it's very difficult. You try to get together, you have 20 people and 20 opinions, and no one is really trained to compromise, so it is difficult.

In sum, émigrés explained that they do not create associations because they have been exposed to an excessively collectivized life, yet simultaneously assert that they have no experience with voluntary organizations. It seems ironic that the Soviet Union—a nation that has so strongly emphasized the value of communalism—should build into its citizens such an individualistic approach to life, especially when these émigrés are Jews, a twice-migrant ethnic group generally noted for their high levels of solidarity and organization.

A final reason as to why Soviet Jews do not create formal organizations in the United States is that their numbers include few leaders whose status was carried over from the country of origin. Immigrant and refugee populations generally feature highly regarded figures whose premigration reputation can consolidate their communities. However, for Soviet Jews, most indicators of prestige within the Soviet Union, such as Communist party membership, are considered undesirable characteristics in the United States because they suggest complicity with the discredited Soviet regime. Even the generally respected émigré rabbis of the Chabad-Russian movement (see Chapter 8) were denigrated as "self-interested businessmen" by various members of the enclave. As a consequence, Soviet Jewish leaders and activists had to establish their reputation solely in the American setting.

In summary, then, the Soviet Jewish enclave was characterized by physical closeness and frequent informal interaction. It was strong in terms of institutional completeness—its diverse activities allowed non-English-speaking émigrés to have active lives. At the same time, however, its members expressed ambivalence about their connections with one another due to their diverse origins and anxiety over lost status. Finally, their paradoxical experience with Soviet organizational life made many regard collectivism as both coercive and alien.

PATTERNS OF FAMILY INTERACTION

With formal organizations receiving little emphasis in the Soviet Jewish enclave, the family became the chief unit of immigrant collectivism. As discussed in Chapter 2, the Russian Jewish family has adapted over the centuries to provide its members with support, comfort, and motivation in a hostile environment. This pattern continues among émigré families in the United States.

Through extended families, refugees obtained a variety of resources from their initial sponsorship in the United States (ORR 1987) to the necessities of daily life, to job referrals and the investment capital required to open small businesses (Gold 1989; Simon 1985). Soviet Jewish families provided assistance and advice to relatives recently arrived from Israel, Europe, and other parts of North America. Through this family-based exchange of information, support, and resources, some of the social, economic, and psychological trauma of the immigration experience was eased. Concurrently, the stability provided by this exchange allowed refugee parents to fulfill some of their traditional responsibilities and hence offered the families continuity that might be unobtainable otherwise. Nevertheless, as is the case among all immigrant groups, problems of family adaptation were major concerns for members of the Soviet Jewish enclave.

Many problems of family adjustment stem from the drastically different values of the United States and the USSR concerning individuality and autonomy. While American families greatly value autonomous functioning (Bellah et al. 1985), both the Russian family and Soviet society encourage a more collective, mutually dependant approach to social life (Hulewat 1981; Cunningham and Dorf 1979).

> The Soviet family structure, which is characterized by family involvement, lack of autonomous functioning, difficulty in managing ambivalent feelings, intolerance of differences, and a manipulative attitude toward authority can become maladaptive in [the] American system where autonomy and competitiveness are highly valued. (Fruchtbaum and Skager 1989:6)

The problems émigré families face include the dependency of the young and old, status loss, and generational differences in adaptation.

Dependent Youth

In the Soviet Union, parents tend to be highly involved in the lives of their children. The peer group, a central force in the socialization of American adolescents, has relatively little influence in the USSR. This is especially true among Jewish families because parents feel their efforts are necessary to shield children from anti-Semitism and to ensure chances for success. Carried over to the United States, this desire to protect children may foster excessive dependence and prevent them from dealing with American life on their own terms (Aronowitz 1984; Hulewat 1981). A Soviet Jew active in her community described problems faced by Soviet émigré adolescents and the overprotective reactions of the parents:

> You know, in Russia how it is so difficult for Jewish kids to go to university. I don't think it's easier here right now. The problem with the kids right now is that we have a lot of dropouts.
>
> Some of the families are kind of supporting these dropouts because the schools here are terrible. And some of our kids cannot get into the good program because they have a problem with language. They can hardly get into the gifted program or at least the above average program so they are stuck with the mentally retarded program.
>
> And parents decide that it's better off that they not go to school. I know some of the families where the kids drop out of school and are working with the family business. And the parents decide if the kids want to get high school diploma, they will go to City College at night.
>
> They are not satisfied with the public education, and they cannot afford anything else, so they say—"don't bother with school, come to work with us."

A resettlement worker observed that many Soviet Jewish adolescents lack a life of their own:

> I have seen such cases of depressing loneliness in a 20-year-old boy or girl. It is easy if they live on the campus—that's a real chance to meet people. But many don't do it. They come and go to City College or a business school for a year.
>
> Then they go to work and they live with their parents. If they don't have friends among other immigrants, it's unbelievable.
>
> I know this one 22-year-old. She's beautiful, she's subtle. I think you would say she is a very intelligent young girl. She spends most of her time at work and then she spends time with her family. There is no outlet to go out because she doesn't know how to.

For some Soviet Jewish children, especially daughters, even adulthood does not offer an opportunity for an independent existence:

My parents don't understand that I am an American now. Nobody lives
with their parents after marriage. I want to have my own life.

Mother is constantly talking about living together in the future. I try to
explain to her it's impossible. (Fruchtbaum and Skager 1989:14).

The above quotes demonstrate that although strong ties yield benefits for émigré families, they also impose restrictions on émigré children and hinder their autonomous functioning.

Dependent Elderly

On the whole, migrating populations are characterized by their
youth (Simon 1986). In contrast, there are elderly individuals in many
Soviet Jewish families. Refugee families experienced problems because the elderly had difficulties learning English, finding employment, and making their way in the United States. Families who had
successfully adapted to American life expressed concern over the isolation of their elderly relatives:

My mother is upset that she can't communicate with the kids and they
are upset that she is forcing them to talk Russian because she couldn't do
anything else. I have to translate at the dinner table when everyone talks
in English and she says "my own grandchildren, and I can't even talk to
them. Maybe I made a mistake when I came here. . . . "

Back home, she was a doctor, she had a career. Here she is just another
old woman who doesn't know English and she is not ready for this role
at all. And nobody really needs her right now.

Another important factor in the development of conflict between
the dependent aged and their families had to do with the relevance of
parental advice. Parents and children alike recognized that the
parents' experience of growing up in the Soviet Union provided few
insights into the problems of children who were living in California
(Eisenstadt 1956; Fruchtbaum and Skager 1989). This problem was
most severe among those families that featured dependent parents,
since their knowledge of and experience with American society was
so limited. Precisely because the parents' attempts to find work and
adjust to life in the United States had been unsuccessful, their advice

was rejected by children. A woman who had been a concert pianist in Odessa described this experience:

> Here I am free but I am still trapped because I lost my friends, lost my position, I lost my social status. You know it's a very difficult question. And another thing, kids grow up and they are different. You cannot share with them your experience. Because, a lot of people forgot what it was like when they were 15, but another side, they forgot even that when they were 15 they were in another society.
>
> I cannot tell my daughter "when I was 15" because she says "when you were 15, you were in Russia." It's not only generation gap, it's a gap of different culture.

Although generational conflicts like those described above are observable among all immigrant families (Eisenstadt 1956; Sluzki 1979), such problems are aggravated among such highly skilled groups as the Soviet Jews. The unprecedented ability of certain émigrés such as Mark and Louis Kushner to adjust rapidly to the United States, while their parents remain dependent and isolated, makes for vast gaps in the levels of adjustment that exist within a single immigrant family.

In sum, despite their high levels of skill and relatively rapid economic integration, families of the Soviet Jewish enclave faced problems in adjusting to American society. In turn, these obstacles often yielded differential adjustment to American life between family members and within the enclave as a whole. While certain émigrés used their skills, education, and resources to "make it" in American society, others (the aged, the young, those who were less skilled or had untransferable skills, and those who were less flexible) found adjustment much more difficult. Precisely because many Soviet Jews did adjust rapidly, the difficulties encountered by others were worsened because they were regarded as the result of personal failure.

THE SOVIET JEWISH ENCLAVE: A SUMMARY

The lives of members of the Soviet Jewish enclave were marked with ambivalence. The following joke, told to me by an émigré, revealed such a position:

A Jew receives permission to leave the Soviet Union. On his way to Israel, as he waits for his papers to be processed, he lives in Paris for several weeks. He migrates to Israel. After living there for 3 years, he
decides it's not for him.

On his way back to Moscow, he again stays in Paris. When he finally
arrives in the USSR, he is summoned to the office of a Soviet official.

"Well, Comrade Bernstein," says the official, "Now that you are back,
decide where you want to live, Russia or Israel."

Bernstein's plaintive reply: "Maybe Paris?"

Like the man in the joke, many members of the Soviet Jewish enclave were seeking a sense of belonging that they have not as yet
found. While these émigrés interacted, they described each other in
negative terms. They were informally close but lacked the desire or
ability to form organizations.

Their resistance to organization notwithstanding, members of the
Soviet Jewish enclave did maintain many of the cooperative and self-
help activities traditional to immigrant groups (Lyman 1974; Wirth
1928). For example, networks of family and friends pooled resources
and exchanged information, thereby providing information, resources,
and a social life that were otherwise unattainable.

Despite the frequency and intensity of intra-group interaction, few
collectivities were formalized. In the chapters that follow, I shall describe Soviet Jewish refugees who have overcome this resistance to
organization. However, the Soviet Jewish enclave appears to be the
model of community for the majority of California's Soviet Jews.
Most obtained jobs and resettlement services through informal contacts or native institutions. Accordingly, these Soviets articulated few
reasons to create mobilized communities. For them, informal social
activities and consumption were the dominant forms of association.

In emphasizing informal and consumption-based communities, the
behavior of these recent immigrants approaches that of certain native-
born Americans. Consequently, it is not surprising that many of
Southern California's most visible immigrant institutions, the Soviet
Jews' included, take the form of the cultural, economic, and social ar-
chetype of American suburbia: the shopping mall.

In recent years, the sociological literature has encouraged scholars
to look for highly organized ethnic communities. While many important community organizations do exist, we cannot assume that immigrant

populations either naturally or easily form such bodies. The case of the Soviet Jewish enclave shows that while an ethnic group may share commonalties of culture, ideology, ecological concentration, and even frequent interaction, these collective features do not directly yield stable ethnic organizations. Further, as will be described in Chapter 8, such organizations that do exist are only created through the extensive efforts of activists. Finally, it is important to remember that the Soviet Jewish community is a recently established one. Perhaps the nature of community will change as this population spends more time in the United States.

NOTES

1. In using the word *enclave,* I merely wish to describe a geographic concentration of Soviet Jews and do not suggest that they engage in the specific entrepreneurial activities that Portes denotes with this term.

2. The occupational patterns of Soviet Jews bear striking similarities to those of Asians in the United States. Because both groups excel in school but are regarded as social outsiders by members of the dominant social group, they are heavily concentrated in technical specialties. By concentrating in such nonpolitical occupations, they are able to avoid being tested against criteria of "ideological purity" that often disqualify minorities from visible positions of leadership and advocacy (Brym 1985).

3. Yiddish-based connections to American Jews were much more important in Los Angeles, home to a sizable and highly concentrated Jewish community, than in the San Francisco Bay Area, where a much smaller and more assimilated Jewish population lacks a specific ecological base.

4. Vietnamese recent arrivals displayed a similar pattern of cheapening the accomplishments of more successful refugees by claiming that in achieving upward mobility, such individuals had "lost their roots."

Unlike other immigrant populations, Soviet Jewish families in the United States are comprised of many elderly persons, especially women, such as those shown here who are working on their English with an émigré language instructor in West Hollywood's Plummer Park.

I met Oleg and Azary, Soviet Jewish émigrés, at a job-finding class at the Oakland Jewish Community Center. Engineers in the USSR, their prospects for finding comparable work in the United States were slim.

The recently educated children of Soviet Jewish families rapidly adapt to the culture and economy of the United States. Two years after arriving in San Francisco, the older son of the family at left has acquired professional employment and started a family of his own. His parents, however, have learned little English and remain dependent on the ethnic community. His wife's younger parents (above) have been able to find work in the United States. Despite these differential patterns of adjustment, Soviet Jewish families remain quite close in the United States.

Although Soviet Jews create few formal organizations, they enjoy interacting with each other. These émigrés are shown dancing to the sounds of a Russian rock band at a wedding in an Oakland synagogue.

A broadcaster in the USSR, Sarge Levin now runs a Russian cable TV program in Los Angeles. Ethnic media build community integration and economic expansion among Soviet Jews.

Along with her husband, this woman from Kiev runs a work clothing store in Los Angeles. She obtains damaged Levis, and with the aid of a Chicana seamstress, repairs them for resale. Like this entrepreneur, many refugee business people hire Latino workers rather than members of their own group.

After being laid off by a major U.S. company, this Odessa-born engineer (at left) purchased an auto repair company and hired immigrants from Moscow and Afghanistan as mechanics.

The religious needs of elderly émigrés in Los Angeles are filled by the Chabad-Russian outreach program, which provides two storefront synagogues with Soviet-born rabbis. Rabbi Estulin is shown here giving a lecture to a group of émigrés.

Elderly Soviet Jews are shown engaged in morning prayers.

This Soviet émigré couple rapidly found professional employment in the United States. The husband has become involved in several community activities in the San Francisco Bay Area.

A Soviet cardiologist, Svetlana Siegel has a practice on Wilshire Boulevard in Los Angeles. Seeking fellowship and continuing medical education, she helped form a Russian doctors and dentists association.

5

Recently Arrived Vietnamese

The Vietnamese community in the United States is much larger and more diverse than that of the Soviet Jews. As noted in Chapter 3, it actually consists of three overlapping groups: the 1975 elite, the boat people, and the ethnic Chinese. In this chapter, I concentrate on a network of boat people of both Vietnamese and Chinese-Vietnamese ethnicity, who entered the United States between 1979 and 1982.

Despite the differences that exist between them and the Soviets, Vietnamese refugees have to solve many of the same problems encountered by the Soviet Jews, and they exhibit patterns of family and community adaptation similar to those which I observed among the Soviets. As in the case of Chapter 4 on the Soviet Jewish enclave in which I presented case studies, I will now introduce the reader to the Vietnamese refugees' experience through case studies. These are drawn from Oakland, California, where I did my most intensive field-work with recently arrived Vietnamese.

CASE STUDIES

The Ung Family

The Ung family lives in a 60-year-old apartment building, occupied by many Southeast Asians, in downtown Oakland, an area that has a high concentration of Southeast Asians as well. In their two rooms live five persons. Three are siblings: Luc, a 24-year-old male; Duc, his 22-year-old brother; and Linh, a girl of high school age. The other two residents are Quy Pham, a second cousin of the Ungs, and Ven Vuong, a young male from Quy's village.

Although the apartment's furnishings are few, they offer clues about the way of life of its occupants. The most prominent object in the room, and the only piece of furniture not purchased secondhand, is a 25-inch Magnavox television. By watching this set, the apartment's occupants learn about American society and sharpen their English proficiency. Connecting a video cassette player to the TV allows the family to supplement their viewing of network programs with Chinese- and Vietnamese-language movies.

The TV is a feature common to any American living room, but other objects in the apartment suggest the links of its occupants to their country of origin. One such object is a small religious shrine. It displays fruit, incense, and a photograph of the Ungs's father, who died since their exit from Vietnam. Placed on the TV is a lacquer and mother-of-pearl fishing scene, sent to the Ungs by their mother. Scattered around the room are Vietnamese books and magazines. Several are adventure novels borrowed from the Oakland Public Library's foreign-language holdings. In the tiny kitchen are a variety of Asian foods and the utensils required for their preparation. On the wall is a calendar advertising a Chinese bank in San Francisco. In the other room are pinups of Hong Kong movie stars.

Ample evidence indicates the difficult financial position of these refugees. Their few chairs and lamps are secondhand, purchased from the nearby Salvation Army. A worn mattress stands against the wall, making room for daytime activities. Each night, family members put aside the folding table and arrange their bedding to make room for sleeping. Since four males rest in this room, leaving the other room for Linh, the household's lone female, they try to use each square foot of space. Also visible are new clothing, fabric, and hardware they will send to relatives still in Vietnam. Showing me the packages, Luc explains, "For me, used clothes, but to send home, always new ones." The financial drain created by the efforts of refugees to support relatives overseas is one reason why they live in such cramped and barren circumstances in the United States.

A final set of objects in the apartment suggests the Ung family's intellectual and organizational competence. In neat folders, Luc Ung has filed the documents that function as the passports and guide maps of modern Vietnamese refugees: Vietnam identity card, visas, health certificate, official correspondence, and the sponsorship application for a brother who is in a Hong Kong refugee camp. Luc has also filed the family's collection of documents pertaining to American matters: welfare and Medi-Cal (a state-funded health care program) forms, unemployment papers, check stubs and business cards from various employers, rent receipts, and the certificate of ownership for Duc's 1972 Datsun. With pride and nostalgia, Luc displayed a book filled with notes his father had made during his training in Chinese medicine. Supplementing this is a three-foot-long acupuncture mannequin, acupuncture needles, and several manuals his brother sent from Hong Kong. On the wall hangs a clipboard, on which the occupants record their household expenses (phone, food, and utilities). In this manner, the costs and contributions attributable to each individual are kept in order.

Laid on a pressed wood bureau in the other room are the books, papers, Vietnamese/English dictionary, and Radio Shack circuit boards that the student members of the household use in their classes. Linh attends Oakland Technical High School, and Luc is working toward his Associate degree in electronics at a nearby community college.

The physical closeness of this dwelling conceals the diversity of its occupants as well as the circuitous routes they took to arrive in Oakland. Quy Pham was the first to enter the United States. A 12-year veteran of the South Vietnamese navy, he was an official enemy to the new administration of his country. While Quy was anxious to flee, his wife was not willing to leave with him. She and the couple's young son remained with her family in Vietnam, leaving Quy with the combined feelings of sadness and bitterness that are the baggage of many refugees.

After a stay in a Malaysian refugee camp, Quy arrived in San Jose in 1980, where he worked in a variety of electronic industry jobs until moving to Oakland in 1982. Quy invited the Ung family, originally settled in Ohio, to join him in early 1982 and sponsored Ven Vuong's arrival to the United States later that year. Quy Pham is currently employed as a driver for a messenger company. He works the night shift, distributing paperwork for a variety of companies.

Two years after Quy Pham arrived in Oakland, the three members of the Ung family, originally from Saigon, joined him. Their father, who migrated from Canton, China, to Vietnam in the 1930s, was a successful practitioner of Chinese medicine and ran an herbalist shop in Saigon. During the 1960s, the family became affluent. They lived in a large house, where Quy Pham had been a frequent visitor. The family's nine children, including the three now in the United States, attended a Chinese school. Both Luc and Duc graduated prior to 1975. When the war broke out between Vietnam and China in 1978, the ethnic Chinese, including the Ungs, became subjected to increasing harassment from local cadres. With their family providing the funds needed to buy their exit, the three Ungs fled Vietnam. After eight months in a refugee camp, Luc, Duc, and Linh were resettled in a suburb of Cincinnati. Although both brothers found the best jobs they have had there, they disliked the cold weather and sense of isolation in a part of the country where there were few Vietnamese. In less than a year, they moved to Oakland to join Quy Pham.

Duc Ung soon found a job as a janitor for a computer company. He was pleased to be employed by a large firm that offered health benefits.[1] For several months, times were good. Luc, as the oldest member of the family in the United States, maintained the serious outlook appropriate to his role as head of the household. His younger brother, Duc Ung, however, felt free to explore American life. With his earnings, he soon acquired a TV set, an electric guitar, and a car. The members of the household experimented with American foods and entertainment, and visited Stinson Beach, Los Angeles, and Reno. Prosperity, however, was short-lived. After the downturn in the U.S. economy in the early 1980s, Duc was laid off and had a great deal of difficulty finding another job. Like Quy Pham, he had to accept work as a driver, delivering newspapers in the predawn hours.

The final member of the Ung household is Ven Vuong, 20, the younger brother of Quy Pham's best friend in Vietnam. Arriving in Oakland in May 1982, Ven, the son of village shop owners, worked diligently at learning English and job-related skills, saying, "I want to get my future started."

Monday through Friday, the members of the Ung household were busy with jobs or school. Conflicting schedules allowed little time for togetherness. Weekends, however, were more relaxed. Quy—who learned to be a skillful cook during his navy years—prepared meals and invited friends to share them. Like many recently arrived Vietnamese, the members of the Ung household were generous and had to be careful not to exceed their limited budget by treating friends to food and drink at many of the Vietnamese coffee shops and restaurants in the neighborhood. Luc pointed out that it was easy to spend too much, since many Vietnamese restaurateurs offer their customers credit.

In summary, the Ung household consisted of a non-nuclear extended family. Its members were of disparate ages and backgrounds, and were resettled in the United States at different times and in different places. While the three Ung siblings were Chinese-Vietnamese, their cousin, Quy Pham, had only distant connections to his Chinese ancestry, and his service in the Vietnamese navy implied a high level of connection to and identification with the Vietnamese nationality. The youngest family member, Ven Vuong, was Vietnamese. Despite broad differences in their backgrounds, members of this household experienced common difficulties in adjustment. They attempted to address these by pooling the limited resources at their disposal.

The Doan Family

Not far from the Ungs lived the Doan family. The members of these two households experienced a common flight from Vietnam and resettlement to the United States. They have similar levels of pre-migration education and even know one another. However, the Doan family has made greater progress in adapting to the United States and, as a consequence, enjoys a better standard of living. Their relatively successful adjustment was especially notable on the wedding day of Thanh's younger sister, Thuy.

In the four months preceding the wedding of Thuy Doan and Nam Van Nguyen, the Doan family, which had been in the United States for three years, opened a restaurant, moved to a larger, rent-subsidized apartment, and saw the birth of its second child. Consequently, the wedding added to the family's list of accomplishments and, at the same time, offered an opportunity for their celebration in the company of relatives and friends.

The social group primarily responsible for the day's events was the members of the Doan household. Like the Ung family, it contained several siblings and more distant relatives. In contrast to the Ungs, however, it featured an intact nuclear family: Thanh Doan, his wife, and their two daughters, Minh, age seven, and Lucy, two months. In addition, it included Thanh's younger brother, his younger sister Thuy (the bride), and Thuy's husband-to-be, Nam.

These refugees shared a common apartment. However, following Vietnamese custom, other relatives who did not live with them were also considered important family members (Haines et al. 1981; Nguyen and Henkin 1984). Thanh felt especially close to a younger brother who resided 40 miles away in San Jose, and his parents and other siblings who remained in Vietnam. Even connections to his older brother, Tao, who died as an infant, were constantly remembered. A portrait of the long-dead sibling was prominently displayed on the family's household shrine.

In turn, other relatives who lived throughout the San Francisco Bay Area demonstrated their responsibility to the family by aiding Thanh Doan. Despite their own financial limitations and difficulties with life in a new country, they have provided much of the economic support that has underwritten the Doan family's recent accomplishments. Thanh, his wife, and his sister all found employment in an aunt's restaurant. Although the family disliked the long hours and subminimum wages provided by their relatives and resented obligations that made them unable to accept better paying employment even when it was offered, they obtained a variety of benefits from this arrangement as well. For example, their aunt provided gifts to Thanh's family, including food and clothing for the children. Also, members of the family were allowed to work odd and sporadic hours, permitting them to participate in other activities. Finally, the aunt's family furnished Thanh with the capital and know-how needed to open his restaurant.

While family-based resources played an important role in facilitating the Doans' resettlement, benefits and services offered by government and resettlement agencies were also vital to their survival in the States. The Doans collected refugee cash assistance (RCA) during their first 18 months in the United States and, because of their children, continued to receive AFDC after their initial eligibility for RCA expired. Several members of the household had taken classes and accepted job referrals offered through Oakland's Asian-Multi Services, a community-based social agency. Their elder daughter, Minh, attended a day-care center, which freed her parents to work and attend classes. This center also provided the girl with lunch and English-language instruction. The family made good use of publicly funded medical and dental services, and obtained a rent-subsidized apartment through Oakland's public housing program.

The Wedding Day

When I entered the Doans's apartment on the wedding day in April 1984, many guests had already arrived. In dressy attire, the adults visited in the living room, passing the time over conversation and appetizers. Thanh Doan and the bridegroom, Nam, wore tuxedos. Unlike native-born Americans who might rent formal attire, Thanh, having entered the country penniless, took pride in being able to purchase these garments. Nam had no family members in the United States and had resided in the Doan household for a long period before the wedding. Thanh, as head of the household and older brother of the bride, occupied the role of father and father-in-law to Nam as well as his natural role of brother-in-law.

Although I had met many of those assembled on earlier visits with the Doans, I did not know all of those present. I soon discovered that unlike the Doans, who had arrived in the States since 1979, many of the guests had entered the United States immediately after the collapse of South Vietnam in 1975. While Thanh Doan had mentioned his well-settled relatives in the two years I had known him (often with ambivalence, since his relationships with them implied dependency that he disliked), this was the first time I met them.

Among the relatives who assembled for the wedding were a couple in their 70s. The man was dressed in Western attire and the woman in traditional garb, her teeth blackened by betel. There are few Vietnamese much over the age of 50 in the United States (ORR 1989; Rumbaut 1989b). However, because the Vietnamese hold great respect for the aged, the presence of this couple, who left Vietnam by air in 1975, gave the gathering a feeling of completeness seldom found within a population suffering so greatly from broken families.

Another couple, the Trans, stood out because of their high degree of assimilation. Attired in impeccable business suits, driving a new Honda, and professionally employed in Silicon Valley, their way of life had more in common with that of middle-class Americans than their recently arrived relatives. They doted over their five-year-old son Stevie, who was upset by a minor fender-bender the family had had on the way to the wedding. The interactions between this family and their only child contrasted dramatically with the autonomy that the Doans allowed their daughter Minh, a puckish 7-year-old who spent her infancy in a Malaysian refugee camp, and now enjoyed the privileged status of the rare youngster among an extended family of adults.

The wedding ceremony itself, which lasted only 10 minutes, seemed to arouse few emotions. These were reserved for the reception that followed. Doan Thanh, the older brother of the bride, head of the household, and organizer of the day's events, appeared to derive a special sense of satisfaction by fulfilling traditional obligations to his family. When the ceremony was complete, the bride retreated into a rear bedroom in order to trade her American-style wedding dress and veil for a Vietnamese *Aó Dài* and *Khan Dong* (crown-like hat). This was the second of three changes of clothing she made during her wedding day. At this time, the wedding party began to leave for the reception.

As we left the apartment, several black teenagers in the hallways and street looked up, noting with some curiosity the group of formally attired Vietnamese filing out of the apartment. These neighbors were a source of concern to the Doan family. While their new apartment was larger and less expensive than the one they had previously occupied in the area of downtown Oakland where most of the city's Vietnamese reside, it was situated in a mostly black neighborhood that was without refugee shops and institutions. The members of the Doan family, especially the females, had learned to be wary of what they termed "the black man." For example, both Thanh's wife and sister described being threatened by blacks while walking near their old building. Because the refugees felt so outnumbered here, their apprehension was great.

The couple's wedding attire and ride to the reception in a white Buick paid credence to the customs of the United States. The reception, however, was more consistent with Vietnamese conventions. As is common among the Vietnamese, the banquet was held in a Chinese-Vietnamese restaurant—this one located on the edge of Oakland's Chinatown. At significant expense, Thanh Doan rented the entire establishment for the evening. Each table was served a seven-course Chinese feast and amply supplied with large bottles of Orange Crush, 7-Up, and Hennessy cognac.

The wedding ceremony was limited to family and close friends (I was the only U.S.-born adult present). However, the reception included an array of guests, revealing the wide range of connections the Doan family had made in the United States. The largest group in attendance were young and middle-aged Vietnamese, especially the young males who account for a disproportionately large part of the refugee community. Some of the young men were in what Thanh and his friends called "disco style" attire. Like Latino and Filipino youth in the Bay Area, they wore shoulder-length, permed hair; baggy, pleated pants; and short, loose-fitting jackets. Another group of guests were dressed in a more conservative style. Their hair was shorter, and they showed a preference for tweed and Italian footwear. The most adept proponents of this style were called "GQ" (after the fashion magazine). Identifying with middle-class Americans, they intentionally separated themselves from the streetwise posture favored by the "disco" types.

In addition to the young Vietnamese, a few young blacks (Thanh's brother's coworkers at an Oakland mattress factory) were at the reception. Also present were resettlement agency staff the Doans had befriended, including a Caucasian couple in their early 20s and Mrs. Pham Van Minh, the director of an Oakland refugee center that provided Minh Doan's day care. During the reception, connections among all of those assembled were honored through a variety of rituals: a silk scarf was signed by all those in attendance, testimonials and toasts were made by family and friends, group portraits were taken, gifts were offered to the couple, guests were thanked, and cake was distributed.

The mixture of events, artifacts, and guests at the wedding ceremony and reception attest to the wide range of connections the Doan family had made during its less than 4 years in the United States. In addition to the "boat people" and 1975 refugees who attended the wedding ceremony, there were working-class Americans, representatives of the refugee resettlement system, and myself. In mobilizing and uniting this array of allies and displaying wide cultural competence, Thanh Doan revealed an impressive network that provides practical and symbolic connections in his new country. Coming from a society that emphasizes the importance of affiliation and loyalty, Thanh Doan has marshaled a significant group of friends in a short time.

The presence of these guests provided Thanh Doan with evidence that he has made major progress in using American society as a vehicle for satisfying his own needs. Through this display, he had made a statement about his own position. No longer "greenhorns," the Doan family had "arrived" in America. They were now able to accomplish desired goals and live in a manner that was acceptable to both natives and Vietnamese alike.

Discussion

This description of the Ung and Doan families reveals many of the central issues in the lives of Vietnamese boat people in the United States. Each family must deal with economic difficulties and broken family status. Each has confronted obstacles in adapting to American life and learning the English language. Despite their consistent efforts, few of these refugees have found stable, good quality jobs in the larger economy. To cope with social and economic problems, each household relied on resettlement services, mutual aid, family links, and connections to the refugee community. The mobility of the Doan family was, to a great extent, the result of their extended family, which provided access to a larger and more affluent network than that available to the Ungs. While the Ung family had little recourse when faced with the lack of job opportunities in the larger economy, the Doan family was able to turn to relatives, who supplied both the capital and the know-how required by the Doans to create their own jobs through self-employment.

Interestingly, Thanh Doan and his family were able to achieve an impressive degree of upward mobility (at least for recent refugees) with only rudimentary skills in English and a minimal knowledge of U.S. legal, financial, and institutional arrangements. Through field-work interactions, I realized the contrast in the degrees of assimilation of the Doan and Ung families. For example, I had a hard time completing telephone conversations in English with the Doans. Further, in helping the family fill out their California state income tax short form, I realized that they had little understanding of bureaucratic rules or written English.

In contrast, members of the Ung family had mastered such skills, yet they had achieved far less mobility than the Doans. For example, Luc Ung, who received an AA degree in electronics at an Oakland community college, had completed several English classes. Similarly, his brother Duc had a great deal of mathematical skill. He could accurately describe which local bank gave the best rates on credit cards, and he solved complex geometric puzzles, using toothpicks on the kitchen table, as a pastime. Despite these linguistic, mathematical, and bureaucratic skills, the Ung family was in worse financial condition in 1984 than during our initial meeting in 1982. The fact that the Doans experienced upward mobility with little linguistic or bureaucratic knowledge while the Ungs made little progress reveals the effects of social structure on refugee adaptation and, at least in the short term, the importance of family-based resources in adapting to the American way of life.

CHARACTERISTICS OF THE RECENTLY ARRIVED

In the mid-1980s, recently arrived Vietnamese in the San Francisco Bay Area, like the Ungs and the Doans, lived in low-rent apartment buildings located in neighborhoods heavily populated by refugees. Two such areas were western Oakland and San Francisco's Tenderloin district. Both regions contained many decaying apartment buildings and welfare hotels where landlords accepted low rent and tolerated many occupants per apartment. These areas were close to the cities' Chinatowns, settings that have received immigrants from Asia for decades. Because of their run-down condition, they offered inexpensive settings for refugee businesses and resettlement offices.[2]

During the 1980s, the development of refugee enclaves in the Bay Area fostered the residential segregation of recent arrivals. This process provided residents with a sense of "turf" and facilitated the establishment of an ethnic infrastructure based upon refugee aid offices, education programs, and small businesses. On the other hand, the large concentration of refugees in a single location placed a heavy burden on social services and made competition for jobs fierce.

Blocked Mobility: A Dominant Theme

Recently arrived Vietnamese refugees in Northern California experienced a great deal of difficulty in finding jobs. This was due to several factors, including their lack of skills and language competence, the severe economic downturn of the early 1980s, poor physical and mental health stemming from the refugee experience, and family-related needs, such as child care and health care (Gold and Kibria 1989; ORR 1989; Rumbaut 1989b).

According to the Office of Refugee Resettlement, "When jobs are not readily available, refugees—even more than the general American population—may be unable to find employment quickly even if they are relatively skilled and actively seek work" (ORR 1988:126). This is illustrated by the fact that labor force participation rates for Southeast

Asian refugees *declined* over time from 55% in 1983 to 39% in 1987 (ORR 1987:131).[3]

While many refugees were unable to find jobs or had given up seeking employment, even those who did become employed tended to obtain low-quality work: positions that paid poorly, were part time, were unstable, and lacked benefits. "A majority of Orange County's Vietnamese work at low paying jobs as assemblers, waiters, dishwashers, clerks and mechanics. They earn about $5 per hour and have no chance of becoming middle class Americans" (Brody 1986:A6).[4] Rumbaut found that 77% of employed Vietnamese in San Diego earned less than $7.50 an hour, and 48% earned less than $5.50 hourly. Additionally, 15.5% had temporary jobs, 29% had no benefits, and 46% had no opportunity for promotion (Rumbaut 1986:Table 3).

Because of low labor-force participation, unemployment, and poor jobs, Vietnamese refugees displayed high rates of welfare dependency. And "while the welfare option may be an alternative means of subsistence, it is not an alternative to poverty . . . welfare income keeps recipients well below the poverty line while conferring upon them a stigmatized status" (Rumbaut 1989:19).

My own fieldwork reflected these disturbing statistical trends. Despite their increasing Americanization, Duc Ung and Quy Pham, refugees who had well-paid jobs in the summer of 1982, were both unemployed by spring 1983. Each spent the next year laboring at a variety of minimum-wage jobs, whose monotony was broken by periods of listless unemployment. Almost every time I visited, I would hear of their struggle with futureless, stupefying jobs like truck salvage, tortilla-chip packer, traffic counter, busboy, clothing assembly, newspaper delivery, or courier. Quy summarized their fate: "If you had a diploma or a good job in Vietnam, you can just throw it away. It won't do you any good here. You can only get a job for $4.50 an hour, so forget about your old one."

Frustrated by their lack of employment opportunities, refugees considered a variety of alternative ways to make a living. According to several sources, thousands participate in the underground economy. While the jobs they find in such a market supplement their government benefits, positions in the underground economy are generally poorly paid and without traditional fringe benefits.[5] Moreover, since they are unregulated, jobs in the underground economy deprive refugees of safe working conditions and public coffers of tax contributions (North 1988).[6] The *Los Angeles Times* claimed that "an estimated 25% of California's refugee families are supplementing welfare payments with in some instances as much as $25,000 a year in unreported income" (Arax 1987:1). Other strategies for earning a living included becoming self-employed, joining the army, or enlisting in the Job Corps. Ultimately, however, few recently arrived refugees were able to support themselves through such alternative forms of employment.

In my two years of contact with these Vietnamese refugees, I found little evidence to suggest that their difficulties in finding work were due to their own attitudes or behavior. Rather, refugees prized decent jobs—those offering a living wage, stability, and, ideally, benefits—and pursued them energetically. Recent arrivals who held desired jobs were identified by their occupations. Quy or Luc would refer to a refugee I had met earlier as "plater," "engineer," or "drafter." In contrast, refugees who worked less-esteemed occupations were never identified as "janitor," "paper boy," or "traffic counter." Refugees' commitment to employment was further illustrated by their efforts to create a good impression for employers even when jobs were poorly paid, unpleasant, and offered no security. For example, Ven Vuong told of stifling his objections when he was unjustly accused of damaging a fork lift. Similarly, Quy Pham offered his technique for managing supervisors: When confused about a task, he always asked co-workers rather than higher-ups to avoid appearing incompetent. Recent arrivals experienced job-related health problems, yet continued to work. Both Quy Pham and Duc Ung complained of respiratory problems and chronic exhaustion. Each consumed Chinese medicines in order to avoid being fired for absenteeism caused by illness. The willingness of refugees to take undesirable jobs and to expend effort in order to keep them, sometimes at the cost of their RCA benefits, suggests their commitment to gainful employment.

Perspectives on Community

Faced with economic difficulties, Vietnamese refugees turned to their ethnic communities for support, information, and diversion. Like Soviet Jews, the Vietnamese were both attracted to and repelled by their fellows. Their community—containing the government elite, working class and rural boat people, and ethnic Chinese—was ultimately more heterogeneous than that of the Soviets, who were nearly all educated and urban. Despite its high level of diversity, the Vietnamese community reveals certain facilitators for organization that are absent from the Soviets' experience.

Lacking the skills and services available to the Soviets, having more experience in self-help activities, and retaining some links from the past, the much larger Vietnamese community developed various forms of organization and solidarity that, especially within subgroups, surpassed those of the Soviet Jews. Experiencing major economic disadvantages and lacking the cultural skills that would permit them to connect to American society, recently arrived Vietnamese developed strong, informal social ties with each other. Recently arrived Vietnamese reinforced links as they shared information, money, and emotional support. For example, refugees relied on these connections to obtain housing, a scarce resource in the Bay Area's tight and costly rental market. During fieldwork, I became acquainted with several families who, due to difficulties with landlords or finances, had to find new housing on short notice. Ethnic contacts provided each of those families with apartments within two days.

In addition to providing one another with housing leads, refugees also supported each other financially. Despite their very small incomes, recent arrivals exchanged hundreds or thousands of dollars with friends and relatives living in the States and abroad. Ven Vuong and Trung Vu told me how they had sent remittances to family members overseas by hiding $50 bills in the battery compartments of pocket calculators. Ven boasted that he was lucky since his package was received intact. Finally, recent arrivals shared the necessities of life on a daily basis. Members of the Ungs's network furnished one another with tools, cars, food, job training, child care, and advice about resettlement services and job opportunities.

Drawing on national pride and homesickness, recent arrivals felt a strong sense of involvement with the Vietnamese community. Following Vietnamese custom, they held that an individual's deeds, good or bad, reflected directly upon his or her family and community. Recent arrivals tried to help those in need and "bring into line" refugees whose actions reflect poorly on the Vietnamese as a group.

In service of this end, recent arrivals invited friends, relatives, and even strangers who had fallen on hard times to live with them. The Doan family's willingness to contribute to needy co-ethnics was illustrated by their support of one particularly unfortunate young man they referred to as "Oklahoma." Oklahoma, a young Vietnamese with no relatives in the United States, was initially resettled in the Southwest. After being laid off in Tulsa, he headed for California. Shortly after his arrival, he was involved in an auto accident that destroyed his car. Intimidated by the police, who he claimed were in cahoots with the other driver, he surrendered his entire savings of $129. Meeting Oklahoma and hearing of his plight, Thanh Doan's brother offered him accommodations in the family's apartment.

As a member of the Doan household, Oklahoma made little effort to earn a living or contribute to household chores and expenses. After spending weeks living off the Doans's support, he still had not found a job. Further, he squandered his general assistance money on Levis outfits. The Doans objected to his taste for "501s" (blue jeans) because he would wear them, rather than more business-like attire, to job interviews. Finally, they indignantly described how he had been taken in by an American hustler who promised to get him a job. Instead of receiving employment, Oklahoma lost the $50 "union fee" demanded by the confidence man and allowed this unsavory character admittance to the Doan's apartment, where he was able to see their prized electronic equipment. Despite their displeasure with his actions, the Doans permitted Oklahoma to remain in their apartment for almost a year. This example reveals the extent to which economically pressed refugees will make sacrifices in order to help co-ethnics in need.

Demonstrating their feeling of responsibility for co-ethnics in a different way, refugees reprimanded other Vietnamese who acted in a shameful manner. Ven Vuong described how his national pride required him to uphold standards of behavior in the refugee community:

When I am in the movie, if other people, Mexicans, Americans, anybody acts impolite, I don't care. But when Vietnamese talk a lot, make noise, put their feet up on the chair, I really don't like it. If Vietnamese people make a lot of noise and don't care about other people, then everyone thinks they are uneducated, that they don't know anything. No one likes them.

I was working as a traffic counter in San Francisco and saw a Vietnamese man asking for spare change. He had his head shaved like a Buddhist and was begging with a bowl. I went over to him and asked, "What are you doing man? You are bigger and stronger than me, why should you beg? Maybe the American people will give you money, but the Asian won't."

A Desire To Assimilate

Despite their concern with ethnic honor and their orientation toward the refugee community, members of the Ungs's network did not maintain an exclusively ethnic existence. On the contrary, most were also concerned with establishing links to the larger society for moral and practical reasons. Because boat people have personally witnessed the transformation of South Vietnamese society at the hands of revolutionary cadres, they are often less nostalgic than the 1975 cohort. While 1975 arrivals often wished to recapture Vietnam, most boat people realized the futility of retaining attachments to a way of life they knew no longer existed. Further, because their experience of migration was so painful, many wished to distance themselves from the past. This position was expressed by Ty Minh, a former supply officer in the army of South Vietnam:

Myself, I suffer a lot in the re-education camp, so I know the value of my life here. I respect it very much, even if I have some hardship. I don't want to say that our Vietnamese people or our Chinese-Vietnamese should forget their roots, but we also have to think that we are member of this society.

One of our responsibilities is to improve this society and if you are always thinking about your own history, you will forget your present. And you couldn't do anything to help society grow.

The feelings of ambivalence on the part of recent arrivals toward their community were especially noticeable during cultural events. On several occasions, I was invited by refugees to attend large Vietnamese festivals. One featured singers of both contemporary and traditional styles, comedians, dancers, and Kung Fu demonstrations. Following the performance, Trung Vu expressed his feelings of alienation. "The singers are not good, the actors do not make me laugh, and the Kung Fu was faked. When they sing the song, 'Saigon I'm coming home soon,' we all know it is a lie."

Because of their economic difficulties, recent arrivals valued attachments to the behaviors, institutions, and individuals of American society. Recognizing the effects of social structure, many recent arrivals described their status as foreigners as a serious disadvantage, one that forced them to accept either the low pay and long hours common to employment in Vietnamese or Chinese firms, or to compete for undesirable jobs in the larger economy. They hoped to overcome these disadvantages by learning English and becoming more Americanized.

Aware of their relations with native and ethnic communities, boat people developed a complex understanding of their ethnic identity. On one hand, these refugees were committed to Vietnamese customs and attached to their countrymen in the United States. On the other hand, they hoped to become more involved in American society, both to achieve economic success and to distance themselves from their recent and painful flight from home.

Although recently arrived Vietnamese sometimes mentioned their confrontations with racial prejudice, they seemed little concerned with racial categories. As noted by Portes and Bach (1985), it was the more assimilated members of the community who, through their higher expectations and extensive interactions with whites, were most aware of discrimination.

Finally, while these refugees lived near concentrations of other Asian groups and sometimes shopped and worked in businesses owned by Chinese or Japanese Americans, they had limited identification with nonrefugee Asians. In fact, several described being exploited by Asian-American employers and resettlement staff. Consequently, among these refugees, there was little identification with the larger Asian–American population.

Reactions to Blocked Mobility

Recent arrivals showed extraordinary restraint under the hardships of social isolation and economic marginality. However, as months passed with little improvement in sight, some refugees revealed their unhappiness. Fed up with their jobs, several quit only to find an equally bad position when limited savings ran out. Ignoring their normally careful efforts to save money, they would sometimes splurge. Duc Ung, for example, who purchased a new Mustang, admitted that he should have chosen a secondhand Honda. Similarly, Ven Vuong and Quy Pham bought a thousand-dollar stereo for their otherwise empty apartment.

Thinking that their luck would improve with a change of scene, recent arrivals traveled around the United States. Members of the Ungs's social circle had been resettled in Alabama, Washington, D.C., and Ohio. These refugees moved west to escape cold weather and to find their fellow countrymen. On the West Coast, many secondary migrants continued to roam. For example, Quy Pham had moved back and forth between Oakland and San Jose several times. Bui Ung and Phouc Nguyen had each lived in Los Angeles but later settled in Oakland. Another member of their network had moved to Oakland from Portland, Oregon. Even local residences were changed with surprising frequency as household structure and economic status varied.

One troubled young refugee, Trung Vu, who had no close relations in the United States, led an especially erratic life. Frustrated by his inability to find work, Vu borrowed $2,000 from a friend and moved from Oakland to San Jose to enter a job-training program. Finding the program difficult and missing his roommates, Vu dropped out and returned to Oakland. Still unable to find work, Vu then took a bus to Washington, D.C., his original place of residence in the United States. Here he worked at a Chinese restaurant for 12 hours a day, six days a week for six months. Saving over $3,000, Vu flew back to Oakland and paid part of his debt. With his remaining savings, he put a down payment on a 1976 MGB sports car, even though he did not know how to drive. With the car stored in a friend's garage, he rejoined the household he had left a year earlier. Having traveled several thousand miles, he had no better chance for employment and now owed money.

Other recent arrivals did not make as extreme attempts to change their conditions as Trung Vu. However, most did complain of the dull sameness of life in the States. While they took their classes and worked at their jobs, they felt little cause for optimism. Older members of the network—those who had lived in Vietnam long enough to remember what it was like in better times—longed to return home. They described Vietnam as nothing short of paradise. Life there, I was told, was simple and rich. Even a poor man took a month off for Tet (New Year). You could build a house yourself. In many rivers, fish would just jump into your boat. And there were no monthly bills.

Contacts With Established Refugees

In recent years, a growing body of research has shown how ethnic communities, originally thought to be malignant holdovers from the old country, provide many immigrants with employment, welfare, and a sense of community (Light and Bonacich 1988; Portes and Bach 1985). If this were the case, connections with the established and educated members of the refugee community should provide a source of support and mobility for recent arrivals experiencing difficulty.

Contacts between 1975 evacuees and boat people do occur; for example, boat person Thanh Doan received many benefits from his earlier-arriving relatives. However, because of differences in background, outlook, and immigration experience, many recent arrivals felt that they had little to gain from links to the refugee elite. In fact, the shared dislike of elite refugees was a basis of social solidarity among recent arrivals that I interviewed.

Conflicts between boat people and the earlier-arriving elite of the Vietnamese community were manifested on many levels. To some recent arrivals, the 1975 cohort was their historical enemy, a corrupt and Westernized urban elite who knew nothing of the rural texture of Vietnamese life. They were described as the sons of colonial administrators who profited from the war and ran before defeat. Recent arrivals also complained that the early-arriving group had created a snobbish and exclusive social environment. The 1975 cohort's many advantages resulted in their establishing standards for success that were beyond the reach of recent arrivals.

Recent arrivals' distrust of the established Vietnamese group was frequently heightened through their contacts with the many members of the 1975 cohort who staff resettlement agencies. Quy Pham, for example, described the refugee elites' involvement with resettlement as a self-serving endeavor—more concerned with securing lucrative jobs and positions of influence than aiding countrymen. Similarly, Ven Vuong referred to his visit to a Vietnamese doctor to illustrate that elite refugees are not always working in the best interest of their countrymen:

> I was sick. I went to Dr. Pham in Oakland. He didn't even want to examine me or talk to me. His nurse gave me a paper and told me to write down the kind of medicine I wanted. They thought I only came to get medicine to send back to my country. Then I got my record from Medi-Cal. The doctor charged them for three visits! Next time I get sick, I will go to an American doctor.[7]

The mistrust and resentment of Vietnamese resettlement staff by recent arrivals was so pervasive that it was generally acknowledged by service providers themselves. Nguyen Ngoc Dinh, a 1975 refugee who was the director of a resettlement center in San Jose, explained why newcomers were wary of service providers who received salaries:

One area of conflict between the refugees who came in 1975 and those who have arrived after 1978 is around what "volunteer" means. In Vietnam, volunteer means no salary or benefits are received, just moral benefits. But in here [in the U.S.], voluntary agency means service provided without cost, like myself. VOLAG workers [government-supported voluntary agencies that resettle refugees] are paid. But in Vietnam, all costs come out of the pocket for volunteer workers, 100% voluntary.

This is the problem between new arrivals and ones who came in 1975. It happens here. The front office staff is asked, "why do you receive a salary?" The new arrival does not understand U.S. society. When I was in Guam [in 1975 after fleeing Vietnam] I thought the same thing.

Recent refugees confirmed Nguyen Ngoc Dinh's explanation. When I would enthusiastically tell recent arrivals about a refugee who ran a resettlement center, they would coolly reply, "Sure, I would like a good job, too."

Solidarity Amidst the Suspicion

Recently arrived refugees frequently expressed cynicism and opposition to their countrymen who arrived in 1975. On a broader level, however, many transcended their conflicts with the elite and maintained a more inclusive definition of ethnic membership. Recent arrivals made use of the agencies run by earlier arrivals, shopped at the businesses they owned, and took pride in those who made noteworthy achievements. To recent refugees, the success of the earlier-arriving cohort was seen as their ultimate future. Recent refugees often respected refugee organizations that were run on a nonpaying, volunteer basis. While the experiences of boat people taught them to be suspicious of those in positions of power, their culture fostered a great respect for the highly educated. For example, despite his frequent deprecation of the elite, Quy Pham often responded to my questions about Vietnamese customs by saying, "I don't know enough about Vietnamese culture; you should get a [Vietnamese] doctor to tell you about it."

Recent arrivals generally accepted the 1975 group's position of leadership. Their major complaint regarding leadership was that there were too many ambitious individuals. Many assert that the Vietnamese community was plagued by an "all leaders, no followers" syndrome. The presence of so many disagreeing leaders and a general lack of

consensus was seen as a problem faced by Vietnamese both in the
United States and in pre-1975 South Vietnam. Ty Minh commented:

> Another problem in our community, we are not believing each other so
> much. Right now, many Vietnamese people are very skeptical. They
> don't believe anyone. Even if you help them, they still think "what's really
> behind that?" The past has taught them a lesson. [Leaders] have to prove
> themselves, prove that they are working for the community. [After
> they] . . . show devotion more and more, so our community will trust
> them.

FAMILY ISSUES AMONG THE
RECENTLY ARRIVED VIETNAMESE

Broken Families

In contrast to the Soviet Jews who retreat from community conflicts to their close and generally intact families, such stable family units were rare among many of the Vietnamese I contacted in
Northern California. Further, while a nuclear family might be considered "whole" by American standards, the Vietnamese are accustomed to large, extended family units. Hence, a collectivity that
American observers might hold to be an intact family is to its
members a fractured unit marked by a significant feeling of separa-
tion and loss.

Vietnamese refugees cherished the family attachments to which
they had access. Quy Pham demonstrated his value for family by living
with cousins in Oakland even though this required a daily 80-mile
commute to his job in San Jose. Quy justified the drive, saying, "If I
lived in San Jose, nobody would take away my body if I died."
Prizing family connections, groups of recently arrived refugees, including both the Ungs and the Doans, created "pseudofamilies"—
households made up of close and distant relatives and friends (Owan
1985). Sharing accommodations, finances, and fellowship, these col-
lectives formed an important source of social support in the refugee
community.

Although male refugees found some comfort in household networks, their ability to establish regular families was often limited by
poor economic status and the scarcity of Vietnamese females in the

United States (Gordon 1982; 1987). They continued, however, to be interested in family-related matters. They maintained ties with family overseas by sending letters and packages, working to facilitate the re-settlement of relatives in the United States, and perusing documents and photo albums.

A major concern for these young, single men was that Vietnamese women in the United States could afford to be choosy and hence avoid involvement with Vietnamese males (like themselves) who were struggling just to survive. Ven Vuong and Luc Ung describe the difficulty of establishing a relationship with a Vietnamese woman in the United States:

> In Vietnam, it was easy to meet a girlfriend because so many men were killed in the war. But in America, Vietnamese lady only likes you if you have good job, nice clothes, good car and plenty of money. They look for money, not for love.

> There was a girl I knew in the refugee camp. We were good friends. I came to United States. She moved to Los Angeles. At first, I used to write to her. I saw her but she is not friendly anymore. She only likes a man if he has a lot of money.

Because of these conditions, the interactions of recent arrivals with nonrelated females were limited to occasional liaisons with "taxi girls" (prostitutes). Despite their status as "new immigrants," the lives of these refugees have striking parallels with those of the Chinese laborers who endured a marginal existence without families in American Chinatowns of the last century (Hong-Kingston 1979; Lyman 1974).

Problems of Intact Families

While intact refugee families were certainly better off than those broken apart by the flight from Vietnam, they, too, experienced serious conflicts. One problem was that housing in the United States simply does not lend itself to the unification of extended families, especially poor ones, under a single roof. A great many refugees I interviewed came from families having nine to 12 children. Unfortunately, the cost of housing that would permit the unification of these families in urban California was beyond the reach of most Vietnamese refugees, whose average household income was $11,955 in 1979 (U.S. Bureau of the Census 1983:Table 97). For example, a refugee described how the availability of housing has affected his own family:

> Before I left Vietnam, 3 generations lived together in the same group. My mom, my family including wife and 7 children, my elder brother, his wife and 3 children, my little brother and two sisters—we live in a big house. So when we came here we are thinking of being united in one place. But there is no way. However, we try to live as close as possible.

Another common problem faced by intact refugee families, especially those with many children, was that of health-care costs. Ty Nguyen, a resettlement worker, described this issue:

> You must realize that refugees here—they really want to work, to be self-sufficient. No one really wants to rely on another person. But why then, do you see most of them still stay on welfare. It's not completely their fault. The policy is not an incentive for them to become self-sufficient.
>
> If they work at the entry level job, they get $3.25, $3.50 an hour. They can make $450, $500 a month. Then why do they stay on welfare for only $240 a month?
>
> This is why. Everyone knows that here, the medical bill is the worst—so everyone has in their mind "how to pay it?" Especially for the refugee who has many children. If they work, then they lose government medical benefit, and low wage jobs don't provide. And that's why, myself, I think that why we still have a lot of refugee on welfare.

Role Reversals

Vietnamese refugees experience various degrees of reversal in the "provider" and "recipient" roles that existed among family members in Vietnam (Sluzki 1979). The most common shift of roles occurred between husband and wife, with the wife taking on the breadwinner role as well as some of the status and power that accompanied it. This occurred because women's jobs, such as housecleaner, hotel maid (a major source of employment for female refugees in San Francisco), and food service worker, were more readily available than the male-oriented, unskilled occupations that the husband sought. In other cases, the wife became the breadwinner as she supported the family by working in a menial job while the husband attempted to find professional employment. Finally, some women had to assume breadwinner roles because of the absence of a spouse in the United States. Role changes also occurred in families in which both the husband and wife worked, since the wife was not employed outside the home before the family came to the United States.

The process by which the mother or children, rather than the father, became the primary source of a refugee family's income indicates the adaptability of Vietnamese families. At the same time, however, the inversion of traditional family roles often provoked hostility and resentment (Liu et al. 1979). Several social workers with refugee clients commented that self-destructive, violent, psychosomatic, or antisocial reactions—such as wife or child abuse, depression, or alcoholism—occurred as a result of family role reversals (Cohon 1981:263-265; Portes and Rumbaut 1990).

Generational Conflict

Like the Soviet Jews, Vietnamese refugees experienced considerable generational conflict in their adaptation to the United States. These conflicts were harsh for Vietnamese refugees because, while their traditional culture is collectivistic and deferential toward elders, American society is individualistic and youth oriented (Brower 1981). A Vietnamese Buddhist monk described how refugee families confronted the issue of self-determination:

Okay, there is some breakdown in the family. Kids are growing and become American and the grandfather and grandmother stick to the old culture. So we have to become involved in this problem.

It's tough. And I think that if you work with the refugees, you will notice that the kids, they are completely American after 7 years in America. They want to date, they want to go out with their boyfriend, girlfriend.

This idea never existed in Vietnam. So the older generation cannot stand this stuff. And the kids feel terribly upset when mother says "Hey—you have to stay home."

Another refugee described his ambivalence toward the rapid rate with which his children are accepting American ways of life:

My mom is 82. She doesn't speak English at all. And the children learn the American way. They come home, and in some cases, they want to imitate American behavior. The children use the wrong terms of address with Grandmother. She says "now you are American and you are impolite to me!"

In the community, criteria have changed. They tolerate children who do not study as hard. But the children still act with discipline at home. Next generation will be different. We are happy we are still in control. We are really afraid that the next generation will fall into a crisis of identity.

In sum, Vietnamese refugees relied on family units to provide support and help them adjust to life in the United States. However, because of their broken family status, selective migration, and severe social and economic disadvantages, these refugee families and psuedofamilies experienced major strains. Even some adaptive strategies that allowed refugee families to survive—such as women and children taking on social and economic responsibilities—were themselves disruptive, yielding role reversals and generational conflicts. Hence, despite their strength and flexibility, traditional families alone were incapable of solving many problems experienced by recently arrived Vietnamese.

RECENTLY ARRIVED VIETNAMESE: A SUMMARY

Recently arrived Vietnamese refugees suffered from ghettoization, broken families, difficulties with English, and a lack of economic opportunity. Drawing on common origins, shared experiences, and mutual feelings of alienation from established refugees, recent arrivals banded together to share social and economic support. In so doing, they developed a unique identity and way of life. Some families, such as the Doans, combined benefits from relatives, the refugee community, and resettlement agencies to allow for positive adjustment to American society. Others, however, such as the Ungs, confronted huge obstacles in their attempts to make a life in the United States.

For many, instability was a major theme. Unable to find decent jobs or establish families, they were deprived of the most vital forms of social connectedness. Periodically dependent on public assistance, they drifted from job to job, went in and out of training programs, entered the underground economy, and moved around the country. In moments of greatest frustration, they spent impulsively or dreamt of an idyllic past. For many, efforts to "get their future started" went un-rewarded.

While a large ethnic community has been established by earlier-ar-riving refugees, this collectivity offered limited benefits to the many boat people. Conflicts rooted in ideology, ethnicity, migration experi-ence, background, and subgroup restricted the development of links between these two cohorts of Vietnamese.

Recent arrivals often described their contacts with elite refugees, such as community leaders, resettlement staff, employers, and doc-tors, as exploitative. While the institutionally complete ethnic Vietnamese enclaves of California offered insulation against culture shock, they also limited the interactions of recent arrivals with main-stream American society, where they might find better jobs (Montero 1979). Even Vietnamese enterprises offered few employment oppor-tunities for unconnected refugees. By 1989, Vietnamese employers in Southern California increasingly preferred Mexicans to co-ethnics as entry-level employees in their businesses.

Despite their economic problems and suspicion toward co-ethnics, however, Vietnamese boat people did maintain feelings of attachment toward the entire refugee population. Perhaps in time, these feelings will lead to the establishment of an integrated enclave.

NOTES

1. While research often emphasizes immigrants' involvement in ethnic businesses, members of the Ungs's network sought employment in large U.S. firms. They believed such jobs offered better pay and benefits, stability, and an opportunity to master the English language. Their employment preference is supported by census data. Employees of Vietnamese-owned businesses earned an average of only $6,066 during 1982 (Bonacich 1987:448).

2. Unlike other cities in the United States where large influxes of refugees were met with hostility, the arrival of a lively community of refugee families and businesses was seen as beneficial by many Bay Area politicians and community activists. In San Francisco, the North of Market Planning Coalition, a neighborhood organization with a wide base of support, praised the refugees as a stabilizing influence in a changing neighborhood. The Coalition considered Vietnamese restaurants and grocery stores an excellent alternative to either the skid-row economy that has dominated the Tenderloin area for years or the luxury hotels and corporate offices that were planned by real estate developers. By the late 1980s, however, many Vietnamese had left the Tenderloin for suburban communities where they could buy homes. While many Vietnamese

businesses remained, the presence of the refugees ultimately failed to resolve the conflict between sleeze and gentrification in the manner that the Planning Commission had hoped.

3. Refugees leaving the labor force cannot be accounted for by death, retirement, or return to the country of origin (Baker and North 1984).

4. Orange County is home to the largest Vietnamese community in the United States and also has the highest housing costs in the nation. The high cost of living in Orange County and other California communities where the Vietnamese are heavily concentrated means that their already scarce dollars have even less purchasing power.

5. While ethnic businesses generally do not provide traditional benefits, such as sick leave and health care, certain nontraditional benefits are provided by employers (Gold 1988; Portes and Manning 1986)(see Chapter 7).

6. According to at least two studies, participation by individual Vietnamese refugees in the underground economy tends to increase the longer the refugees are in the United States. Baker and North (1984) found that between 1976 and 1980, Vietnamese males between the ages of 20 and 24 disappeared from FICA rolls by 8%, and their contributions to Social Security dropped by 18% between 1975 and 1978. Ruling out other causes, they concluded that the entrance of refugees into the underground economy was the plausible explanation for shrinking contributions (Baker and North 1984:100-113).

7. A much-publicized investigation of fraud by Vietnamese doctors in early 1984 proved that Ven's experience was not unique (Leba 1985:137-144).

I visited this network of Vietnamese boat people, shown in Liem's apartment, for a year-and-a-half. Although its members were of very different class, regional, and ethnic origins, they formed a "pseudofamily," sharing accommodations, money, and advice in Oakland.

Some skilled and educated refugees rapidly achieve middle-class status in the United States. However, others, like these children in San Francisco's Tenderloin, live in a manner similar to that of immigrants who came during the last era of great migration—from 1880 to 1920.

Having reestablished family links thousands of miles from their homes in Vietnam, this family celebrates a marriage in their Oakland apartment. Their clothing and decorations suggest the group's immersion in various cultures.

Many Vietnamese families retain links to their traditional culture and religion by establishing a household shrine. The baby in the picture at right is the girl's uncle, who died as a child.

The styles of dress and self-presentation of these three women indicate the diverse patterns of adaptation that can be found within the Vietnamese-American community.

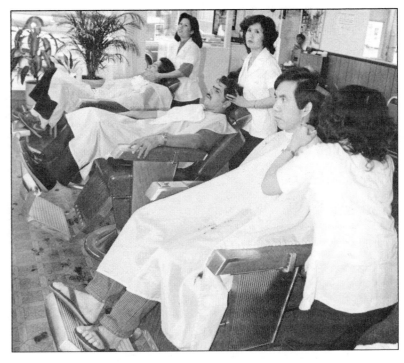

Van's barber shop, located in San Francisco's Tenderloin (home to 10,000 refugees in the early 1980s), relies on women barbers who, in the Asian style, provide massages as well as haircuts to a male clientele.

Although most Vietnamese businesses cater primarily to the Vietnamese community, this San Francisco bar has a native-born clientele.

In contrast to the inner-city locations typical of most immigrant enterprises, Vietnamese entrepreneurs have established a new shopping district in suburban Orange County.

Many entrepreneurs within the Vietnamese community are of Chinese ethnicity. Relying on family and ethnic connections retained from Vietnam, these partners have established a chain of restaurants in Los Angeles and Orange County.

Companies such as this food import and processing business are among the largest enterprises created by Vietnamese refugees. Relying on ethnic links for capital, labor, and customers, they foster economic integration in a manner conducive to the development of an ethnic economic enclave.

Some political organizations within the Vietnamese refugee population are concerned with activities in the homeland. This demonstration, organized by a San Francisco resettlement agency, protests the communist takeover of Vietnam on the eighth anniversary of the Fall of Saigon, April 30, 1983.

Expatriate Vietnamese leaders, such as Ha Phan, re-establish positions of visibility and influence as they find employment in the refugee resettlement system.

Vietnamese students, especially the children of the 1975 first-wave refugees, have made remarkable strides in the United States. This group is receiving college scholarships from a Japanese-American association as a commemoration of funds the association received in the 1940s that permitted Japanese-Americans to leave internment camps to attend East Coast colleges. Most of the scholarship recipients planned to major in pre-med.

6

Resettlement Agencies and Refugee Communities

A key factor distinguishing the experience of Soviet Jewish and Vietnamese refugees from that of most other migrant groups is the elaborate programs devoted to their resettlement. Extensive legislation, millions of dollars, and countless hours of paid and volunteer effort have been expended in order to smooth these groups' settlement in the United States (Baker and North 1985; Caplan et al. 1985; Eckles et al. 1982; Lewin and Associates 1986).

Policymakers and the researchers they commission to study resettlement have generally defined the relationship between service providers and recipients as a one-sided affair, with refugees depicted as passively lining up to receive services. It is only much later, when such problems as noncompliance with regulations, abuse of services, or nonutilization arise that the makers of resettlement policy finally realize that resettlement is a two-sided relationship (Arax 1987; Cichon et al. 1986; Lewin and Associates 1986; Zahler 1989).

Of course, refugees cannot help but react to resettlement based upon their own values, expectations, alternatives, and needs. They approach resettlement in ways that reflect their own purposes rather than those of the bureaucrats and staff members who create and carry out resettlement policy (Desbarats 1986a; deVoe 1981; Finnan and Cooperstein 1983; Gold 1987; Gorelick 1982; Indra 1987, 1989). This chapter relies on an interactional approach to consider various effects that refugee resettlement services, policies, and agencies have upon Soviet Jewish and Vietnamese communities in California.

THE NATURE OF REFUGEE RESETTLEMENT

Resettlement agencies are intended to facilitate the adaptation of Soviet Jewish and Vietnamese refugees by providing them with advice, guidance, training, and other services, ideally, in a close personal context (Brower 1981; Dorf and Katlin 1983; Indra 1987; Murray and Associates 1981; ORR 1982a, 1989). However, the inherently awkward nature of resettlement often prevents these goals from being accomplished to the degree hoped for by both the framers of policy and the recipients of services (Wilson and Garrick 1983).

The difficulties involved in resettlement result from the near impossibility of the task at hand: delivering elusive elements of social membership on demand. No matter how well funded a resettlement agency or how skillful its staff, the major goals of resettlement (economic self-sufficiency and cultural adjustment) are difficult to attain. Economic self-sufficiency is largely dependent upon economic factors beyond any resettlement worker's control. Similarly, cultural adjustment, learning English, and resolving the mental trauma brought on by the refugee experience can only be achieved through the efforts of refugees themselves, expended over protracted periods of time (Lappin and Scott 1982; Owan 1985; Schuetz 1944).

Further complicating matters, resettlement interactions frequently take place in an environment of extensive cultural incompatibility between providers and recipients of services (Brower 1981; Caplan et al. 1985; Lewin and Associates 1986). Recent research has shown that between 50% and 70% of refugees did not know how to obtain such vital services as legal help, free emergency medical care, ESL (English as a second language) training, free emergency food, or low-income housing, that were available to them (Wilson and Garrick 1983:13). And those refugees who do consume services tend to be among the elite of the community:

> Those with little education and who held low status or skill occupations in Southeast Asia are much less likely to be receiving the services they need than the more advantaged refugees. (Caplan et al. 1985:242)

Finally, the institutional constraints faced by the resettlement agencies, including limited staff, scarce and unstable funding, and various bureaucratic obligations and restrictions, make resettlement all the more difficult.[1]

THE REFUGEE SERVICE DELIVERY
ESTABLISHMENT

Since the mid-1970s, a number of programs have been enacted by
Congress to encourage the smooth adjustment of refugees. The most
important of these is the Refugee Act of 1980 (Public Law 96-212).
This legislation was intended to provide "transitional assistance to
refugees in the United States," to make "employment training and job
placement available in order to achieve economic self-sufficiency
among refugees as quickly as possible," to offer refugees English language training, and to ensure "that cash assistance is made available
to refugees in such a manner as to not discourage their economic self-
sufficiency" (Section 311, quoted in Murray 1981).

The services provided for by the Refugee Act of 1980 as well as other
legislation are delivered and administered by a diverse network of government, religious, nonprofit, and profit-making agencies and organizations.
In addition to services funded by federal, state, and local government,
charitable contributions support resettlement activities as well.

A major role in the resettlement of refugees is carried out by 13
voluntary agencies, or VOLAGs, that are funded by the federal government (ORR 1984:ix). The largest number of Vietnamese have been
resettled by the United States Catholic Conference (USCC). In fiscal
year 1982, for example, USCC settled 37,270 Southeast Asian refugees, a figure that accounted for 52% of all Southeast Asian refugees
entering the United States in that year (ORR 1983). Nearly all Soviet
Jews (75,331 from 1976 to 1981) as well as some Southeast Asians
have been resettled by the Hebrew Immigration Aid Service, or HIAS
(Eckles et al. 1982:27). Refugee cash assistance (RCA) is not offered
through resettlement agencies. Instead, it is distributed by county
welfare departments.

Services available to Soviet Jewish and Vietnamese refugees from
their resettlement agencies include job training, job placement, physical and mental health programs, instruction on cultural adjustment
and cultural preservation, English as a second language, and assistance in opening small businesses.

The Soviet Jews' Resettlement System

There is a major contrast between the agencies that provide service
to Soviet Jewish refugees and those resettling the Vietnamese. Soviet

Jewish resettlement agencies are highly centralized and integrated, long established, well funded, and few in number. They enjoy a level of funding per refugee that is considerably greater than that allocated for each Vietnamese arrival. While the federal government gave each VOLAG $525 per Southeast Asian refugee, Soviet Jews' resettlement agencies, which had access to nongovernment funds provided by Jewish charities, received $1,000 per refugee from a federal matching grant program (Eckles et al. 1982).

Vietnamese Refugees' Resettlement System

In contrast to agencies resettling Soviet Jews, those for Vietnamese are decentralized, often overlapping, have few professional staff, and are subject to severe fiscal problems. Vietnamese refugees' agencies generally provided only short-term and survival-type aid. Because most are directed specifically toward the problems of Southeast Asian refugees, few existed prior to 1975. Further, after the peak of migration in the early 1980s, many agencies experienced heavy cutbacks in staff and funding or were phased out altogether. In contrast to the native-born employees of the Jewish resettlement agencies, most Vietnamese resettlement agencies employ several refugee staff members (Hein 1988). Vietnamese resettlement programs were frequently plagued by disorganization. For example, the *California State Plan for Refugee Assistance and Services, 1983,* published by the Department of Social Services (DSS), was critical of federal refugee resettlement policy, claiming it to be a "patchwork program . . . causing" states and counties to "constantly contend with operational confusion, inconsistencies and inefficiencies" (DSS 1983:7-9).

In addition to other differences, Soviet Jewish and Vietnamese resettlement programs maintained contrasting numbers of resettlement agencies and a vastly disparate degree of integration and centralization among service providers. In 1983, there were over 40 agencies resettling Vietnamese refugees in San Francisco alone, with 15 or more in surrounding counties (Murray 1981:3). This compared dramatically to the three agencies providing services to Soviet Jews in San Francisco at the same time (three more were located in neighboring Alameda County). The large number of resettlement agencies providing service to Vietnamese refugees was inefficient in terms of coordination and allocation of funding, and sometimes created interagency competition and hostility.

EFFECTS OF RESETTLEMENT POLICY

Some of the ways in which resettlement systems have shaped refugees' adaptation and community formation are described below. This topic will be addressed in terms of several resettlement activities, including job placement, the provision of psychological therapy, and religious and ethnic socialization. This discussion is not intended to be all-encompassing or conclusive. Rather, its purpose is to reveal certain processes that occurred within refugee communities due to the effects of the resettlement system.

Socialization and Negotiation in Service Provision

To do their job at all, resettlement agencies must engage in a great deal of client socialization. For many refugees, resettlement staff were the first representatives of American society with whom they had any significant contact. As a consequence, even the most basic interactions between refugees and resettlement staff involved various forms of cultural conflict (Wilson and Garrick 1983). In the words of one government resettlement report, "There are aspects of the American life with which refugees must simply learn to cope." (Cichon et al. 1986:87).

Job Placement

The development of economic self-sufficiency is one of the major responsibilities of the refugee resettlement system. Staff and clients alike agreed that refugees should find jobs. However, the two parties to this interaction often had contrasting notions about the job-finding process. Further complicating these interactions was the fact that the U.S. economy and the means of finding jobs within it are not easily understood by recently arrived refugees who lack competence in English. Finally, because many Soviet Jewish and Vietnamese refugees entered the U.S. job market during the early 1980s—a period marked by a recession and the highest unemployment rate in decades—jobs were scarce (Rumbaut 1989b; ORR 1989). All of these factors (the need for jobs, the scarcity of job opportunities, and refugees' lack of understanding of American job-finding practices) came to a head during face-to-face interactions in the job placement units of refugee resettlement agencies.

Interpreting job-finding through Soviet experience. Because of the vast differences between Soviet and American procedures for finding employment, recently arrived émigrés had particularly difficult interactions with American job placement workers. For example, émigrés who were seeking jobs often interpreted their interactions with the Jewish Vocational Service in light of past encounters with *Raspredelenie,* the Soviet state employment agency. Drawing upon their Soviet experience, wherein desired services were delivered by bureaucrats in exchange for favors, émigrés who were not referred to jobs of their liking sometimes assumed that agency staff were holding out in order to receive a payoff. Accordingly, émigrés occasionally attempted to bribe staff or offered indirect payment in the form of contributions to the Jewish Federation.[2]

In addition to using bribes, émigrés also tried to acquire jobs through Soviet-style political machinations involving *blat* (influence) and *sviazy* (connections). I was informed of this technique while teaching a job-finding class to a group of Soviet engineers. During each of the first four meetings, participants would assert that the best way to find jobs is through the application of influence with the right persons:

All of this training, it's no good. This is what we should do. Do you know the director of the Jewish Federation? Does he make appointments with people like us? We will talk to him. He could go to the president of big engineering company, Jewish president, and tell him to hire some of us. There are only a few of us. He could hire one of us each week.

These émigrés saw American institutions through the lens of their Soviet experience. Rather than following the suggestions of agency staff, they hoped to apply job-finding techniques that had worked in the USSR.

If American service providers were to carry out their assigned duty and help émigrés find jobs, they had to resocialize clients, making them understand that Soviet job-finding techniques would not work in the American context. However, given the high rates of unemployment and scarcity of good entry-level jobs that have plagued the U.S. economy in recent years, American-style job-finding techniques sometimes appeared to émigrés as no more effective than those retained from the Soviet Union.

Agency versus client in job placement. Even when refugees accepted American approaches to finding work and adopted the roles that resettlement agencies established for them, conflicts between refugees and resettlement agencies continued to occur (ORR 1982a) because agencies and clients had very different conceptions of what job placement should involve. Each refugee sought the most desirable, well-paid, and prestigious job that could be acquired. In contrast, agencies approached the job referral process en masse. They hoped to place a large number of clients with a minimum of effort in order to develop a record of accomplishment that would favorably impress funding agencies and supervisory boards.

I observed this conflict while working at Refugee Center, an independent San Francisco resettlement agency. Its staff hoped to ensure continued funding by consistently exceeding contractual quotas for its government-funded job-placement service. Job developers determined that the most efficient way to secure placements was by developing good relations with sizable firms capable of employing many refugees. Bill Le described the agency's strategy of emphasizing initial contacts, pointing out that early efforts would be rewarded with easy placements later on. However, staff efforts to impress employers frequently conflicted with the interests of individual refugee clients. For example, to convince an employer of the quality of the agency's referrals, a job developer would send an overqualified worker—one who had clerical skills and was fluent in English—to perform a poorly paid menial position such as janitor or assembly-line worker. While the quality of the worker impressed the employer and thus ensured future requests for referrals, such workers were often angered because they had been placed in a position far below their level of skill. The fact that resettlement agencies often referred clients to poor jobs soured many Vietnamese refugees' views of resettlement agencies and job-placement units. Although finding employment was a major problem for newly arrived Vietnamese, many were uninterested in using employment referral services they knew existed.

Soviet Jews were also frustrated by their experiences with the job-placement units of their resettlement organizations. Conflicts were heightened because many Soviet Jewish refugees were professionals. With university educations and years of experience, they strongly identified with their occupations in the USSR and were often unwilling to accept the less-than-desired positions to which they were referred.[3] A Soviet Jewish activist explained how job-placement interactions angered some Soviet Jews to the point of alienating them from the entire American Jewish community:

> Many people are still complaining about ways they were treated by American professionals of Family and Vocational Services. I believe that people feel not enough attention, not enough guidance, not enough personal involvement [was applied]. Career counseling was not adequate. People were pushed to accept low level jobs as opposed to giving them a chance by actively seeking middle-level.

> Some of the complaints are justifiable and some of the expectations were realistic. And yet for many, there is a one or two time exposure to a counselor of Family or Vocational Service. For many, it cast a negative reflection on the whole Jewish community in America.

Refugee networks versus resettlement services. Soviet Jewish and Vietnamese refugees were uncomfortable with and unimpressed by resettlement agencies because they compared the benefits and style of service delivery offered by agencies with those available through their own ethnic networks. As noted in Chapters 4 and 5, grass-roots refugees' networks provided their members with many forms of emotional and economic support in a personable and trust-based context. Most Vietnamese recent arrivals I interviewed found the quality of service available through their own networks superior to that obtained from agencies. This conclusion is supported by a University of Michigan study of almost 7,000 post-1978 Southeast Asian refugees, which found that "the indication is that the refugee networks provide the most aid in gaining jobs, while organizations help to some degree" (Caplan et al. 1985:223).

Working the system. Not all refugees rejected the services available through resettlement agencies. Some became adept at "working the system" and combined the services and information available from several agencies with informal networks to achieve an optimal standard of living. Occasionally, these refugees maintained addresses in different cities or counties in order to maximize eligibility for benefits. For example, in early 1983, one Vietnamese recent arrival, Loc Mai, had job applications on file at two job-placement services and attended a paying job-training program sponsored by a third Comprehensive Employment and Training Act (CETA) agency. Loc's preschool-aged daughter attended a day-care center at a local church, thus freeing Loc to attend classes and allowing Loc's wife to work at a restaurant. (Mrs. Mai was also on the waiting list for a paid training program for clerical workers.)

Loc used several publicly funded sources of medical and dental treatment for his family. He inconsistently attended an evening English class at a local community college that provided him with numerous social contacts as well as language training. By mixing the services of several agencies, Loc maximized available benefits. At the same time, he lessened his dependence upon any single agency. Thus he could avoid coercive relationships with agencies that tried to exchange their services for his compliance with institutional goals.

Through his interactions with agencies, Loc mastered an area of American life. However, this is surely not the type of assimilation the framers of resettlement policies had in mind. Many studies suggest that Loc's manipulation of the welfare system was not unusual. Thousands of Southeast Asian refugees work in the underground economy while simultaneously collecting public assistance and other benefits (Arax 1987; Baker and North 1984; North 1988; Rumbaut 1989).

A network of recently arrived refugees of which Loc was a member maintained a consensus as to which needs were best filled through contacts with resettlement agencies and which were better satisfied through personal contacts. These refugees agreed that job referral and job-training programs offered by resettlement agencies were of little value. They explained that training programs took too long and often offered "skills" like sewing machine operation or janitorial training that led to undesirable jobs. Job referrals available from resettlement agencies were usually minimum wage, part-time, and offered few opportunities for advancement. Also, if a refugee refused to accept an agency-referred job or quit one, he or she would be subject to reprimands or denied eligibility for further referrals.

On the other hand, recent arrivals generally felt that day-care, immigration, and sponsorship services were valuable. Such services helped refugees save both time and money, were staffed by Vietnamese-speakers, and did not maintain the authoritarian style recent arrivals associated with employment-related programs. Well over half the Vietnamese clients of a church-sponsored resettlement office in San Francisco where I did fieldwork came to obtain aid completing various immigration and social service documents. Most common were applications to sponsor relatives in refugee camps, Green Card applications, and releases required for arrivals from other states to receive cash assistance or aid to families with dependent children (AFDC).

Like the Vietnamese, some Soviet Jews learned to work the system and to combine selected services from agencies together with those from other sources in order to maintain the highest possible standard of living. Soviet Jews also exchanged information within their communities and subgroups to determine the best sources for satisfying various needs. However, because they were able to meet needs through intimate connections, many Soviet Jews berated agencies. With the exception of highly dependent groups, such as the aged, teenagers, or those with health problems who regularly used resettlement agencies, many émigrés considered resettlement services as an alternative that was "better than nothing, but not great."

Training refugees to receive therapy. In addition to job placement, another area in which extensive cultural conflicts and misunderstandings arose between resettlement staff and their Soviet Jewish and Vietnamese clients was the provision of psychological therapy. Health assessments have shown that refugees suffer from a variety of mental health problems. Consequently, the government has funded a number of mental health programs for this population (Cichon et al. 1986; Efron 1990; Lappin and Scott 1982; Owan 1985). Unfortunately, most Soviet Jews and Vietnamese lack the cultural prerequisites of a successful, American-style therapy interaction, such as a willingness to confide in bureaucrats, a belief in the unconscious, and the ability to openly criticize parents. Finally, most refugees do not see a connection between the process of therapy and the problems that, for them, are most pressing (Brower 1981; Gold 1987; Owan 1985; Slote 1972). The following quote, addressed to a social worker, illustrates a Soviet client's refusal to take therapy seriously:

> I like you. You're a nice lady and this way I can practice my English. But I don't really understand how talking about this will help me. (Dorf and Katlin 1983:152).

Because refugees were not prepared to engage in therapeutic interactions, resettlement workers had difficulty in developing a clientele of cooperative therapy consumers. Thai Nguyen, a Vietnamese-born, American-educated social worker, described his efforts to train refugees to become involved in therapy:

From a mental health professional point of view, whether we can successfully work with these people depends on how well they are willing to work with us. This method of problem solving is rather new to the population; we really have to work, to, you know, educate them, to inform them what our role is.

So whatever the cases that we have, they mainly come from in-patient unit, from schools, from Children's Services at the Department of Social Services, through the Probation Department and through the San Francisco Trial Diversion Program.

I think the difficulty is that there is a lack of understanding of mental health as it is understood in this country. For an average Vietnamese, mental health would immediately mean that the person is crazy, acting crazy, saying crazy things. But to us, a mental health problem could also be that the person is experiencing marital problems, a person is having difficulty to deal with a co-worker, for an adolescent having difficulty establishing or maintaining peer relationships, you know, to have friends. These are the kinds of problems that we would work with.

Social workers who were aware of their clients' lack of interest in psychological therapy, yet still felt that refugees would benefit by discussing problems in a neutral and supportive environment, engineered situations that permitted issues of interest to refugees to be discussed in a manner that emphasized therapeutic content. These included classes and workshops on women's issues, health, raising children in the States, and adapting to a new economy (Coughlin and Rosenberg 1983; Cunningham and Dorf 1979). A Jewish Family Service social worker described a class offering both information and therapy:

We have just completed a "coping with stress" workshop. We called it something like "Finding your own job and coping with the anxiety in the interim." They [Soviet Jews] are not used to talking about their feelings. I just read the evaluations . . . very concrete job search issues were most important [to them]. And the feeling piece was not their interest. But our counselors felt that a lot of stuff was happening in that there were other people in that boat and it was okay to talk about that. It was okay to be anxious.

In sum, clients of refugee resettlement agencies were constantly exposed to American cultural forms. Much of the activities of resettlement workers actually involved training their clients how to understand American society and receive services. In this way, even if the services rendered by agencies were themselves of relatively little importance to a refugee's adaptation to the United States, the interaction through which such services were provided was rich in information about the host society. However, refugees were not passive recipients of this information. By exchanging their impressions in ethnic networks and combining services from several agencies with those from their own communities, refugees sought an improved standard of living while limiting coercive and frustrating relations with agencies.

Resettlement Policies and the Creation of Ethnic Communities

Rejecting the assimilationist model of immigrant adaptation that was dominant during earlier waves of migration, the framers of both public and private resettlement policy now endorse ethnic pluralism. Refugees are often encouraged to retain and build upon their ethnic identity and community membership as a means of coping with life in the United States (Finnan and Cooperstein 1983; Gorelick 1982; Herberg 1989; Lewin and Associates 1986; Reimers 1985; Rischlin 1962). This perspective is institutionalized in such programs as the MAA Incentive Grant Initiative, which funds community-based ethnic MAAs (mutual assistance associations) to provide services to fellow refugees in an indigenous cultural environment (Lewin and Associates 1986).

The direct provision of resettlement services by refugees was generally exclusive to the Vietnamese. Soviet Jews receive resettlement services from co-ethnics (American Jews) but few Soviet émigrés were involved in the delivery of services and none ran their own agencies.[4] Vietnamese mutual assistance agencies frequently maintained their own ideological agenda for the refugee community in the United States (Finnan and Cooperstein 1983:49). They were involved in such activities as cultural preservation, political socialization, community relations, and the development of economic self-sufficiency.

Refugee Center:
An Ethnic Mutual Assistance Association

Refugee Center, an independent agency run by highly committed Vietnamese, epitomized the active MAA that was involved with the ethnic community. Refugee Center workers exhibited a high degree of social and ideological unity that fostered organizational effectiveness. Due to its independent status and motivated staff, Refugee Center was able to grow through the mid-1980s, securing grants to provide long-term services, while many other agencies suffered cutbacks. In contrast to the bureaucratic apathy and feeling of decline that characterized many resettlement agencies after 1982, Refugee Center had a dynamic atmosphere. Loc Pham, Refugee Center's job placement coordinator, articulated the Center's ideology of refugee resettlement:

> My motivation to work for refugees is based on concern for my people, not ideology. This is a hard job with lots of problems and few successes, so I don't stand to gain. We do it out of pride in country. Our goal is for the Vietnamese to participate in all levels of American society and to become self-sufficient taxpayers.

Building constituencies. To apply its ideology, organize the refugee community and promote its own visibility, Refugee Center constantly worked to build constituencies among government agencies, political figures, foundations, private industry, mass media, other resettlement services, and members of the refugee community. These connections were used to enhance organizational effectiveness and ensure continued funding under conditions of declining resources.

Responsive, well-socialized clients were mobilized to prove the Center's grass-roots support, consume its services, and participate in its events. Because an agency's ties with the ethnic community were valued by the Office of Refugee Resettlement in awarding refugee service contracts, Refugee Center was able to use its constituencies to successfully compete for grants against more experienced, American-run agencies[5] (Lewin and Associates 1986; ORR 1982a).

Refugee Center sponsored a Democratic club, an elderly association, an organization of boat people, a small business development program and loan fund, and a Vietnamese language class for refugee children. In addition, Refugee Center carried out several activities to demonstrate that Vietnamese refugees were contributing members of society, not just recipients of government aid. Its benefits for African refugees and Amerasian refugee children were attended by refugees, prominent citizens, and a number of American political figures.

In conjunction with its community activities, Refugee Center was skilled in the art of public relations. It employed an expert in this field who advertised the agency's activities and got plenty of favorable press for its benefactors. Through constant publicity, the Center's director came to be regarded—at least in the English-language media—as a spokesman for Bay Area Vietnamese.

Finally, Refugee Center also maintained good relations with other agencies. Toward this end, its staff participated in local refugee forums, loose associations of agency staff, social service administrators, and academics. Agencies used these forums to exchange information and client referrals, alert each other of community developments, and create multiagency protests against funding cuts or negative media coverage.

By supporting ethnic MAAs, resettlement policy underwrites this kind of community mobilization and development among Southeast Asian refugees.

Jewish Socialization and Resettlement

Vietnamese resettlement agencies used ethnicity as a basis for motivating staff and building constituencies. Soviet Jews' resettlement system also sought to enhance ethnic ties in the course of resettlement; the entire program of resettlement for Soviet Jews was directed toward involving émigrés in the American Jewish community. From their time of exit from the USSR, Soviet Jews were encouraged to participate in religious activities and plan the location and style of their resettlement on the basis of religious values (Carp 1990; Panish 1981; Schwartz 1980).

In contrast to Vietnamese ethnic socialization, however, Soviet Jews' resettlement policy has been directed at religious integration. The goal was not to develop independent refugee organizations but to include Soviet émigrés in American Jewish activities (Goldberg 1981). The executive director of Jewish Family Service of Akron described the "assimilation task" for Soviet exiles:

If our program succeeds in its goal of awakening Jewish consciousness, then these new Americans, in the near future, should become vital, responsible, and contributing members of our Jewish community. (Schwartz 1980:55)

This concern with Jewish religious socialization was a point of great emphasis in interactions between émigrés and resettlement workers. For example, since the early 1970s, several articles in *The Journal of Jewish Communal Service* have provided resettlement staff with hints on how to bring Soviet émigrés into the American Jewish community:

> It is absolutely essential to exploit ESL [English as a second language] classes . . . where they are actually a captive audience. . . for inculcating Jewish attitudes and values . . . to foster a positive Jewish self-concept while developing Jewish cognition, Jewish language expression and Jewish life skills. (Schiff 1980:45-49)

As a fieldworker, I personally experienced the efforts of agencies to provide émigrés with religious training. Before I was put in contact with an émigré family as a volunteer English teacher, the program supervisor of the local Jewish resettlement agency made sure that I was a Jew and was willing to discuss basic aspects of Judaism as part of English training.

Some Soviet émigrés responded positively to the Jewish socialization component of resettlement. They joined synagogues, sent their children to Jewish day schools and camps, participated in Jewish community activities, and raised funds for Jewish philanthropic activities. In general, however, émigrés were not highly involved with American Jewish activities (Markowitz 1988). A recent survey found that 70% of Soviet Jews who have been in the United States at least eight years attended a temple or synagogue less than three times a year, and 37% go only when invited to a bar mitzvah or wedding (Kosmin 1990: 51). The response of émigrés to Jewish socialization was so minimal that in 1987, the Los Angeles Bureau of Jewish Education seriously considered closing its Soviet émigré program.

Although officially there was a strong emphasis on the inculcation of religion within Soviet Jewish resettlement activities, many of the resettlement staff I interviewed were extremely uncomfortable with this task. Social workers realized that émigrés' most immediate interests involved achieving economic stability and ensuring secure careers for their children, not studying Hebrew or going to temple (Zahler 1989). Noting their clients' resistance to religious indoctrination, many resettlement workers downplayed the role of religion in resettlement. A Southern California social worker commented:

> And for our lay people, if our board people were really to hear that . . . [Soviet Jews came to the U.S. for other than religious reasons] I

don't think that they would be really thrilled. I think they really think they rescued them . . . they think about it in terms of the refusenik.

But I tell you, as far as I'm concerned, it doesn't really bother me. They are people, they want to restore their lives, they want to live in the United States. You can't work in this business and sit in judgment of people.

By the late 1980s, there was official acknowledgment that most Soviet Jews were not religiously active. Initial hopes to "create a Jewish need" or "foster Jewish language skills" and make Soviet émigrés into "vital, responsible, and contributing members of our Jewish community" were replaced by a more realistic acknowledgment of Soviet émigrés' secular and ethnic identification, as opposed to a religious one (Carp 1990; Kosmin 1990; Zahler 1989).

In summary, both Soviet Jewish and Vietnamese resettlement agencies sought to develop ethnic identity and membership among their clients. Vietnamese-run agencies, such as Refugee Center, seemed to take this goal seriously and fostered a variety of ethnic values, activities, and constituencies in the course of resettling clients. Soviet Jews' resettlement agencies also received a strong mandate to inculcate Jewish values during resettlement interactions. However, this was a different kind of ethnic relationship because while both staff and clients were Jews, they had contrasting cultural, linguistic, and national origins. Social workers and other staff who had direct contact with Soviet Jews realized the ethical problems and futility of foisting unwanted indoctrination upon émigrés. Consequently, most downplayed this goal in the course of client contact.

At the agency level, resettlement activities can foster the development of ethnic solidarity through the support of MAAs and the community-building activities they provide. At the same time, however, coercive, "preachy," or unsatisfying interactions—those involving low-quality job referrals, culturally alien therapy sessions, or unwanted religious socialization—alienated refugees from resettlement agencies. Under such circumstances, clients pragmatically worked the system or avoided it altogether.

Working the System From Within

An important, but seldom-mentioned, impact of the refugee resettlement system is that through employment within that system, refugees find positions of income, power, and visibility that would be unavailable otherwise. The government's commitment to funding ethnic-based agencies and the necessity of hiring refugees as service providers due to their cultural and linguistic skills has allowed a fairly sizable number of refugees to work within the resettlement system (Hein 1988). Further, in making refugees eligible for medical care, job training, and other benefits, the state provides refugee entrepreneurs who deliver such services with a captive market of subsidized customers.[6]

Employment Within Resettlement Agencies

The existence of refugee resettlement programs has provided a small but significant number of refugees with stable, white-collar jobs and, as such, has facilitated the development of a refugee middle class. While few Soviet Jews are employed as resettlement staff, many Vietnamese refugees have found jobs as service providers (Hein 1988:473). This pattern was most evident among two groups: Chinese-Vietnamese who were trilingual in English, Vietnamese, and Chinese (Cantonese or other dialects) and Vietnamese activists who had college degrees.

Multilingual refugees had the skills required for frontline staff in resettlement agencies dealing with Southeast Asian refugee clients of diverse linguistic backgrounds. For example, Thuy Chau, a 19-year-old Chinese-Vietnamese refugee who had finished high school and one year of junior college in the United States, realized the employment potential in her language and clerical skills. By working as a volunteer in a resettlement office, she developed contacts with resettlement staff that were instrumental in her being hired for a comfortable job with a $1,200-a-month salary plus benefits, a far better position than would be generally available to a refugee of her age and education.

College-educated Vietnamese refugees revealed a similar pattern of developing contacts with agencies through volunteer work that ultimately resulted in full-time employment. Their education qualified them for management-level positions. Because of the unstable nature of agency funding, such contacts were also useful for obtaining work if one's own agency was a victim of cutbacks.

Government Funds Support Refugee Entrepreneurs

The eligibility of refugees for government-subsidized health benefits provided a major source of income for Soviet Jewish and

Vietnamese health professionals. Having obtained their licence to practice in the United States, these refugees directed their practices toward co-ethnics and were reimbursed for services by government programs. Refugee business districts always featured several such medical offices. In turn, refugee medical professionals supported the ethnic media, ethnic business directories, and various support services, thereby creating a venue for further ethnic interaction.

Other refugee entrepreneurs cashed in on refugees' entitlements by opening trade schools and beauty colleges. Located in refugee enclaves, they served an exclusively ethnic clientele, with tuition paid by the government. I observed one such operation, a beauty academy located in an Orange County mini-mall. It functioned symbiotically with a Vietnamese coffee shop next door, where students spent their breaks and lunch hour.

Community Segmentation Is Enhanced
Through Competing Agencies

Ethnic resettlement agencies encourage Vietnamese solidarity by organizing members of the refugee community. However, when viewed from a broader perspective, this solidarity appears largely local in impact. The underwriting of numerous, competitive agencies often gave birth to "ethnic fiefdoms" that accentuated the already segmented and conflict-ridden nature of this refugee population (Finnan and Cooperstein 1983; Lewin and Associates 1986; Nielsen 1985).

Competing Vietnamese activists often used resettlement agencies as positions to air their views, compete for followers, and build a community power base. Each agency director and his staff used their connections with American institutions, manipulating traditional symbols and current issues in order to attract followers. However, because Vietnamese refugees have a long history of being deceived by corrupt leaders, they are not easily persuaded to follow political movements. As a consequence, they regard displays of political ambition with cynicism, thereby yielding a vacuum of leadership. This condition was widely acknowledged by observers as well as refugees themselves:

> In general, the Vietnamese communities seem to have too many leaders
> . . . . One former government official described organizing a festival as
> "nearly impossible" due to the lack of "obvious leaders." . . . There were

numerous examples of prominent refugees working together at first, then splitting to form rival organizations. (Finnan and Cooperstein 1983:65).

While historical circumstances, culture, and personalities predisposed the Vietnamese toward a segmented pattern of community formation, a resettlement policy that generated numerous, overlapping, and competing agencies furthered this lack of unity. In the words of an Orange County activist:

> The Vietnamese political leaders all have the same ambition, they want to be striking out for himself or herself, but in fact, not the community. I know most of the leaders are an American creation.

It seemed that no agency was immune from political subversion and conflict. As a result of factionalism, Refugee Center's highly influential, effective, and well-connected executive director was dismissed by its board of overseers in 1984. In protest, several of the Center's most committed, skilled, and experienced staff resigned, removing much of the organization's vitality and depriving the refugee community of some of its most effective activists.

In sum, while the creation of ethnic-run resettlement agencies yielded many positive effects for the Vietnamese community, it tended to discourage community-wide unification by empowering competing elements of an already factionalized population. Despite the segmentation brought on by support of local MAAs, several government-funded reports have shown them to be an effective means of mobilizing communities and serving unmet needs. As such, their continued support has been endorsed (Lewin and Associates 1986; Cichon et al. 1986:109).

Reactive Solidarity

When Soviet Jewish and Vietnamese refugees felt frustrated by their interactions with American or ethnic-run agencies, they sometimes created their own organizations as alternative sources of services, or as a basis through which they could assert their own perspective. Ivan Light (1980) describes this process as reactive solidarity.

While both Vietnamese and Soviet Jewish refugees were grateful for the services they received, many resented the paternalistic manner in which resettlement policy was devised and delivered.

Resettlement workers and activists were especially resentful of what they felt was their exclusion from the creation and provision of resettlement services. As refugee communities became better established in the United States, comments regarding such exclusion became more frequent and passionate. An Orange County activist commented:

> I am on the County refugee forum. It has 12 members—all of them are white except me and Mr. Tran. We love the help Americans have given us, so we don't say anything. But when they have programs for the black American or Mexican American, they never have the group almost all white. We have been here over 10 years. We have many doctors and educated people. Why can't we make for ourselves?

Similarly, a Soviet Jewish activist who engaged in protracted struggles both to organize his own community and to be heard by American resettlement staff stated:

> Many people still have been complaining about ways they were treated by American professionals of Family and Vocational Services. Then we come with beautiful ideas and nobody wants to listen to us. And then they push us, you know "you go to this place."

> I've been a client of Jewish Vocational Services, I have been a peer and I run an agency, but I cannot get a job with the Jewish Federation saving [resettling] Soviet Jews. The Soviet Jews are predominantly served by non-Russian-speaking Americans.

As a result of resentment toward agencies, members of Vietnamese and Soviet Jewish communities developed ethnic associations that functioned as alternatives to American service providers while simultaneously acting as power bases through which refugees asserted their demands.

Reacting against both American and co-ethnic resettlement agencies, Vietnamese refugees organized volunteer associations to help co-ethnics. These were especially important among the ethnic Chinese subgroup. Few ethnic Chinese had college degrees or spoke English fluently. Consequently, as a group they lacked the skills, credentials, and connections required to take leadership of government-funded, refugee-run resettlement agencies. In addition, Chinese-Vietnamese were highly suspicious of the Vietnamese (Peters 1988).

Finally, both Vietnamese and Chinese-Vietnamese informants claimed that Chinese-Vietnamese were not treated fairly by Vietnamese-run resettlement agencies.

As a consequence, the views and needs of the Chinese-Vietnamese were not met by existing MAAs and agencies. Relying on their long history of minority self-help in Vietnam, the Chinese-Vietnamese created various associations, often based on dialect and regional origins. In the words of a Chinese-Vietnamese resettlement worker:

> I feel a lot of discrimination from the Vietnamese. They did it in Vietnam and they do it here, too. We know from experience that Local Agency won't do too much to help us.

> So now we can come out. We describe our background as Chinese, not Vietnamese. We thought "we are people in a common position, we have to join together." Because in any country, especially here in the United States, the government cannot hear the individual, so you need to join an organization and have some information. So that's why we joined together and raised this Association for Indochina Chinese Refugees.

Soviet Jewish activists also made several efforts to organize. As a group with special knowledge, interests, and concerns with Soviet Jewry, they wanted to be heard by the American Jewish agencies that developed resettlement programs. As already mentioned, the issue of religious socialization was one source of contention. Soviet Jews were also displeased by the American Jewish community's views on the destination of their co-ethnics' resettlement.

As a means of supporting the Jewish state, many American Jewish organizations favor Israel (rather than the United States) as the official destination for Soviet émigrés and have endorsed policies requiring mandatory settlement in Israel (see Chapter 2). Saying "let my people go, indeed," émigrés pointed out the hypocrisy of American Jews, who enjoy the wealth, freedom, and security of the United States, telling Soviets to live in Israel—a country they associate with limited freedoms, few economic opportunities, and impending war. Whenever Jewish agencies discussed measures to force Soviets to settle in Israel, émigrés expressed their displeasure. In the words of a Los Angeles activist:

> This is a very sensitive problem, but we have to face it and be honest, because unfortunately, I have to say that I've heard a lot of statements on

behalf of American Jews, okay, which I can only describe as a double standard. Why should they sit in Beverly Hills and accuse me of not going over to Israel and I left Russia with $120 and he has all the money in the world?

Consequently, disputes over resettlement policy, including religious socialization, job placement, and nations of refuge, left many Soviet Jews with feelings of resentment toward the American Jewish community.

Moreover, as Soviet Jews have become established in the United States, they have complained that they are being directed into predetermined roles for religious participation, community support, and ideological commitment (Markowitz 1988). Feeling that their desires and input were ignored, they established autonomous associations. A Soviet Jewish activist commented:

Now when they [the Jewish Federation] contacts the Soviet Jews for support, they [the Soviet Jews] summarize the point like this:

"I am not a poor man any longer and I would have been glad to support your organization. But when I was a nobody and when I came to my counselor for Jewish Vocational Service, she told me that I have to sweep the streets and I would never be a doctor over here. So now I am established, I say forget this [fund drive]. I don't want to give you any [money]. I don't want to be affiliated in any way with those people [Jewish Federation of Los Angeles]."

Due to conflicts between Soviet Jews and their American sponsors, the Jewish organization in Los Angeles that has received the most attention from Russian Jews has not been an established American congregation. Rather, the Chabad-Russian Outreach Program—an immigrant-oriented storefront synagogue staffed by Moscow-born rabbis—has been a focal point of numerous Soviet Jews' attendance and contributions (see Chapter 8).

Although the staff of resettlement systems often feel threatened by their clients' autonomy-seeking actions, research indicates that refugees' reactive organizations have yielded positive results for refugees and service providers alike. These community initiatives have been able to identify and serve isolated client constituencies, encourage responsibility, and mobilize communities in a way mainstream agencies cannot (Lewin and Associates 1986; Cichon et al. 1986;

Finnan and Cooperstein 1983). In addition, their independent efforts have accessed sources of nonfederal funding and established new connections for the refugee community:

> Through their requests for funding from United Way, local foundations and local government agencies, MAAs have brought the needs of their members to the attention of policy makers. Even if their own appeals for funds do not succeed, others may be able to build on the MAA efforts to obtain needed support—financial and otherwise—from these civic institutions. (Lewin and Associates 1986:613)

In sum, reactive solidarity occurred when resettlement policies and interactions angered refugees to the point where they chose to create their own associations as a vehicle to challenge the existing structure. While efforts to achieve ethnic autonomy threatened the established resettlement system, these refugee-based groups often yielded benefits for their communities.

CONCLUSIONS

Interactions between resettlement agencies and refugees are frequently characterized by cross-cultural conflict and negotiation. Oftentimes, those refugees who need service most cannot obtain it because of difficulties in communicating with resettlement staff. Some clients are successfully socialized to receive services. Others, however, find interactions with agencies unbearable. As an alternative, they acquire help from ethnic networks. Finally, a number of refugees learn to work the system, obtaining services from multiple sources, including various agencies and ethnic networks, to maintain an optimal standard of living.

Soviet Jewish and Vietnamese resettlement involves activities intended to develop ethnic communities. The Vietnamese refugees' resettlement system subsidized ethnic-based mutual assistance associations; Soviet Jews were linked to the American Jewish community. For the Vietnamese, this policy occasionally led to the creation of effective, culturally informed, and highly motivated resettlement agencies. However, given the segmented nature of the Vietnamese population, this policy also discouraged community unification as contentious MAAs competed with one another for followers and funding.

Although some Soviet Jews participated in the religious training offered during resettlement, many others were turned off by this approach. As a result, the reactions of clients required the resettlement system to downplay and reframe its initial emphasis on "Jewish programming" in favor of a more consumer-oriented approach. Finally, negative reactions to resettlement agencies provoked reactive solidarity among some Soviet Jewish and Vietnamese refugees. These refugees created their own networks, organizations, and grass-roots movements as alternatives to mainstream resettlement agencies.

In conclusion, the effects of refugee resettlement must be understood in light of interactions between service providers and consumers in a community context. Refugees react to resettlement according to their own resources, values, and priorities. Perceived as disruptive by service providers, these reactions often yielded benefits as well. They reduced cultural conflicts, enhanced organizational effectiveness, promoted self-reliance, and caused policies to be revised for the better. To best achieve such positive outcomes, resettlement services might consider clients as able partners, not dependent adversaries.

NOTES

1. Although this discussion focuses on negative aspects of refugee resettlement interactions, it is not intended in any way to detract from the significant accomplishments made by dedicated staff in providing necessary services to refugees.

2. This approach to finding work was also retained by émigrés who had successfully found employment in the United States. For example, a personnel manager of an engineering firm that employed many Soviet Jews described regularly receiving gifts from the men he had hired.

3. This is partly due to the fact that the Soviet Union has little if any unemployment and a highly centralized job-placement agency. Hence, the complex and uncertain experience of applying for a job in the United States is totally unfamiliar to Soviet Jews (Gitelman et al. ND). These interactions are also difficult for American service providers. I interviewed two staff members of Jewish Vocational Services—the job-finding agency that aids Soviet émigrés—who readily admitted that they had little experience placing professionals before the Soviet Jews arrived.

4. Since the late 1980s, the Los Angeles-based Association of Soviet Jewish Émigrés has received grants from the City of West Hollywood and Los Angeles County to aid recently arrived émigrés.

5. So much so, that activities devoted to establishing a constituency of clients, referred to as "outreach," are considered legitimate expenses in agency budgets.

6. In this way, resettlement agency jobs for recent refugees bear a marked similarity to the role played by ethnic political machines for turn-of-the-century immigrants. In each case, the state offered jobs to recent arrivals in a manner that helped to establish an ethnic middle class (Glazer and Moynihan 1963).

7

Self-Employment
and Refugee Communities

This chapter examines how Soviet Jewish and Vietnamese refugees shape their own communities through involvement in small businesses.

In recent years, sociologists have devoted a great deal of attention to the study of ethnic self-employment. Drawing on studies of contemporary groups, like Cubans and Koreans, and historical cases, such as Jews, Chinese, and Japanese, scholars have emphasized the ability of recently arrived immigrants to provide themselves with jobs, community solidarity, and protection from discrimination. This body of research has been instrumental in demonstrating to academics and policymakers alike that ethnic communities are not just supportive, culturally rich environments, but viable units of economic organization as well.

The idea of self-employment as an effective basis for ethnic community has been widely accepted because it is compatible with a broad spectrum of political outlooks, ranging from Reagan Republicans' Urban Enterprise Zones to Louis Farrakhan's calls for black economic development. Even Marxists—who would seemingly abhor the capitalist ethos of small business—have warmed to the notion of ethnic enterprise, seeing it as rooted in community-based collectivism rather than individualistic self-interest (Cummings 1980; Russell 1985). In this manner, the idea of immigrant enterprise—backed up by research on selected groups that have been especially successful—has become an appealing approach to the economic and social problems of immigrant and minority groups in American society.

However, like all influential ideas, that of ethnic self-employment is surrounded by controversy. One body of scholarship challenges the degree to which the widely trumpeted "success stories" are really successful (Sanders and Nee 1987). Another asserts that these successes have been achieved only through the "superexploitation" of customers, workers, and family members (Bonacich 1987, 1990; Zhou and Logan 1989).

A third critique—the one most relevant here—questions the generalizability of immigrant entrepreneurial success. More specifically, it asks to what extent groups without unique resources, connections, and environmental facilitators can also reap major rewards—in terms of economic mobility and community development—from self-employment.

The following pages examine the nature of small business activities among Soviet Jewish and Vietnamese refugees in California. Rather than simply considering the viability of refugee enterprises, I focus on the relationship between ethnic community and ethnic business.

SELF-HELP AND THE ENCLAVE

Sociological and anthropological studies of successful ethnic enterprise have consistently shown a symbiotic relationship between an ethnic community and its businesses. Rather than simply being interested in their own short-term profits, ethnic business owners help each other and members of their community, providing social welfare benefits, advice, credit, jobs, leadership, goods, and support for the community's institutions. At the same time, members of ethnic communities supply their business owners with investment funds, patronage, low-cost labor, loyalty, and prestige (Silverman 1988).

Each party to this relationship may exploit the other: Business owners might pay workers substandard wages and local toughs may demand protection money from entrepreneurs (Katz 1988; Light 1972; Lyman 1974). However, each also returns benefits as well: Exploitative owners help workers start their own businesses and ethnic gangs will harass a business' competitors (Gold 1988; Katz 1988; Waldinger et al. 1990). As a symbiotic relationship, these exchanges are not simply charitable but, rather, are reinforced by broadly defined, shared interests (Cohen 1969; Cummings 1980; Gorelick 1982):

[I]mmigrants may be vulnerable and oppressed, but, because they can draw on connections of mutuality and support, they can also create resources that offset the harshness of the environment they encounter. (Waldinger et al. 1990:35)

The ideal type of symbiotic relationship between ethnic business and ethnic community has been called the ethnic enclave (Portes and Bach 1985; Portes and Manning 1986). Based upon studies of Cubans in Miami, Portes and his colleagues argue that under such conditions, ethnic self-employment provides immigrants with better jobs than they would likely find in the larger U.S. economy.

Although Portes's findings have been criticized (Sanders and Nee 1987; Johnson 1988; Zhou and Logan 1989), they offer a model of the context through which refugees and immigrants have been able to create a sizable number of jobs and mobilized communities. Consequently, the notion of the immigrant enclave will be used herein to assess the viability and community-generating potential of Soviet Jewish and Vietnamese entrepreneurship.

FACILITATORS FOR SUCCESSFUL ETHNIC ENTREPRENEURSHIP

According to the enclave model, the most central feature of a viable ethnic economy is the ability of its entrepreneurs to sell goods and services to members of the larger society (Cohen 1969; Light 1972; Min 1988; Portes and Manning 1986). Ethnic-specific demand for native language services and traditional products does play a key role in the development of the ethnic economy because it shields the newly established proprietor from competition with more experienced and better capitalized native businesses (Light 1972). However, immigrant populations are generally too small in number and too limited in spending power to support more than a handful of ethnic-oriented entrepreneurs. Among Vietnamese entrepreneurs, for example, excessive competition for co-ethnic customers has been discussed as a source of business failure (Leba 1985). Further, as Portes and Manning (1986) note, almost every immigrant population, even those with low rates of self-employment, supports some ethnic restaurants, bars, travel agencies, and other small shops. Rather, it is those groups that are able to provide goods and services to members of the larger society that have achieved significant rates of self-employ-ment. Such has been the case among Chinese restaurateurs and laundrymen (Light 1972; Lyman 1974), Japanese truck farmers (Light 1972), Jewish retailers (Sowell 1981; Wirth 1928), and, most re-cently, Korean retailers (Min 1988) and Cuban light manufacturers and construction firms (Portes and Manning 1986).

As the occupational specialization in the above list suggests, a sec-ond important factor in developing a viable ethnic economy is eco-nomic integration (Bonacich and Modell 1980; Cummings 1980). Immigrant entrepreneurs facilitate success through horizontal and vertical integration (Wilson and Martin 1982). Horizontal integration involves ethnic business owners cooperating to choose store location, avoid competitive pricing, pool information, and engage in collective buying. Vertical integration occurs when a whole package of business services (ranging from credit, wholesale goods, and maintenance to parking, transportation, real estate, manufacturing, and import/export concessions) are provided by co-ethnics. Through vertical and hori-zontal integration, ethnic entrepreneurs can support each other, strengthen co-ethnic ties, share information, avoid cannibalistic com-petition, and generally contribute to the interlocking business orienta-tion of the entire immigrant community.

A third factor associated with ethnic success in self-employment is geographical concentration. Close physical proximity facilitates ex-changes of information and access to ethnic sources of credit, labor, and raw materials. It is telling that those immigrant groups that have been most successful in small business (Jews in New York, Chinese in San Francisco, Japanese in Los Angeles, Cubans in Miami, and Koreans in New York and Los Angeles) tend to have highly concen-trated (as opposed to diffused) populations in the United States (Kim 1981; Light 1972; Light and Bonacich 1988; Portes and Manning 1986).

Of course, geographical concentration alone is not enough to foster the creation of an ethnic economy. While seemingly an aspect of a group's cultural or political organization, rather than its economic life, ethnic solidarity is central to the development of high levels of ethnic self-employment. Ethnic institutions and an environment of trust, loyalty, and cooperation are required for immigrants to create a sizable ethnic economy (Cohen 1969; Kim 1981; Lyman 1974; Portes 1987).

Finally, several other factors have been noted as important for the establishment of entrepreneurship. These include the availability of labor and capital, expertise in production and management, the presence of conducive cultural traits (work ethic, norms regarding family economic cooperation, rotating credit associations), and access to international business connections. These ethnic resources will be discussed in detail later in this chapter.

MOTIVES FOR OPENING ETHNIC BUSINESSES

As recently arrived refugees, Soviet Jews and Vietnamese lack many of the resources needed for running a successful business: investment capital, secure credit histories, U.S. business experience, and knowledge of the English language and American culture. Further, for refugees, immigrants, and natives alike, owning a small business can be considered a difficult occupation, requiring long hours of dull work, responsibilities that do not end at 5 p.m., risk of robbery, and a high chance of failure (Dun and Bradstreet 1983). Given these many disadvantages, why, then, do Soviet Jewish and Vietnamese refugees become entrepreneurs? The growing body of research on ethnic economic activity offers many explanations for the propensity of immigrants to become self-employed. Light (1980, 1984) suggests that for the sake of parsimony, all can be reduced to either of two forms of argument: culture theories and disadvantage theories (Light 1980:33).

Culture Theory

Culture theory claims that certain ethnic groups, such as Jews, Chinese, Japanese, Greeks, Armenians, and Parsis (Bonacich 1973:583), possess cultural attributes that encourage and facilitate their participation in business activities. These groups are said to have access to cultural institutions for raising capital, controlling family labor, and ensuring economic cooperation (Ward 1986; Min 1988). Many are noted to hold religious or cultural values similar to the Protestant Ethic that yield character traits of future orientation, acquisitiveness, and thrift that are conducive to entrepreneurial activities. Finally, it is suggested that such groups see small business ownership as a prestigious and worthwhile activity (Light 1985).

Cultural explanations for the preponderance of certain immigrant groups in business follow two different forms: orthodox and reactive (Light 1980). Orthodox cultural theories claim that certain groups, such as Jews and Chinese, are, by nature, business oriented. Reactive cultural theories claim that the "facilitators" that encourage small business ownership "emerge from the minority situation" (Light 1980:34). Reactive theories are context based, and so combine disadvantage and cultural approaches. They explain why immigrant populations, such as the Koreans or Soviet Jews, who had no prior business experience become self-employed in the United States in large numbers (Min 1984:17). The notion of reactive entrepreneurship is embedded in the concepts of the middleman minority (Bonacich 1973) and pariah capitalism (Weber 1927:360).

While cultural theory explains why certain groups tend to go into business more often than others, it can be criticized as a tautology: If a group is well represented in business, then one concludes its culture fosters entrepreneurship.

Culture theory applies most directly to the experiences of refugees who open small businesses out of choice, despite opportunities for employment in the larger economy. Such was the case of several Soviet Jews in my sample who had found high-paying employment as structural engineers but preferred to work in small business instead. A Soviet Jew linked ethnicity to entrepreneurship:

> I worked just maybe a month as a coach for a girls' school. You know, I just quit because I didn't see my future in that. I have a family that I have to support and I decide "what are Jewish people doing when they don't have a profession? What are they doing? They should sell something."

A Vietnamese refugee, Mrs. Nguyen, who has recently purchased her second business, reveals a similar predisposition toward business activities:

> My parents had a business (in Vietnam) restaurant and hotel, and when I married, they gave some to me, so I have been in business all my life. As soon as I get here, I say I make money and I save money to buy the business. I want to buy my restaurant again.

The importance of culture as a factor contributing to entrepreneurship among Soviet Jewish and Vietnamese refugees is confirmed by the fact that the subgroups of each population that are considered the most entrepreneurial in character—Soviet Jews from the Ukraine and ethnic Chinese from Vietnam—are overrepresented in the small business activities of their respective communities. According to émigré lore, Ukrainian Jews, especially those from the port city of Odessa, are marked by a "hustling" mentality. Since the Ukraine is regarded as the most anti-Semitic republic in the USSR, these entrepreneurial skills may have been developed as a survival technique. Similarly, the ethnic Chinese of Vietnam, long noted for their business skill, are heavily involved in self-employment activities in the United States (Purcell 1965; Rose 1985; Rumbaut 1986, 1989; Tran 1986; Ward 1986). Culture theory does a good job of explaining the actions of immigrant entrepreneurs who are excited about and skilled and resourceful in business. It does less well in helping us understand the experience of refugees who open businesses solely as a source of income. Their experience is better codified by disadvantage theory.

Disadvantage Theory

Disadvantage theory asserts that certain immigrant and minority group members go into small business because they are disadvantaged in the general labor market due to poor English, inferior education, lack of American credentials and licenses, and discrimination (Kim 1981; Min 1988). Disadvantage does play a major role in motivating Soviet Jewish and Vietnamese refugees to enter business. In fact, many of the business owners I contacted indicated that disadvantage was a reason for opening their operation (Gold 1985). These respondents included Soviet Jewish engineers who owned bagel shops, auto repair businesses and real estate concerns, and Vietnamese refugees with advanced degrees from U.S. universities who owned restaurants and gardening services, an ex-bank manager who owned an ice cream parlor, and a former military officer with a psychology degree who ran a dry goods shop. A representative of the Vietnamese Chamber of Commerce described how self-employment permits Vietnamese engineers to avoid the "glass ceiling" that restricts corporate promotions:

Well, I don't want to say discrimination, but I attended a top American university, and I feel there isn't room past a certain level for a Vietnamese. Like right now, most of the Vietnamese engineers can't wait to get out of the corporate rat race and open their own company. They can't get into the upper level of established corporations.

Although disadvantage theory describes the motives of such individuals for opening small businesses, I found little evidence to indicate that self-employment was a direct alternative to unemployment (Light 1972; Min 1988). The experience of Soviet Jewish and Vietnamese refugees suggests that few individuals can move from a status of unemployment to that of successful business owner. Running a business requires a great deal of capital, knowledge, and commitment. Those Soviet Jewish and Vietnamese refugees who opened businesses only out of desperation often lacked these resources. Hence, businesses that were created by refugees short on skill and assets, solely for the purpose of creating a job for oneself, were very likely to fail.

Grisha Goldberg, a structural engineer from Moscow, exemplified this position. Having searched for work as an engineer for three years, both in Chicago and in the Bay Area, Grisha was convinced by his friend Arkady Levy to join three other Soviet émigrés and one American in starting a business. They leased a windowless, dingy basement adjacent to a university, remodeled it, and opened a "beer and sandwich" restaurant. Almost immediately after start-up, Goldberg and his partners realized the business was destined for failure and put it up for sale. On many days, receipts totaled less than $100. The final blow occurred when they were caught selling beer to minors. Because they refused to pay a $700 fine, their liquor license was revoked by the state. At last, a buyer was located. After the partners agreed to reduce the price by $25,000, the business was sold. Despite each partner's losses in the thousands of dollars, they were grateful to be out of business. Disillusioned by this attempt to become an entrepreneur, Goldberg renewed his search for employment in engineering.

Nghi Le, who had been a lawyer in Saigon, had a similar experience. After failing the California bar exam three times, he borrowed money from family and friends and bought a large restaurant and nightclub in San Jose. Although he enlisted the aid of an experienced Vietnamese manager, the operation never turned a profit. Nghi Le was saved from bankruptcy by a fire that destroyed the restaurant.

Instead of functioning as an alternative to unemployment, owning a small business was more often an alternative to underemployment among Soviet Jewish and Vietnamese refugees. Refugees experienced their disadvantages in terms of the low quality of employment that was available. While initial jobs were considered undesirable, nevertheless they provided refugees with cultural socialization, English language proficiency, and investment capital. (Such was the case for Anna Gomberg, described in Chapter 4).

Entrepreneurship and Independence

My research indicates that several refugees started businesses because they felt that contact with and regulation by members of the larger society was, in itself, a disadvantage. These refugees entered business because it offered the independence needed to fulfill goals that would be unattainable through other conditions of employment. A study of Vietnamese food businesses emphasizes the importance of independence in refugees' decisions to become self-employed in the United States:

> Our data show that the Indochinese define success differently than Americans in food-related enterprises. Profit . . . is not the sole or even the main criterion for success. . . . The enterprises provide employment and social contact for family and kin . . . provide the basic nutritional needs of one's family. Working together provides the family with a setting in which positive adjustment [to the United States] can be made. (Indochinese Community Center 1983:9)

Refugees who opened businesses in order to escape the disadvantages associated with employment in the larger economy referred to three major reasons why they opted to do so: (1) to limit contact with an unfamiliar culture, (2) for family-based reasons, such as providing employment for relatives, and (3) to enjoy unique opportunities or relationships within the refugee community.

Limiting Contact With an Unfamiliar Culture

As refugees, Soviet Jews and Vietnamese have less control over their exit from their native country than do immigrants. Accordingly, they may be especially likely to enter small business because of the high degree of autonomy such a business provides. The director of a

Vietnamese association referred to the value of independence as he describes why so many Vietnamese refugees open businesses in Orange County:

> It doesn't mean Vietnamese are successful in business in here. . . .
>
> We don't spend as much as American so we save some money. We use this money for a small business. To make about $1,000 a month and to be the owner, we control our own life, it feel more easier. That why there a lot of businesses come up. They try to survive some other way. They don't have to come to the company.
>
> If you work for yourself, you can work 14 hours. You don't feel tired. But if you work in the company, 8 hours is too much.

Many Vietnamese entrepreneurs found Orange County's Little Saigon—the world's largest overseas Vietnamese community—to be a desirable and prestigious location because of its immersion in Vietnamese culture. Basking in this enclave's institutional completeness, they were willing to deal with its high rents and cutthroat competition.

My interviews and fieldwork suggest that independence-oriented businesses are common among Soviet Jewish and Vietnamese refugee populations. Refugees who opened these types of enterprises spoke little English and maintained minimum contact with American society. Certain Soviet Jewish and Vietnamese refugees intended their businesses to be inconspicuous in order to conceal income from agencies that provided RCA, AFDC, food stamps, unemployment insurance, or welfare. Other operations were hidden because they were thought to be illegal by their proprietors. For instance, several Vietnamese refugees involved in informal credit and banking arrangements and rotating credit associations believed that such activities were akin to "pyramid schemes" and hence against the law. Others who did not understand tax or licensing laws or health codes tried to remain inconspicuous for fear of being cited for violations (Leba 1985).

Further, some independence-motivated businesses were "cottage industries." Located in refugees' homes, they often went unobserved. For example, members of both ethnic groups prepared foods; assembled clothing; repaired electronic equipment or automobiles; taught a variety of skills; and ran translation, photographic, and videotaping services out of their apartments. Because many Soviet Jews have backgrounds in building and engineering, several were involved in unlicensed construction businesses.

A recent *Los Angeles Times* article confirmed this finding regarding the existence of an underground economy. "The underground economy is found in Southeast Asian communities throughout the state. Officials estimate that as many as half of the state's Southeast Asian families on welfare—about 22,000 families numbering 100,000 refugees—are earning illegal income." Much of this income is derived from working in sweatshops and selling at swap meets. (Arax 1987:1, 3).

Family Factors

Soviet Jewish and Vietnamese refugees often chose small business employment because it allowed them to provide for the needs of family members and/or to make use of family-based resources in a way impossible under other conditions of employment. For many refugees, small businesses function as an extension of the family itself. Within Vietnamese culture, the role of small businesses as an extension of the family is bolstered by the tradition of business and financial activities being the responsibility of female family members (Finnan and Cooperstein 1983:31).

> There are some women who manage two, three and up to five *Ho* [savings and mutual lending societies] simultaneously and know how to manipulate the funds of all without a hitch. (Nguyen 1949:i,9)

Drawing upon this tradition, Vietnamese families frequently utilized a system of division of labor in which the husband took a job while the wife opened a small business, such as a grocery or restaurant. This arrangement offered families a high degree of economic security and minimized risk. The husband's income supported the family while the wife's business became established. He also helped by working at the business during the evenings and on weekends. If the husband was laid off from his job, income derived from the wife's business could support the family. In addition to providing a stable source of income, this arrangement also allowed the family to act in accordance with Vietnamese norms regarding family life, thereby easing some of the difficulty of resettlement and maintaining a good reputation within the refugee community (Gold 1989; Kibria 1989, 1990).

While Soviet Jewish women do not have a tradition of business pro-
prietorship, they are accustomed to participation in the family's economic life as wage earners (Simon et al. 1982). Consequently, several
Soviet Jewish families also maintained a family-based division of
labor in which one spouse would be self-employed while the other
worked in the larger economy.

Another family-based reason why certain Soviet Jewish and
Vietnamese refugees opened small businesses was that such endeavors could be passed on to children. Coming from countries where jobs
were often lifelong, both Soviet Jewish and Vietnamese refugees
were extremely upset by the frequency with which workers in the
United States lost or changed their jobs. By creating small businesses
that could be passed on to children, they hoped to spare the younger
generation the trauma of instability which they, as refugees, suffered.
For example, Mr. and Mrs. Tran opened a grocery store that bore
their teenage daughter's name. They planned to give it to her as a
wedding gift. A Soviet Jewish entrepreneur voiced a similar goal as
he described his future plans:

> I don't wanna depend on nobody. For this business, I have a 15-year
> lease. Then I'm gonna own this building. So when I buy this building, I
> will protect myself and my kids because we will have business and prop-
> erty and nobody can kick me out.

Small Business and Community Visibility

A few Soviet Jewish and Vietnamese refugees engaged in their own
small business enterprise because its independence allowed them to
earn a living while accomplishing political or community-service
goals within the refugee community. For example, the president of a
Vietnamese veterans' association boasted of one its members, an ex-
general living in Texas, who purchased three convenience stores as a
means of providing jobs for unemployed Vietnamese veterans. In this
manner, he was able to earn a living, help veterans, and maintain a
highly prestigious position in the refugee community. Refugees in
this category found that small business ownership allowed them to
take advantage of their special connections to the refugee community.
For example, Sasha Doctorovich, a Soviet Jewish electronic engineer
who was the manager of production for a computer company, assembled a staff of engineers, many of whom were Soviet Jews. When the
operation was sold to Japanese investors, Doctorovich formed his

own company in order to keep his staff together as a functioning unit. Similarly, a Vietnamese doctor left employment at a San Francisco hospital and started his own refugee-oriented practice. The independence of this operation allowed him to earn a substantial income while simultaneously maintaining a high degree of visibility and influence within the refugee community.[1] These examples reveal how the independent nature of small business allowed Soviet Jewish and Vietnamese refugees to make use of resources and to fulfill goals that would be unattainable otherwise. In so doing, they can escape the disadvantages inherent in employment within the larger economy. While these refugee business owners are earning a living, they are also accomplishing noneconomic goals that they feel are important.

ETHNIC RESOURCES
AND SMALL BUSINESS

As recent refugees, Soviet Jews and Vietnamese have many disadvantages (limited English ability, lack of capital, no credit histories, little knowledge of American culture, and few connections) when compared to the average American business owner and to other immigrant populations as well (Chan and Cheung 1982; Kim 1981; Light and Bonacich 1988; Min 1988; Portes and Bach 1985; Willette et al. 1985). Consequently, their chances for business failure can be considered quite high. However, refugee entrepreneurs also possess various advantages by virtue of their status as refugees and their connections to refugee communities.

The following list, though not exhaustive, includes some resources that Soviet Jewish and Vietnamese refugees used in running their operations. These are investment funds, ethnic labor markets, ethnic consumer markets, ethnic supplier networks, and programs offered to refugees by public and private agencies.

Funds

Because Soviet Jewish and Vietnamese refugees enter the United States with few financial assets, they are without the capital required for business start-up. Lacking stable jobs, credit histories, and collateral, they are unable to obtain small business loans from banks. Therefore, refugees must find alternative sources of capital. Community connections are frequently used to provide this capital.

A study of Vietnamese businesses in Orange County found the following sources of initial capital: own savings, 37%; family sources, 27%; "money lenders" (rotating credit associations), 13%; and financial institutions, 13% (Trankiem 1986:60). Totaling own savings, family, and money lenders, a full 77% of these business owners used sources of start-up capital rooted in the refugee community. The most common form of community that provided aid to refugee businesses were informal social circles of family and close friends. Such networks ranged in size from the two persons (mother and uncle) who helped finance Alex Kogan's electronics shop to the more than 30 friends and relatives who provided funds, as well as labor, child care, and advice, to the two Vietnamese owners of "Saigon Lunch." In the following quote, an émigré businessman describes his dependence on other Soviet Jews for financing:

> We came from a different world. I would say that in Russia we could trust each other more than here in America. I have over 30 relatives in San Francisco and they didn't have a choice [about giving money], they were my relatives . . . I just said "I gotta have it."

> We do take each other's word in many cases. At one point, I asked for a loan from a guy I hardly knew. He came up with a big amount of money without a paper [a contract] or without anything signed. Probably, I'd do the same thing if somebody wanted my support.

Similarly, an established Vietnamese entrepreneur pointed out that trust-based lending is facilitated by the Vietnamese tradition of regarding the entire family as a single fiscal entity: "Among the Vietnamese, you can borrow with less worry because if I cannot pay, my children will pay for me. So makes for easier lending. We trust each other, so we lend money."

The networks refugee entrepreneurs rely on for capital are most often small. Intimate ties involving relatives or close friends are central because social solidarity in Soviet Jewish and Vietnamese communities exists within localized subgroups and not among the entire refugee population. Further, because most Soviet Jews and many Vietnamese resist organization, capital formation networks are generally informal. In the following quote, a Vietnamese entrepreneur described the limited advantages of the rotating credit association:

> When I first came here, it was hard to get credit. I got turned down for Visa [card]. And at the bank, they ask for collateral, which is hard for a refugee to get. Even if I could get a bank loan, interest rates can be so high. I remember when they were 21%—interest would eat up your profits. You work for the bank, not yourself.

> So we have some other ways. Family members can lend each other money. Also, we have a custom called *Hui* [rotating credit association]. Every month, the members put in $100. We can borrow the money and pay low interest to do whatever we want. We used to do this in Vietnam, but here it is not so good because *Hui* cannot produce enough money to start a business. To start a business, you need $40,000. *Hui* cannot produce this amount. The most you could get would be about $6,000 or $12,000.

Whereas this man regarded rotating credit associations to be of limited value, other refugees prized these capital formation networks. For example, the owner of a large electronics shop said he regularly used the *Hui* to solve cash-flow problems.

While the capital formation networks of refugees are usually small, many are also quite effective because many Soviet Jews and some Vietnamese are able to find work in high-paying occupations. For example, I interviewed several professional Soviet Jewish couples (engineers, doctors, and the like) who earned close to $100,000 a year. Having few expenses, these families had significant disposable income available to aid relatives. Similarly, Chinese-Vietnamese entrepreneurs have been able to work out deals with Chinese-Americans and overseas Chinese to develop extensive projects, such as ethnic mini-malls in Los Angeles, Orange County, San Jose, and Seattle. While these networks were also small in size, they provided ample investment funds (Brody 1986; Gelernter 1990). Because of their intimacy, these networks offered a degree of flexibility and responsiveness unavailable in larger collectivities.

While informal business networks were starting to develop within Soviet Jewish and Vietnamese communities, many refugee entrepreneurs commented on the limitations of these collectivities. Because ethnic networks are rooted in personal trust and cooperation, businesses suffer when relations sour. For example, several refugees opted to sell out because they could not get along with partners (Leba 1985: 132-136). Others described being swindled by co-ethnics whom they had too easily trusted:

After I moved to San Francisco, I met a guy from Russia who had a tiny coffee shop on Montgomery Street. He told me that place does tremendous business. So I borrowed from a private source and I got involved in that little place. I found out that it was not making any money at all. In fact, it was losing money. And what was worse was that I found out the place was to be demolished in 4 years, in the moment the lease expires. I sued the guy and I won the case, but he took off. As far as I know, he is in Italy someplace. What we found out later is he is a professional crook. He did many things like that throughout the States. From Detroit to Florida to here [San Francisco] to L.A., you can trace him doing things like that.

Finally, refugee entrepreneurs sometimes felt that co-ethnics lacked the resources that American business associates could provide. A successful restaurant owner stated, "I'd rather not get involved in something serious with Russians, to say truthfully. Only because I believe they don't have enough experience yet and in many cases, connections. Let's face it, that we need sometimes."

As refugee entrepreneurs became better established, they were able to obtain credit from banks and investors. Most large-scale Soviet Jewish and Vietnamese operations depended on these sources of funds. Relying upon ethnic ties, Vietnamese (especially Chinese-Vietnamese) entrepreneurs have acquired investment capital from overseas sources. A Chinese-Vietnamese publisher described this relationship:

Say I am Chinese, I come from Vietnam. Example, you are Chinese and you come from Taiwan or maybe Singapore, or maybe Hong Kong. I need money—I need your help to support my business. How come you help me? I would like to tell you.

Because I, I have good experience and I have good credit. You have the money, but you don't know how to run a business. So you check on my credit and ask the other people. I want to buy this restaurant. You help me, maybe you become partner, because you believe me. Maybe you are partner, or maybe I give you interest after 6 months.

Vietnamese and Chinese-Vietnamese entrepreneurs, as well as banking and real estate officials who served them, asserted that Asian-style business transactions occur in an environment of greater flexibility and negotiation than would be accepted in U.S. commercial circles. This flexibility, they felt, facilitated economic expansion. In fact, a large number of Asian and American banks are located in and directed toward California's Asian enclaves. Even U.S. financial institutions, such as Cathay Bank and Security Pacific Asian Bank, employ Asian-born staff to encourage business with an Asian clientele.

Labor

Soviet Jewish and Vietnamese entrepreneurs made frequent use of workers from three major sources: family, co-ethnics, and other immigrant populations. While all three categories represent ethnic labor markets, refugee employers have special access only to the first two sources.

The use of family labor was common among Soviet Jewish and especially Vietnamese refugee entrepreneurs in California. A recent study of Vietnamese business owners found that 87% preferred relatives over nonrelatives as business associates (Trankiem 1986:Table 18). In the following quote, a Vietnamese shop owner described the use of family labor:

> Southeast Asians are hard workers. We work long hours and our family backs us up. We are not like Americans—when the children are 18 years old, the parents kick them out. For us, it is common for the children to stay at home until they are married. So we rely on family to help during early years of business operation.
>
> In our family, the wife runs the small business. I help out on weekends and with the accounting. We get no pay, so it is easier to cover our expenses and avoid bankruptcy. We also help our children get started in business so they can have some income.

The use of family labor helped refugee business owners minimize labor costs while also providing loyal help. However, it could also limit the growth and employment-generating potential of refugee enterprises because businesses were sometimes specifically designed to employ relatives rather than turn a profit. "Extended family relations could also act as a disincentive to effort, saving and investment since extra returns will be largely appropriated by increased demands from members of the extended family" (Trankiem 1986:64). I found Trankiem's observations to be true during my fieldwork. On several visits to Vietnamese restaurants, I was initially impressed by the many customers present. However, as I ate my meal, I noticed nearly all the "customers" going behind the counter, clearing dishes, and doing other tasks. It became apparent that these were not customers at all, but the owner's family and friends, who had been on break when I entered.

A final disadvantage associated with employing relatives was that hiring decisions were made on the basis of family obligation, rather than worker skill. Since many refugee enterprises are already hampered by a lack of skilled workers, hiring decisions can sometimes be a serious problem (Trankiem 1986:68).

Among more affluent refugee entrepreneurs, notably Soviet Jews, there frequently existed a generational determination of involvement in family businesses. I observed several cases wherein parents would work in the store, while limiting their childrens' connections with the operation, hoping that higher education would yield a more prestigious professional occupation (Gold 1989). When such businesses grew, employees were selected from the larger labor market rather than the immediate family.

In addition to family members, Soviet Jewish and Vietnamese refugees hired nonrelated, co-ethnic labor. The relationship between immigrant employers and workers has long been noted as an asset to ethnic business owners (Glazer and Moynihan 1963; Gorelick 1982; Lyman 1974; Waldinger 1986; Ward 1986). Mr. Tran, a Vietnamese entrepreneur and advisor to a refugee business development program, describes the use of co-ethnic workers by Vietnamese entrepreneurs:

Gold: I have heard from some refugees that Chinese-Vietnamese hire them for sub-minimum wages.

Tran: I understand this. It is a rumor that refugees get hired for long hours and low wages. We have to understand the employer's position—they need to make a profit. It doesn't look nice if the employee is not treated properly. But if we are on employer's side—they are doing the right thing. If there is an agreement between the employer and the employee, they cannot expect to get the same wage as a unionized worker. But they accept the offered wage and work hard and make money. It is good for employer and for the employee. At least it looks fair.

The wage is not as good—but they couldn't apply for a job in another company due to their lack of English. They might have a skill, but cannot understand the instruction of their supervisor, so it is a minus point for them. It is good business to pay as little in wages as possible.

In contrast to the enclave model that stresses the rewards of co-ethnic employment, job-seeking Soviet Jews and Vietnamese members almost universally preferred jobs in large U.S. companies to those in ethnic businesses (Johnson 1988). They held that such jobs were preferable because they offered better wages, fewer hours, more security, health benefits, and opportunities to learn English.

Whereas Tran's comments, refugees' preferences, and the history of immigrant labor suggest an image of harsh exploitation (Howe 1976; Lyman 1974), my fieldwork and interviews indicated that direct exploitation of co-ethnic workers was generally moderated by ethnic customs. Within refugee businesses there often existed a paternalistic exploitation relationship between owners and workers (Portes and Manning 1986). As Tran's quote describes, both employers and workers understood the latter's disadvantages in the larger labor market. Taking this into account, refugees would work for lower wages or for longer hours than would be accepted by non-ethnic workers.

At the same time, however, refugee employees enjoyed advantages from their employers that are not extended by U.S. businesses to their staff (Portes and Manning 1986; Trankiem 1986; Werbner 1984). For example, to offset low pay, Vietnamese workers often received gifts of food and clothing from their employers. In other cases, workers were permitted to bring their children to the workplace. Thus childcare problems were solved, and children were taught business skills. Soviet Jewish and Vietnamese refugee employees reported receiving "under the table" wages from refugee employers that would not jeopardize their RCA, AFDC, or unemployment benefits (Arax 1987). Poorly compensated employees sometimes received aid from former employers to start their own businesses. Finally, refugee employers I interviewed were less concerned with enforcing strict discipline among workers than is the case with American employers. Refugee bosses did not mind if workers kept irregular hours or worked on their own projects while on the job. For instance, the Soviet Jewish owner of an auto repair shop permitted his mechanics to restore their own used cars during slow periods.

One reason refugee employers must extend these privileges is that refugees, unlike other immigrant groups, are entitled to a variety of benefits upon their arrival in the United States, including instruction in the English language, job training, and, most significantly, 18 months of refugee cash assistance (Rose 1985). (Prior to 1981, the period of eligibility for RCA was a full three years). Hence, in the time period when other immigrants are most exploitable by ethnic employers, by virtue of their economic needs and lack of knowledge of the English language and American society, refugees are supported by public assistance and do not need to work.

Although refugee entrepreneurs often used co-ethnic workers, several Soviet Jewish and Vietnamese business owners relied on out-group labor. The advantages of nonrefugee employees included lower cost, greater skill, and obedience. For example, Soviets frequently claimed that émigré workers would challenge their authority in ways Americans would not. A Soviet Jewish engineer who ran his own electronics firm comments on this difficulty:

Gold: What problems would you say exist in working with Soviet employees versus Americans?

Doctorovich: We question each other's motivation. There is an element of jealousy that doesn't exist with American employees. I am president of this company and I hire American employees and have no problems. I hire them, they work for me. They don't question if I rightfully have this position or whether they are more clever or less clever than I am.

With Russian employees, that element is always present. [They think] "why is he president and I am just . . . ?" and psychologically, I understand that. But it is very distractive.

As a consequence, there was a growing reliance on out-group labor among large-sized operations run by Soviet Jews and Vietnamese in Southern California. Rather than employing fellow refugees, members of both groups increasingly relied on Mexican, Chicano, and Central American workers. In interviews, entrepreneurs associated several advantages with Latino employees: they were physically strong and worked very hard, lacked legal residency, were easy to control, and, as cultural outsiders who did not speak the owner's language, were unlikely to open a competing enterprise or use their job as an opportunity to engage in "inside job" crimes (such as embezzlement or protection rackets).[2] Finally, Latino workers could not demand favors based upon common ethnicity.

In contrast to their positive characterizations of Latino labor, Soviet Jewish and Vietnamese employers described co-ethnic workers as disrespectful, overly ambitious, unwilling to do hard physical labor, potentially criminal, and generally more difficult to manage and fire. By 1989, reliance on Latino workers had become so common in Orange County's Little Saigon (an area where almost all signage was in Vietnamese or Chinese) that many stores posted "help wanted" placards in English. The manager of several properties that house ethnic businesses in Little Saigon commented:

> As far as the labor pool, I sure don't see a lot of the Southeast Asian people doing real labor. All the big companies here hire Mexican labor. In the workplace here, it's not uncommon to see Hispanic laborers going from door to door asking for work in the Vietnamese stores.

A Chinese-Vietnamese journalist offered a similar explanation: "Mexican, no green card, so you pay cheap. I pay you $5 an hour, but I pay Mexican $3 an hour. And Mexican are strong, and if I need to fire him, he just goes."

Since the mid-1980s, a growing number of Vietnamese entrepreneurs have become involved in the garment assembly businesses in Southern California. As a highly competitive, labor intensive industry, it relies heavily on a low-cost labor force that is made up of refugees and Latinos. Recent reports document various abuses in this industry, including child labor, home work, subminimum wages, and nonreported earnings (Bonacich 1990). A *Los Angeles Times* article noted some 400 garment businesses in Orange County that employed over 5,000 workers (Efron 1989:P1). Industrial sewing equipment was sold in several refugee neighborhoods, and I saw these machines in several refugees' homes. According to the manager of one sewing machine shop, Vietnamese entrepreneurs frequently purchased machines on a time payment plan. The availability of a low-cost and marginal labor force consisting of Vietnamese refugees and Latino immigrants was central to the existence of this growing sector of refugee enterprise.

The involvement of Vietnamese refugees in the garment industry is important in terms of sociological theory because it marks their first large-scale participation in providing goods for a non-ethnic market —a major criterion of ethnic business success according to Portes's enclave model (Portes and Manning 1986).

In summary, the ethnic bonds uniting owners and workers are an important resource for Soviet Jewish and Vietnamese entrepreneurs. However, these bonds also oblige bosses to extend special privileges to ethnic workers, especially relatives. Further, some ethnic entrepreneurs avoid ethnic labor for reasons of profitability, customer rapport, or authority relations. The ability of recently arrived refugees (those most disadvantaged in the job market) to collect RCA makes them less ripe for exploitation by co-ethnic employers than is the case among recently arrived immigrants who are ineligible for such benefits and hence must find immediate employment. Finally, the availability of low-cost Vietnamese and Latino workers is a major resource for refugees' growing involvement in the garment industry.

Ethnic Consumer Markets

Several Soviet Jewish and Vietnamese refugee businesses relied upon co-ethnics as consumers for their goods and services. This was especially evident among grocery stores and restaurants located in refugee neighborhoods. Service, entertainment, and retail goods businesses, such as nightclubs, barber/beauty parlors, and clothing stores, were also common. These shops provided the basic needs of refugee consumers. Many Vietnamese shops offered air freight services that permitted refugees to send in-kind remittances to their relatives back home. These companies often specialized in such items as electrical generators, motor scooters, boat motors, mini buses, and fabric that could be resold or used for income-generation in Vietnam.

By the late 1980s, Vietnamese ran over 2,000 businesses in Southern California, with the largest concentrations located in Orange County (Little Saigon), and Los Angeles County's Chinatown and Monterey Park/Alhambra areas. Most of these businesses were directed toward Asian consumers. This heavy reliance on co-ethnic customers violates the ethnic enclave model's prescription that sales to out-group members are necessary for ethnic economic success. However, the large influx of Asians to Southern California in the 1970s and 1980s provided a huge number of often affluent co-ethnic consumers. As of 1985, Los Angeles and Orange Counties included 1,225,000 Asians (Billiris 1990)—certainly enough patrons to support a large number of enterprises.

As time passes, it appears that Chinese-Vietnamese are assuming a major role as marketers to a broadly defined Asian-American population.

For example, major groceries and restaurants located in L.A.'s Chinatown and Monterey Park—areas with a multinational Asian clientele —are now owned by Chinese-Vietnamese. Two Chinese-American city officials explained that the Chinese-Vietnamese are taking over businesses in an ethnic-succession process. Elderly Chinese-Americans are reaching retirement age and selling their operations. However, affluent and educated immigrants from Taiwan and Hong Kong are often unwilling to purchase and run these operations, especially because Asian businesses are faced with crime and anti-growth city administrations (Vigil and Yun 1990). This leaves a huge, unfilled demand for Asian goods. The Chinese-Vietnamese, already accustomed to running businesses, are willing to accept the risk and effort involved and so have been quite aggressive in opening ethnic-oriented retail operations in Asian neighborhoods.

Soviet Jewish enterprises have also evolved over time. Most were directed at the general population rather than other Soviet Jews. Soviet Jews have been resettled throughout the United States, thus impeding the development of large-sized ethnic enclaves like those underlying the success of Cuban and Korean ethnic entrepreneurs (Min 1986; Portes and Bach 1985; Wilson and Martin 1982).

However, since the glasnost era, large numbers of Soviet émigrés have continued to settle in areas like West Hollywood in California and Brighton Beach in Brooklyn, New York. Thousands of Soviet Armenians and Pentacostalists have added to this consumer market (ORR 1990). In these neighborhoods, a growing number of Cyrillic-language signs offer Russian-style products to the local community. Further, as relations have warmed between the United States and Eastern Europe, more products from those countries, such as food, beverages, and cultural goods, are now available. By 1990, West Los Angeles featured a number of groceries, ranging from tiny delis to full-sized supermarkets, that offered a variety of goods imported from the USSR and Eastern Europe.

Soviet Jewish and Vietnamese real estate agents, accountants, investment counselors, tax preparers, doctors, lawyers, and dentists utilized ethnic consumer markets. Doctors were especially dependent upon ethnic customers because, as immigrants, they found it almost impossible to obtain the certification in a medical specialty that is required for employment in most hospitals and HMOs. Private practice, then, became the only option for employment. Taking advantage of refugees' eligibility for Medicare and Medi-Cal, the practices of refugee doctors were directed toward refugee communities.

In addition to supporting themselves, physicians and other professionals provided a windfall for other sectors of the ethnic economy, such as medical supply companies, office buildings, dental labs, pharmacies, and, most notably, ethnic media industries whose newspapers, magazines, cable TV programs, and ethnic "Yellow Pages" carried their advertisements (Leba 1985; Trankiem 1986). For example, a quarter of the 900-plus businesses listed in the *1988 Vietnam Business Directory of Southern California* were medical professionals, including 133 doctors, 66 dentists, and 21 pharmacists.[3] Nearly half (45) of the 115 advertisements in the 1988 *Los Angeles Russian Language Telephone Directory* offered various medical services. A Soviet-trained physician described the role of the ethnic media in her practice:

> I got my office and I make my advertisement in our newspaper—*Panorama*. I was working in a famous institution in Russia, so a lot of patients from Russia, they have already known this institution very well. I even have my own patients from over there in Russia, they come to here. It also helps because you know how much they went through.

Although many successful Soviet Jewish and Vietnamese entrepreneurs took advantage of refugee customers, others did not use the ethnic consumer market. Instead, they directed their operations toward the society at large or other ethnic groups. In so doing, they found they had access to more customers, experienced less competition, and were able to charge higher prices than would be permissible with a refugee clientele. Because refugee businesspersons who directed their operations toward non-ethnic consumers utilized their knowledge of the larger society to make decisions about store location and marketing, for them, assimilation was an important business skill.

Finally, Soviet Jewish and Vietnamese businesses faced competition from nonrefugee entrepreneurs. Various Asian businesses market their goods and services to Vietnamese consumers. As of 1989, the largest import company, restaurant, and grocery in Little Saigon were owned by immigrants from Thailand, Hong Kong, and Taiwan, respectively. Similarly, Southern California's largest purveyor of Russian-style foods was owned by Armenians. While the businesses of ethnic outsiders drain customers from refugee-run operations, they also attract consumers to ethnic shopping districts and make available goods and services that benefit Soviet Jewish and Vietnamese enterprises as well.

In summary, co-ethnic customers are a resource for many Soviet Jewish and Vietnamese business persons. This is especially true among Vietnamese shopkeepers and professionals of both groups. However, many of the most successful Soviet Jewish and Vietnamese businesses do not use their own ethnic group as a consumer market. Instead, they use their knowledge of the larger society to gain access to more numerous and, often, more affluent native consumers. Finally, Chinese-Vietnamese entrepreneurs appear to be directing their goods and services at a broadly defined Asian-American consumer market.

Supplier Networks

Many immigrant groups benefit from integration between ethnic wholesalers and retailers. Ethnic-based arrangements provide credit and can lead to an ethnic near-monopoly over the distribution and sale of certain goods (Kim 1981). Benefits provided through integration "shed light on the unique success of the Cuban enclave" in Miami, Florida (Wilson and Martin 1982:156). Because ethnic-based links exist between wholesalers and retailers, credit that would be unavailable otherwise is extended. For example, Vietnamese suppliers of groceries, cookware, air-freight-to-Vietnam services, and Vietnamese-language publications and video and cassette tapes offered special deals to Vietnamese retailers. The same relationship existed between the suppliers of Russian-style prepared foods and the owners of Soviet Jewish delicatessens. In addition to local networks, refugee tradespeople sometimes had access to international financial and supplier networks that provided capital and advantages in import/export operations.

However, because access to the country of origin is restricted for refugees, the benefits provided by such arrangements are limited when compared to those enjoyed by many voluntary immigrant groups. In fact, as evidenced by the cutthroat competition that exists among small shops and restaurants in refugee neighborhoods, horizontal integration does not approach the level associated with other ethnic enclaves (Kim 1981).

The one refugee group that appears to have more extensive ethnic integration is the ethnic Chinese. By maintaining ties with overseas Chinese in the United States and abroad, and by creating their own organizations in the States, Chinese-Vietnamese were able to integrate their economic activities (Trankiem 1986). Retaining the strong dialect and region-based associations they had developed in Vietnam, Chinese-Vietnamese imported products from Asia and offered each other advice, assistance, credit, and employment. Relying upon ties to overseas Chinese in several Asian nations and the United States, they were able to access goods and capital in a climate of ethnic-based trust, cooperation, and negotiation. A Chinese-Vietnamese manager of operations for one of Little Saigon's largest entrepreneurs comments:

> Actually, I think the Chinese [Vietnamese] they can success more than Vietnamese because they can gather together and once you gather together you build up real easy, right?

> First of all you get a better deal. Second thing, you get better quality. Third thing, which is very important thing, is credit.

However, even among the ethnic Chinese, cooperation exists within groups of common regional/linguistic or familial origins, and not at the level of the broader Chinese-Vietnamese population.

Cannibalistic competition was a serious problem for refugee entrepreneurs, but there were certain efforts to regulate this through horizontal integration. To accomplish this, both Vietnamese and Chinese-Vietnamese entrepreneurs developed chains, locating several branches of the same store in close proximity. For example, in Southern California, a single company selling *Pho,* a popular Vietnamese noodle soup, had 3 branches in Little Saigon, 2 in Chinatown, 2 in Long Beach, and 1 in Monterey Park/Alhambra. I observed a similar loading of locations among various grocery chains and a tailor shop. A Southern California Vietnamese commented:

> In their association, they would divide the area to be a section or district or zone which they think "okay, this should be good for one market, and two restaurant and three coffee shop" and things like that. They are individual ownership, but they do sort out that area, they try to group it and they try to divide the area into sections.

Problems of competition over co-ethnic customers were also confronted by Soviet Jewish doctors. While those in Northern California were unable to unite, Los Angeles émigré physicians created a large mutual-support association that offered its members social activities, investment advice, and continuing professional education (Gold in press).

Special Refugee-Aid Programs

Public and private agencies, charitable groups, and foundations provided Soviet Jewish and Vietnamese refugees with programs to help them start small businesses. Such programs offered low-cost or no-cost technical assistance in many aspects of business operation, including obtaining business licenses, renting storefronts and equipment, determining appropriate locations, packaging loans, marketing, accounting, and legal advice. In addition, loan funds themselves were sometimes available through federal grants for minority business owners (for Vietnamese), the Hebrew Free Loan Association (for Soviet Jews), or other sources. These resources provided Soviet Jewish and Vietnamese refugees with advantages unavailable to other entrepreneurs (CSEARR 1984; Lubin 1985). As noted in Chapter 6, government entitlements that make refugees eligible for health care and job training often subsidize refugee-run medical offices and, occasionally, training programs that deliver services in a culturally familiar setting.

Refugees who ran various resettlement and refugee-aid agencies can also be seen as entrepreneurs. Like other refugee business people, they use ethnic connections and ethnic labor and consumer markets in order to obtain funding for their agencies. They also used their cultural and linguistic knowledge and access to the refugee community in order to impress agencies and foundations. The entrepreneurial character of resettlement activities was revealed by the fact that many Vietnamese involved in service provision refer to their occupation as "the refugee business" (Gold 1987).

In summary, Soviet Jewish and Vietnamese refugee business owners provided themselves with economic, organizational, and motivational advantages over native or other ethnic group business owners by virtue of their status as refugees and membership in an ethnic community. These resources were vital because refugee entrepreneurs had less capital and experience and fewer connections than their competitors.

Certain patterns of refugee enterprise—especially those associated with the size of business networks, proprietors' motives, and the effects of resettlement programs—distinguish Soviet Jewish and Vietnamese refugees from ethnic entrepreneurs with different national origins. Other business practices, however, are common to both refugees and immigrants. Finally, while nearly every refugee business utilized sources of capital from the refugee community, the use of other ethnic-based advantages is highly variable, reflecting the diversity of motives, resources, and social ties that exist within these refugee populations.

SOVIET JEWISH AND VIETNAMESE BUSINESSES COMPARED

Although both were refugee groups, Soviet Jews and Vietnamese exhibited distinct styles of entrepreneurship. More frequently than Soviet Jews, Vietnamese entrepreneurs revealed patterns traditionally associated with immigrant businesses. These included formal rotating credit and mutual assistance associations, captive labor and consumer markets, family labor, sweatshops, and a propensity toward small groceries and restaurants (Bonacich 1973; Light 1972; Lyman 1974). This may be due to the larger numbers of Vietnamese refugees, higher levels of residential segregation, greater experience with traditional business arrangements in the country of origin, and a larger family size.

Soviet Jewish business activities contrasted with those of the Vietnamese in terms of the nature of business networks and the use of ethnic consumers. While Soviet Jewish business networks did exist, such arrangements were generally smaller than those of the Vietnamese and were always informal. The earning power of professional Soviet Jews allowed these compact networks to contribute considerable sums to émigré entrepreneurs. Because Soviet Jews have been resettled throughout the United States, the development of large-sized ethnic enclaves associated with Vietnamese refugees, as well as the most business-oriented new immigrant groups—Cuban and Koreans (Min 1986; Portes and Bach 1985)—has been limited. Finally, fewer Soviet Jewish entrepreneurs consistently relied upon ethnic consumers. These were generally limited to cultural services, the food industry, and professional services (doctors, dentists, income tax preparers, accountants, real estate brokers, investment advisors, and those involved with Russian language media).

CONCLUSIONS

Soviet Jewish and Vietnamese refugees display several patterns that distinguish their entrepreneurial activities from those associated with immigrant groups. Because refugees come from diverse origins and have less opportunity to participate in long-term chain migration, their ability to form large-scale and formal self-help networks is less than that of many immigrant groups. Instead, their networks are small and informal. Rather than developing integrated ethnic economies, many Soviet Jewish and Vietnamese refugees maintained a highly individualistic style. For example, when I asked a Vietnamese entrepreneur if he relied on ethnic suppliers for the goods sold in his shop, he passionately asserted his independence: "We don't care who we buy from—Filipino market, Korean market, Mexican market—we don't care. We like to have our merchandise move. Whatever the consumer needs, we will buy that and resell. Make money."

State-mandated policy has unique effects upon Soviet Jewish and Vietnamese entrepreneurs. Because refugees are eligible for cash assistance and training upon arrival in the United States, the ability of refugee employers to exploit the recently arrived is more limited than is the case for economic immigrants who are ineligible for these benefits. Further, refugee business owners can receive technical assistance from resettlement agencies. Finally, refugee doctors and trade school operators are indirectly subsidized by their clients' entitlements.

Refugees, unlike immigrants, come to the United States involuntarily. Consequently, many enter the realm of small business because of its ability to provide them with a level of independence, prestige, and flexibility unavailable under other conditions of employment. Small business helps refugees limit their contact with an alien culture they do not choose to confront, allows them to care for family members in a manner consistent with ethnic traditions, and permits them to maintain a position of visibility within the refugee community. For certain refugee entrepreneurs, these "independence" reasons appeared to be as important as financial considerations in their decisions to open their own business. Finally, U.S.-based business experience is crucial for the success of refugee-run enterprises. Lacking the resources, links, and preparation of voluntary immigrants, few Soviet Jews or Vietnamese could successfully run a concern without obtaining first-hand experience with relevant forms of U.S. economic life.

Soviet Jewish and Vietnamese businesses had various effects on community formation. Many of the symbiotic relationships between entrepreneurs and community members associated with classic ethnic enclaves did exist within these refugee populations, although at limited levels of development. For example, refugees pooled capital and shared information to support their communities' businesses. Grassroots members provided enterprises with patronage and low-cost labor. At the same time, refugee businesses supported the ethnic media and developed geographically concentrated, institutionally complete ethnic communities that enhanced ethnic solidarity on a broader level. Entrepreneurship sometimes unified refugees with potential competitors—Vietnamese with Chinese-Vietnamese, or Soviet Jews with Soviet Armenians, American Jews, or Israelis. However, ethnic-based business competition also heightened conflict among these groups, most notably between the Vietnamese and Chinese-Vietnamese. In general, ethnic businesses reinforced solidarity among groups that were already united on the basis of ethnicity, region, past occupation, and, especially, family and social networks.

On the other hand, refugee businesses seemed to do little to unify unaffiliated or conflicting members of the refugee population. Most businesses relied upon small, preestablished networks for capital, labor, and advice, and had few ties to the larger community. Further, as their companies grew, many refugee entrepreneurs appeared to become even less dependent upon community-based resources, resorting to banks for credit, relying less on family labor, utilizing Latino workers, and exploiting nonrefugee consumer markets (Waldinger et al. 1990:36). As is the general pattern of association among these refugee communities, close interactions and community existed at the subgroup level, unifying small groups, but having limited broad impact.

The vast diversity that existed within Soviet Jewish and Vietnamese business communities must be acknowledged. I interviewed refugee entrepreneurs ranging from manicurists and coffee-shop owners to commercial real estate developers and computer company owners, and I observed only a few areas of ethnic business specialization. Self-help organizations are unlikely to develop among entrepreneurs involved in such highly dissimilar businesses.

Finally, while some refugee enterprises were deeply involved in the ethnic community, others had only the most minimal ethnic basis. With this broad spectrum of business activities located within segmented populations, entrepreneurship—or any social institution—has a long way to go to foster community unification. Given the short period these groups have been in the United States and the limited resources at their disposal, the effects of refugee businesses on economic development and community organization were impressive. Nevertheless, refugee entrepreneurship must grow significantly before it can fill the needs of Vietnamese and Soviet Jews for good jobs and stable community ties.

NOTES

1. Piore (1986:29) comes to a similar conclusion in his analysis of refugee economic activity: "Sometimes they manage to preserve status structures from their communities of origin as a substitute for status that is unavailable in the place of refuge."

2. Gangs and crime were identified as the number one fear in a recent survey of Orange County Vietnamese (Emmons and Reyes 1989).

3. Vietnamese refugees in the United States often use ethnic physicians to obtain medications for relatives in Vietnam as well as themselves, thereby providing practitioners with access to another captive market.

8

Patterns of
Community Organization

Throughout this book, I have stressed the segmented nature of Soviet Jewish and Vietnamese communities. Such factors as diverse origins, the role of resettlement systems, factional conflicts, political cynicism, and a generally individualistic outlook have resulted in a paucity of inclusive organizations within each of these two groups. Nevertheless, groups within each population do work to organize their members. In this chapter, I review some of the ways in which Soviet Jewish and Vietnamese refugees have overcome community atomization and created groups.

COMPETITION AND ETHNIC SOLIDARITY

In recent years, a growing body of literature has demonstrated the importance of group competition as the basis for ethnic collectivism in modern societies (Nielsen 1985; Olzak 1983; Olzak and Nagel 1986; Patterson 1975). Competition is central to mobilization because the ethnic group acts as an interest group through which its members compete with others for desired social and economic goods. Moreover, in competing for resources, a group's identity is defined and boundaries between it and others are clarified.

By looking at ethnic competition in political and economic institutions, we can better understand how ethnic boundaries form institutional networks that can be transformed into viable social movements. (Olzak and Nagel 1986:ix)

For example Padilla (1986; 1987) shows how two distinct Spanish-speaking nationalities (Puerto Ricans and Mexicans) increased their influence by assuming a common Latino ethnicity in order to demand Affirmative-Action-mandated jobs from Chicago corporations.

The competition model of ethnic mobilization is valuable for the study of Soviet Jewish and Vietnamese refugees because it shows how these two groups, heavily segmented and with few country-of-origin links, can become unified in the American context. In fact, economic and political issues do facilitate much of the mobilization and creation of organizations that occur within Soviet Jewish and Vietnamese refugee populations.

However, as we have seen throughout this book, ethnicity and group identification are complex and deeply felt issues. As emphasized in the chapters on grass-roots communities, refugees described their affiliation in light of motives that were moral and affection as well as economic and political. Ideologies, cultural orientations, antipathies, commitments, and abstract principles shaped their group behavior as much as their pursuit of political and economic ends.

To see group identification simply and solely as a vehicle for resource mobilization depicts social actors as excessively utilitarian and, consequently, misunderstands the social importance of ethnicity in political, economic, and cultural realms. Accordingly, models of affiliation that hold "that ethnic loyalties reflect, and are maintained by the underlying socioeconomic interests of group members" (Patterson 1975:305) offer an incomplete description of refugees' collective lives. They fail to capture the ability of ethnicity to motivate feelings of group belonging and action in a manner more fundamental than can be explained by calculations of cost and reward alone (Isaacs 1975).

An alternative conception of ethnic activism is needed to understand how cultural concerns can provide a basis for ethnic solidarity. Woldemikael's (1987) notion of "assertion and accommodation" offers such a model, emphasizing cultural concerns while retaining a competition-based explanation of ethnic group formation and activity. Woldemikael defines assertion as

a process in which persons resist imposition of new cultural or institutional relationships. Accommodation is considered as a process in which individuals submit to a cultural or institutional imposition. Through assertion, groups struggle to maintain their culture and institutions. Through accommodation, groups change to adapt to social relationships and cultures that are imposed. In contact situations among groups, each group will pursue mainly one of the two opposites. (Woldemikael 1987: 416)

Most Soviet Jewish and Vietnamese refugees outwardly accommodated to American cultural patterns. However, many simultaneously asserted themselves by retaining and passing on traditions. This is a complex, multilayered process because there is no clear consensus regarding Soviet Jewish or Vietnamese ethnicity (Markowitz 1988). Battles over ethnic identification occur, not only between refugees and the larger society, but also among various factions within the refugee population itself.

EXTENT OF COMMUNITY ORGANIZATION AMONG SOVIET JEWS AND VIETNAMESE

Their differing propensity to create organizations was among the most dramatic contrasts between Soviet Jewish and Vietnamese refugees. Soviet Jews formed few independent, formalized organizations. In the Bay Area, I was aware of one formal group, as well as an informal business network (Gold 1988). In Southern California, I enumerated about nine Soviet Jewish associations: a religious congregation, three veterans groups, two professional societies, an activist group, and two leisure clubs.

In contrast, Vietnamese associations were abundant. For example, in 1981, Bui, Le, and Nguyen enumerated 340 Vietnamese associations nationwide. During fieldwork in 1983, I counted over 58 Vietnamese associations in the 7 counties of the greater San Francisco Bay Area (IRAC 1982; ITAP 1981). Most recently, the *1990 Vietnam Business Directory* for Los Angeles and Orange Counties contains listings for a broad variety of community organizations. Included are 98 "associations," 33 churches (Christian, Catholic, and Baptist), and 39 Buddhist pagodas. In addition, the *Directory* lists 42 newspapers and magazines, which are often tied to activist groups. Finally, it advertises 21 language schools, relevant bases of community organizations in terms of Woldemikael's notion of cultural assertion.

These listings tell nothing about an organization's size or viability. However, the sheer number indicates the Vietnamese propensity to create organizations.

Although the Vietnamese have created numerous associations, I have seen no evidence that indicates the ability of these organizations to unify large numbers of refugees. For example, in their report on Vietnamese communities in the United States, Finnan and Cooperstein described a pattern of affiliation based upon numerous but small organizations:

> None of the Vietnamese organizations, however, represented a very large segment of the community. In part, this proliferation of ethnic organization among the Vietnamese reflects their numbers, as well as their multiple goals, interests and backgrounds. It also relates to the historical fragmentation among the Vietnamese, as well as to their war-bred distrust of leaders. (Finnan and Cooperstein 1983:53)

ORGANIZED GROUPS IN SOVIET JEWISH AND VIETNAMESE COMMUNITIES

Despite the contrast in involvement of Soviet Jews and Vietnamese in community activities, the formalized associations created by these two nationality groups revealed equivalence in terms of structure, goals, and constituencies of support. For example, both populations exhibited large, relatively unmobilized grass-roots groups and smaller, more organized collectivities consisting of entrepreneurs, veterans, professionals, religious followers, and activists. Several of these have already been discussed in previous chapters. In the section that follows, I describe three kinds of groups that provided an important basis for community organization among both refugee populations: entrepreneurs, religious traditionalists, and political activists.

Entrepreneurs' Groups

An extensive literature demonstrates how immigrant groups reinforce social connections through forms of economic cooperation, ranging from the survival-based traditions of "sharing and caring" practiced by inner-city American blacks or recently arrived refugees (Haines 1981; Kibria 1989; Willie 1988) to international networks of cooperation that distribute and exchange a wide array of economic goods and services (capital, labor, manufacturing, transport, construction, and support services) within a single ethnic population (Cohen 1969; Kim 1981; Portes 1987; Purcell 1965).

A well-documented form of economically based solidarity is ethnic entrepreneurship. Perceiving a common economic fate, entrepreneurial communities reinforce ethnic ties as they cooperate in various economic endeavors, generally in competition with natives or other immigrant populations. In the course of earning a living, ethnic ties and economic interests become intertwined. Attacks on a group's economic activities often initiate a self-feeding cycle of ethnic cooperation, leading to economic success, which precipitates outgroup hostility, which, in turn, fosters greater ethnic solidarity and cooperation (Light and Bonacich 1988).

Economic cooperation is a common, if relatively informal, activity among refugees. As noted in Chapter 7, this phenomenon is most highly developed among the Chinese Vietnamese, a group that exemplifies economically reinforced ethnic solidarity (Bonacich 1973; Chen 1987; Reimers 1985; Teitelbaum 1985). Less extensively developed economic ties also unify Vietnamese and Soviet Jewish entrepreneurs.

Soviet Jewish Entrepreneurs' Group

Like the entrepreneurs of other ethnic groups, Soviet Jewish businesspersons mobilized their colleagues for mutual benefit—sharing information and capital and finding partners (Cummings 1980; Light 1972; Orleck 1987). The benefits provided by business organizations were especially valuable for émigrés because upon arrival in the United States, they lack two of the most important resources for entrepreneurship: capital and business experience (Gold 1988; Min 1988; Orleck 1987).

In Los Angeles, the businesspersons' group grew out of two taxi cooperatives (Russell 1985). Through these, émigrés developed the connections, skills, and capital sources that allowed their eventual movement into more extensive self-employment activities. The Moscow-born vice president of one cooperative described his experience as typical for a Soviet Jewish cab owner:

> When I got here first, I got a job in East L.A. in a garment factory. I worked very hard by the way, always sweating. Just moving around

cloth—I sure wasn't satisfied. And then I found out about cab association. It's got 201 members, 94 are Russians. And I found out I can make
a little more money driving a cab. I worked as a lease driver at first, and
in 1978, I bought my own cab. Now I lease it at nights to other Russian
driver.

I'm not going to drive my cab for all my life. I'm planning for the future
to go to some kind of different business—a shop or restaurant. My wife
already has a beauty parlor.

So that's why we have so many Russians. Most of them—like me—are
business-minded people. Driving a cab is a start. In the future, a lot of
them will go into other businesses. A lot are already in businesses—
stores, restaurants, body shops. They rely on partnerships.

Similarly, the producer of a Los Angeles Russian radio program described relying on ethnic connections to build his enterprise:

I organized KMNB radio station and translation service. It stands for
"multinational broadcasting." I opened the service almost 6 years ago for
old people who did not understand English. We translated American television programs.

We got money from people who would be our future clients—Russian
store owners and even people who wanted to use the service. Then my
show grew, we got bigger shares of money from advertisers because we
had the Russian audience. Now I have a cable TV show. We have Armenian, Polish, Russian, American viewers. And a lot of businesses like to
have advertisements on the show. They get good publicity and I make
money.

These networks provided Soviet émigrés with a variety of resources
useful in opening and running a successful operation. Well-established
entrepreneurs often gave novices advice about contracts, licenses, and
appropriate store locations (Lubin 1985). Members also offered each
other opportunities for investment. For example, in San Francisco, a
Soviet Jewish realty company distributed information about available
storefronts and supplied real estate speculators with lists of homes
that could be purchased and refurbished for resale. As noted in Chapter 7, Soviet entrepreneurs also supplied one another with investment
capital and an active social life (Gold 1988; in press).

For many members of the businesspersons' subgroup, self-employment
provided not only a source of income, but also a sense of personal and

ethnic identity, a means of access to American society, and a social
life. As such, ethnic identity and solidarity were reinforced through
economic cooperation (Light 1972; Chan and Cheung 1982; Silverman 1988).

Because these émigrés came from a secular society, their understanding of Jewish identity draws more from the accomplishments of
Jews in general than religious teachings and practices (Markowitz
1988). Consequently, they see a predisposition toward business as a
central component of Jewish ethnicity (Kosmin 1990; Zenner 1983).
For example, Joe Crystal, the owner of a laundry plant and several
Laundromats in San Francisco, saw entrepreneurial ability as a product of the Soviet Jewish experience:

Gold: Coming from a communist country, how did you know how to run a
      business?

Crystal: I feel that it is my feeling. Mostly Jewish they have a good living in
      Russia. Discrimination and all stuff like this, but they living economical
      highest level than another. So they learned some ways. And after I left
      Russia, I go to Italy for 7 months. I survived. Now I am still here, I sur-
      vived. You put me on Alaska, I'll survive there too, believe me.

      I have a lot of examples of friends of mine. Here, in New York, Chicago,
      San Francisco, L.A., sometimes they are successful, sometimes not.
      What is help in mine point of view: we are much more aggressive than
      people who were born here. That's for sure. We are fighters. I know so
      many people here who fall down, go up again, fall down, go up again.

Although Soviet Jewish entrepreneurs received benefits from ethnic
business networks, they also noted the liabilities of these arrangements. For example, given the contentious environment of the Soviet
Jewish enclave, several émigrés described conflicts that arose among
co-ethnics. Again, I quote the taxi cooperative vice president:

   Our previous vice president, he was a Russian too. We had a problem because he started taking bribes from fellow Russians who wanted to drive
   cabs even though they couldn't speak English, which is against regulations. So they kicked him out and they elected me instead. Now we have
   some people who are against me. We never sing the same song.

Despite such reservations, the businesspersons' network continued
to function and provide benefits for its members. In the words of an

entrepreneur, "We know each other—we all live in the Russian Jewish area in West Hollywood. It's not necessary to be friends, but we can work together."

In summary, Soviet Jewish businesspersons were able to overcome the general feeling of disconnectedness that characterized the Soviet Jewish enclave. United by common economic purposes and consciously drawing upon their Soviet-based survival skills, they cooperated in business and pleasure. Further, they saw their way of life as rooted in Jewish ethnicity. Because this outlook was shared, it allowed for the establishment of a business network that provided its members with economic and informational resources (Cummings 1980; Light 1972; Portes and Bach 1985). However, the business network remained informal. It was unified by pragmatic needs and personal relationships. Thus entrepreneurial cooperation was limited in its ability to unify this community.

Vietnamese Business Networks

In addition to organized ethnic Chinese entrepreneurs, other elements of the Vietnamese population also participated in solidarity-reinforcing networks. For example, in the San Francisco Bay Area, I interviewed several Vietnamese restaurant and shop owners who participated in rotating credit associations to raise capital. Many were well-established, 1975-era refugees whose reputations made them good credit risks: able to borrow from co-ethnics they had known prior to migration.

In both San Francisco and Los Angeles, business-minded Vietnamese created associations to promote refugee entrepreneurship. While occasionally serving the ethnic Chinese, these organizations, created by ethnic Vietnamese, appeared to function as bureaucratically based counterparts to the associations indigenous to the ethnic Chinese refugee population. Relying upon resettlement funds and professional experts, they provided ethnic Vietnamese entrepreneurs with some of the resources that the Chinese enjoyed by virtue of their ethnic membership. For example, the Vietnamese Chamber of Commerce in Orange County (a group consisting of highly educated Southern California refugees) provided seminars to refugee business people and published the *Vietnam Business Directory*. The existence of distinct Chinese-Vietnamese and Vietnamese business groups reveals a clear ethnic boundary between these two subpopulations.

In sum, among both Soviet Jews and Vietnamese populations, shared economic and entrepreneurial interests united groups of refugees and, in so doing, reinforced social ties. While these organizations provided valuable services, they reached only a small fraction of the greater community. Moreover, the Soviet Jewish group remained informal, and many of the Vietnamese involved in business networks already shared links based in common ethnicity or country-of-origin acquaintance. As suggested in Chapter 7, economic cooperation has yet to unify large numbers of Soviet Jewish and Vietnamese refugees.

Political Activists

A second basis for ethnic community-building is found in the realm of politics. Immigrant groups have a long tradition of political activism (Lyman 1974; Wirth 1928). Since the 1960s, however, politics have been an area of special relevance for ethnic groups because of the state's increasing use of ethnic categories as a basis for the distribution of benefits under its control (e.g. jobs, development projects, contracts, and educational opportunities). Newly powerful and mobilized ethnic groups throughout the world have used their political clout to demand redistribution (Nielsen 1985; Olzak and Nagel 1986).

Following the example of blacks, an entire series of U.S. ethnic groups have used the political system to enhance their competitive position. As a result of these movements, ethnic solidarity and awareness as well as conflict have been heightened (Ahrari 1987; Padilla 1987; Wilson 1978). Political activists have engaged in a lively, if not altogether successful movement for ethnic mobilization among Soviet Jewish and Vietnamese populations in the United States.

Soviet Jewish Activists

Soviet Jewish activists were the most ideological, ambitious, and culturally assertive group in the émigré community. Well established and highly educated, they expressed more moralistic and idealistic concerns than other émigrés. Taking their status as refugees seriously, activists hoped to become full participants in American democracy and to remind other Soviet Jews of this mission as well. Activists often functioned as intermediaries between the Soviet enclave and the larger American Jewish community. Several were involved in voluntary efforts to resettle just-arrived émigrés and held various positions in Jewish-American community bodies.

The most ambitious undertaking by Los Angeles activists was intended to unite several interest groups within the émigré population—veterans, doctors and dentists, the elderly, religious and secular constituencies, and ethnic media—in an umbrella organization called The Association of Soviet Jewish Émigrés (TASJE). The most recent and successful in a series of émigré organizations dating back to the early 1980s, it was initially headed by Felix Ryback, a social service worker. After several years of frustrating involvement with the Jewish Federation of Los Angeles (the body that raises money and provides services to the greater Jewish community), Ryback, along with several other influential émigrés, organized TASJE and applied to the city of West Hollywood for funds to resettle and serve Soviet Jews. After being turned down in 1986, the organization was finally awarded a grant in 1988 in direct competition with the politically influential Jewish Federation.

As noted in the discussion of reactive solidarity in Chapter 6, many Soviet Jews were aggravated by their interactions with the American Jewish community. In response, they sought to create organizations through which their own prerogatives could be expressed. Felix Ryback described this:

> The degree of tolerance demonstrated by those people [in the American Jewish community] who are supposed to be tolerant, okay, is very insignificant. For example, back a few years, Mr. Kogan, he organized a club [of Soviet Jews]. It was the first attempt to get the community organized and it worked, it worked well. But the club is actually more Russian oriented than Jewish oriented.
>
> So they have some misunderstandings with our Jewish Community Center which would not allow them to use facility and some support, so they have alienated [Russian Jews] and they don't want to deal with Jewish community and the Jewish Federation.
>
> I sit on various boards with Jewish Federation. Many times, I would not be given the floor, many times they would play political games and so forth. Many times they would not put my motion to vote. So I just said "hey, this is not Russia. If the chairman happens to disagree with my suggestion, it doesn't mean that the committee disagrees with my suggestion. Put it to a vote, okay."

Another official of TASJE shared these feelings of exclusion from the Jewish Federation:

The reason we came here is because 20 years ago, people like you just shouted in the streets, "let our people go." But here we are, we are already considering ourselves like Americans. Not just immigrants, but already Americans with good experience.

A position of irony is that we still treated as boys and girls. We are not even close to policy making in this country. The whole decisions are made without us. They just use us as bait for raising money. So what's going on right now, it's a process of recognition of the Soviet Jews as a power. And I'm doing a lot of things in this matter just to help establish ourself as a real strength.

Precisely because of the close ties émigrés have to American Jews (the majority of whom share Russian/Eastern European origins and have been crusading for the Soviets' right to emigrate since the 1960s), Soviet Jews have been given little opportunity to assert their own political, cultural, and religious identities in the United States. In fact, several émigré activists described expending significant efforts just to demonstrate to American Jews that they had a unique and positive culture. A woman from Oakland complained:

I remember, even when I didn't know the language so well, I could hear the question "How do you know you are a Jew if you didn't do this and you didn't know that." And "why didn't they go to Israel?"

I tell you, each family have some that died in the Ghetto. That's the kind of experience that you grow up with as a kid. Not long ago, we had a discussion on Jewish religious education with American Jews and we told them "We are Jewish enough and sometimes more than enough."

American Jews, primed by decades of anti-Soviet propaganda and having heard numerous tales about religion-seeking Soviet Jewish refuseniks, are unprepared to acknowledge that most Soviet Jews love the Russian culture and landscape, enjoy aspects of the Russian lifestyle, and have a degree of pride in the accomplishments of the USSR. Instead, according to émigré activists, American Jews often assumed that the Soviets would happily give up their inured perspectives for typically American ideologies, forms of Judaism, and styles of community membership. When émigrés were reluctant to do so, American Jews repudiated them: "As American Jews found some of the ways that Soviet Jews act to be alien, they came to label these behaviors and the individuals associated with them not 'Jewish' but

'Russian'" (Markowitz 1988:84). It was this outlook that activists challenged in asserting their own prerogative. A Bay Area activist commented:

> I want the American community to understand who we are, because I feel personally a lot of our problems and a lot of our, you know, negative feelings toward each other is because people don't understand each other.
>
> First of all, we are not like your grandparents, people from Sholom Aleichem. We are educated, professional people.
>
> If you talk about the community in general, it's a nonreligious community and that's it. Because we don't have religious ground. You have to form this ground first, but I don't think this will be an overnight thing. Right now, I try really to impress to American community, for us, Jewishness is nonreligious.

As noted in Chapter 6, many conflicts between Soviet émigrés and their well-meaning American Jewish hosts concerned the Soviet Jews' resettlement. Issues of contention included religious socialization, job placement, nation of refuge, community representation, fund raising, provision of psychological therapy, and scholarships for émigré children to attend Jewish schools.

Recently, Jewish émigrés have also become politically active in a manner that challenges the American Jewish community. While American Jews tend to be Democrats, most Soviet Jews are politically conservative and, when naturalized, join the Republican party (Noonan 1988). A Soviet Jewish journalist and publisher commented on Soviet Jews' differences with their American counterparts:

> Most American Jews are used to being liberals. But Russian Jews, having very tough experience, know what socialism does mean. They are very close to the right wing, politically. We have gotten involved with the campaigns. I think that almost everybody voted for Republicans.

By emphasizing political differences with their co-ethnic U.S. sponsors, Soviet Jews are demonstrating their unique identity and are building an independent leadership with links to larger American institutions beyond the established Jewish community.

Despite their efforts, activist émigrés faced a great deal of difficulty in organizing the Soviet Jewish enclave. In both San Francisco and Los Angeles, early attempts to create Soviet Jewish organizations failed. A Los Angeles activist noted that émigré groups have many "different agendas." In Southern California alone, there were three Russian veterans' associations. One merged with American veterans, a second remained independent, and a third focused on the problems of the disabled.

Similarly, ethnic identification was contested among Soviet émigrés. While some were religious Jews, others saw themselves as Russians. Further, despite the general trend toward conservatism, ideological conflicts sometimes prevented unification. For example, two of the most powerful figures in Los Angeles's Soviet Jewish media—the publisher of the community's major newspaper and the producer of a weekly, Russian-language television program (their offices were located in the same building)—refused to cooperate because of their divergent political views. While the publisher was conservative and anti-Soviet, the producer held a middle-of-the-road outlook and made frequent visits to the USSR.

Activists often found themselves trapped between antagonistic and ill-informed groups representing émigrés on one hand, and the American community on the other. They had to educate American Jews about the outlooks held by Soviet immigrants, and at the same time, teach fellow émigrés about the complex of Jewish organizations and agencies that make policy and offer services:

Obstacles all over, personal ambition and tension and jealousy. But the biggest victory what I consider in our organization that the old, existing organizations all became members. The Veterans War Organization, Handicapped Veterans, Engineer and Scientists Club, Non-profit Olympic School and Poetry Club, so this is recognition.

My mentality is that we should not waste time for fights or arguments, we should work harder to get recognition. We have thousands of experienced people. The goal is to continue to make a unit of our community to involve more and more people. To give them a chance to express their talents and serve another people. And in the tradition to be a Jew. To help our friends, our relatives in Israel, to help our friends and relatives in Russia, because this is a new issue which the West doesn't know.

Nobody knows better than we our needs. We collect clothing and furniture for immigrants here, we have connections with local and state politicians. Right now, I've made connections all over—in Russia, in Israel, in Canada and Australia.

Finally, the desire of Soviet Jewish activists to separate themselves from American co-ethnics, while an immediate concern, was limited. Their goal was not secession from the American Jewish community but, rather, the assertion of Russian/Jewish identity with Americans accommodating them. Émigré activists hoped for a reconciliation with their sponsors as soon as the Americans showed more respect.

> Our number one goal is we are building a strong bridge between the Russian island and the American society and the Jewish community. It is a bridge that should be strong enough to let a thousand people come through.

> We like our people to be integrated, to be recognized as Jews—don't lose our identity which we barely have. We'd like our kids and our grandchildren come to the Russian culture.

> We received grants from the city of West Hollywood, we receive some help from City of Los Angeles, from County, looks like from Jewish Federation and we are applying for more and more, so we get recognized in time.

Downplaying the distance between immigrants and natives, émigré activists contended that their conflicts were not with American Jews in general but, rather, with Jewish Federation bureaucrats who did not want their resettlement programs challenged.

> We are trying to establish our community and to educate the Federation. The real Federation—the community volunteers is people like you and me—all kinds, hundreds of associations and people. It's not tension with the Federation, but tension with the administrators. They just filter information and there is no integration with the community. The mentality of all bureaucrats is very much the same. Don't shake my boat because I might fall over. So [they think] it's better not to do anything.

In summary, activists within the Soviet Jewish population have worked to organize their community. They were interested in aiding Soviet Jews, developing an American power base, and preserving their Russian and Jewish identity and culture. Confronting many obstacles along the way, they now feel their efforts are being rewarded.

Although the adaptation of Soviet Jews is a contemporary issue of concern to émigrés and American Jews alike, it is important to note that a similar conflict occurred between Russian immigrants and American sponsors some 70 years ago. "German-American Jews, who feared for their recently achieved middle-class status . . . took a compassionate, though largely condescending view" toward Russian Jewish immigrants. The established community was "interested in helping to 'Americanize' them, . . . feeling that the quicker they become indistinguishable from the rest of America, the better" (Farber et al. 1988:404). In response, immigrants created their own organizations that were rooted in Eastern European Jewish belief, tradition, politics, culture, and language (Gorelick 1982; Rischin 1962).

Following this precedent, we can assume that as time passes, Soviet Jews will cease being the subjects of the American Jewish community. Instead, like the Russian Jews who were resettled by German-American co-ethnics early in this century, they will become yet another subgroup of a diverse population. Their presence will color the Jewish-American community and, eventually, they will take dominant roles alongside their one-time hosts (Gorelick 1981; Rischin 1962; Wirth 1928).

Vietnamese Activists

Vietnamese activists came from a variety of backgrounds and held a diversity of opinions regarding the development of the refugee community in the United States, but they shared common characteristics. As a group, they were sophisticated, professionally employed, upwardly mobile, and familiar with Western life. All had attended a college or university for at least two years. Their education was obtained in Vietnam, France, Japan, and the United States. As their high levels of education would indicate, refugee activists were generally from the middle to upper classes of Vietnam, a position they generally maintained in the United States. Finally, drawing on their education and multilingual ability, activists frequently found employment in the refugee resettlement system.

Sharing common class position and political ambition, Vietnamese activists were divided on many issues. The clearest basis for their division was generational. The older generation of activists had lived in Vietnam until they were 30 to 50 years of age. Many were involved with the military and/or the government of South Vietnam. Others were academics. With few exceptions, all of the men I interviewed in this group were veterans. The one woman in this group was married to a Vietnamese soldier and had been employed in the U.S. embassy in Saigon.

The young generation of activists came to the United States during their teens or early 20s. All of the younger activists attended college or university in the United States. Because they came to the States when they were young, none held positions of high status in Vietnam. However, many were members of affluent and powerful families. Members of the younger generation were well integrated into American life. They frequently drew from the experience of American minority groups in shaping their perspective on resettlement.

Older-Generation Activists. Older Vietnamese activists were accustomed to occupying positions of institutional and political power. Many had high military ranks and had planned the policies of South Vietnam. They often knew each other before coming to the United States, enabling them to initiate mutual aid activities upon arrival. A Vietnamese professor described forming a refugee association:

> When we were in Camp Pendleton in 1975, we were aware we needed to have something done for intellectuals. I was assistant dean of the Saigon University. My friends were judges, attorneys, and professors. They elected me as head of the group.

Because they had occupied important positions in South Vietnamese society, older activists were concerned with the erosion of their personal status, as well as their collective loss of legitimacy as the leaders of Vietnam. Their organizations sought to reaffirm their position as the rightful leaders of the Vietnamese community. A Vietnamese professor described the loss of status felt by his cohort:

> As intelligence people, intellectuals, we deal with status problem. One who was in Vietnam an attorney, a judge, a medical doctor, a professor like myself. It's something else. Now in here, we have to drop to the bottom of society and to work our way up to gain status.

The older-generation activists were well equipped in their efforts to regain status and lead the Vietnamese refugee community. They had been in the United States several years, knew English well, and had

created a variety of organizations. Further, many were financially secure, and several retained war-era links with Americans.

Despite these many advantages, older-generation activists also experienced liabilities in their efforts to reestablish community control.
Most importantly, they had to fend off accusations that the Saigon
elite was a corrupt, incompetent, and brutal group. Further, detractors
saw their tradition-based model of resettlement and community development as undemocratic and of little benefit to needy refugees in the
United States. Finally, because these older activists were passionately
anti-communist, they faced difficulty in establishing links with the
liberal groups in American society (many of whom were anti-Vietnam
War activists in the 1960s and 1970s) that are the traditional allies of
urban minority groups.[1]

To counter accusations of corruption among the Saigon regime,
older-generation activists made special efforts to demonstrate their
good intentions in the United States. Some alluded to the suffering
they experienced in fleeing Vietnam, while others accepted partial
blame for South Vietnam's defeat. For example, a former government
official described his motivation for working in resettlement: "Well,
we are losers and I am a loser. I lost my country. I spent more than
two thirds of my life in Vietnam and now I want to spend the rest of
my life helping my people."

Older-generation activists retained their identification with the
country of Vietnam and dreamed that someday the communists
would be defeated. Until that time, they sought to help Vietnamese
in camps overseas. This agenda provided a base for movement building. I interviewed many refugees who supported and contributed to
various military groups. Alex Huynh of the Vietnamese Veterans Association stated:

> We have a lot of veterans among the Vietnamese boat people. They can-
> not go to United States quickly. They must spend months, years in refu-
> gee camp. They need help. Most of these people have suffered in one
> way or another.
>
> So we urge veterans here who can make a living and assimilate to
> American society already to think about over there and contribute over
> there. Write letters over there, encourage them in their depression. If
> they need, send them money, clothes.

We ask governments in the Free World to use power to ask Communist government to let people out. Because no country in the world still keeps their prisoners of war after seven or eight years. Inhuman circumstances.

In contrast to the older activists, younger ones who identified more with the United States were less concerned with freeing Vietnam.

As a group, older activists were also more interested in making a good impression on Americans than were the young. They often referred to the Vietnamese concept of "face" (roughly equal to maintaing a good reputation) in describing their efforts to encourage high standards of behavior among refugees (Ho 1976). A former professor described his view of conformity, prestige, and social control among refugees in the United States:

If other refugees in the United States do something wrong, it is very shameful and we feel very hurt. We try to do something to help so we won't be criticized by the American public.

[We feel:] he's a Vietnamese, he does something wrong. We are Vietnamese, so we feel hurt. That is why we have to do something to help each other. Esteem by the community spreads: news, rumors, others hear that. My friends hear that my children did well, so they are proud of you. [They say] "You deserve, because you are in a high position before in Vietnam." [On the other hand,] if somebody else doesn't do well, he loses face, society looks down on him and nobody likes him. So he goes somewhere else.

Alex Huynh alluded to similar motives as he described his veterans association's efforts to sanction deviant refugees:

We do have veteran minority who came here and had wrong idea about United States government. Those people do not like to work. Then, when welfare is cut off, they do some wrong things—stealing, crime.

If we detect, we give them warning: "If you do like that, you give a very bad image to American people." And if they cannot [stop] . . . then we will turn them in or ask the police or we can take care of them. Not kill them, but we have many ways to do this, yeah, we have to do this.

In their efforts to make a good impression on Americans, older-generation activists were especially concerned with welfare and other public expenditures on refugees. Many commented that welfare robs refugees of their dignity and makes Americans view them as "free-loaders." Older activists hoped to reduce the numbers of Vietnamese relying on public monies in order to convince politicians that additional arrivals would not be an imposition. Young activists, on the other hand, generally wished to maximize benefits so that newcomers' suffering might be eased.

In sum, older activists used their knowledge of Vietnamese tradition, together with the fact that they occupied prestigious positions in Vietnam, to impose their leadership over the refugee community. Older activists reminded their fellows that if they really wished to preserve Vietnamese customs, they must support the old elite—to put another group into power would be a violation of tradition. In this way, older activists created a definition of Vietnamese ethnicity that was inherently conservative, one that claims that "to stray from the social arrangements of the past is to deny one's nature and nation." Drawing upon Vietnamese traditions of Confucianism and ancestor worship, its influence was sometimes considerable in a community marked by homesickness. However, the proposals of older activists were not universally accepted. They had little appeal for assimilationists, young activists, the ethnic Chinese, and those who were too overwhelmed by immediate problems to worry about cultural preservation or recapturing Vietnam.

Young activists. Younger Vietnamese activists had a perspective that was based in the United States rather than Vietnam. Comfortable with American social and political perspectives, their image of the ideal refugee community was less hierarchical than that of the old generation. Younger activists were under 40 and had attended institutions of higher learning in the United States. With the exception of a cadet in a Vietnamese military academy, none were military veterans. Several came to the United States as students or immigrants prior to South Vietnam's 1975 collapse.

Although only about 2% of all Vietnamese in the United States today were in the country before 1975, those early arrivals were very well represented among management-level employees of resettlement agencies, especially in the San Francisco Bay Area. Of the 11 Vietnamese I interviewed who were agency directors or managers of a unit within an agency, 9 were in the United States before the fall of South Vietnam.[2] Because of their concern with community and their American education, young activists were active in the resettlement system.

Unlike many of the older refugee activists who arrived in the United States with English competence, professional skills, and families, among thousands in a similar position, the young activists came as students without resources or support networks. To young activists, the experience of going through a painful period of unaided adjustment and the high degree of knowledge about American life that resulted served as ideal preparation for work in refugee resettlement. Because they suffered, they could empathize with recent arrivals; because they know the American system, they could offer newcomers excellent advice. Tran Van Duc, a social worker, described his position:

> Well, after being here for about 17 years, I believe I understand how the system works. So by choosing to be a service provider to the community, with the experience that I have in this country, I think that I can make some kind of contribution to the growth and development of the community.

Many younger activists were ambivalent or even hostile toward the former rulers of South Vietnam. Several explained that while the mass of Vietnamese, themselves included, had no say in the policies of their country, they had to pay the greatest price for the mistakes of the Saigon administration. Ty Nguyen described the views of Vietnamese who arrived in the States before 1975:

> I have to tell you this, that some of these old mentalities, and I am not going to say who, they are not going to work. They have the bureaucratic mindset of the old sinecure Saigon government. They were corrupted. The Saigon government was to a large extent corrupted by Thieu.

> You know, there are so many different categories, but I think that most people who were here before '75, in fact all of the people, I don't really know any one who are for Thieu and his henchmen. But that doesn't mean that all of the people who were here before '75 were for the Communists either . . . they weren't rooting for the other side. They were just against the killing and the war and like that.

Because of their mistrust of "the sinecure Saigon elite," many young activists were opposed to its members gaining power and influence within the Vietnamese community in the United States. They feared that links between the smooth-talking Saigon elite and American bureaucrats, so destructive to the mass of Vietnamese during the war, would be reestablished in the United States through resettlement programs. Young activist Michael Tran stated: "If someone was a senator or a colonel in Saigon, I don't care, it means nothing to me. They had power in Vietnam and due to their corruption, they blew it."

Younger activists saw the older generation's efforts to fight communism as evidence of their inability to provide the community with effective leadership. Not only did they consider this a hopeless endeavor, but, further, they felt that it wasted the limited economic and moral resources of the refugee community, resources that should be directed toward disadvantaged refugees in the United States. Tran Van Duc commented:

> Of course we need to develop more in community resources. We don't need the people to be on top, we need to expand the base, to bring it up. I think that's very important.

> I believe we are here to live and to die here, so I believe that it is more important for us to somehow improve the community here rather than spending energy and time and effort somewhere else. I'm talking the community here instead of what's going on in Vietnam.

Young activists suggested that the older generation's emphasis of traditional Vietnamese culture as the means to successful adaptation was a self-interested endeavor. For example, Nguyet Pham criticized the older generation's concern with saving face:

> So I'm here and just starting all over again. They [the old generation activists] say "Oh Vietnamese culture" and that is supposed to be. You never put down a parent, because of their pride, because they are afraid [that] people [will] know that bad thing [about someone]. It won't work.

Members of the older generation often retained traditional hostilities toward Vietnam's Asian enemies and disliked the ethnic Chinese; young activists, in contrast, found attractive the idea of forming coalitions with other Asian-Americans. In the words of a community mental health worker:

> In terms of growth and development, we cannot afford to be separate. It is the same thing with other Asian groups. We need somehow to be included with Asian-American or other ethnic minority. Instead of

Vietnamese minority or ethnic Chinese minority or Japanese we cannot afford to do that. Despite our differences, I think we would be better off getting together.

Like other American ethnic groups, young Vietnamese activists wished to limit paternalism from outgroup members, notably native-born Americans. Just as they sought to escape the influence of the Saigon elite, so they also hoped to avoid being controlled by American bureaucrats. In fact, precisely because they were highly assimilated and had extensive contact with Americans, young activists were more aware of discrimination than were members of other refugee subgroups. An American-educated Orange County activist claimed: "I don't know if there is room at the top for a qualified [Vietnamese] person, so I'm going to tell my son to get an education in business and be self-employed." Similarly, Ty Nguyen described his encounters with prejudice in the resettlement field:

I was appointed the director of Refugee Employment Project. It didn't work out because . . . they thought I was going to be a token. But for the good of the agency, I suggested a lot of changes. They thought I was too usurping. They asked me to resign after only 3 or 4 weeks.

But then the [Vietnamese] community was really angry. You know, letters were written, words exchanged. And individuals said "If you do that again, we are not going to talk with you again, because that is spit in our face."

In summary, younger activists competed with the traditionalistic older generation. Acknowledging their Vietnamese origins, younger leaders were comfortable in the American setting. They were especially concerned with grass-roots co-ethnics (boat people), whom they sought to aid through involvement in resettlement agencies. While small in number and too liberal and Americanized to appeal to the mass of older refugees, young activists maintained power and visibility by virture of their involvement in resettlement. However, because refugee youth often adopt outlooks similar to the younger activists as they reach adulthood in the United States, the power and influence of the young activists has expanded with the passage of time.

Merging of the generations. While the two generations of Vietnamese activists had many conflicts, these did not preclude the possibility of unification. Several older activists, for example, were critical of their peers' obsession with tradition. On the other hand, most young activists valued Vietnamese traditions and several esteemed older-generation leaders above those of their own group. While conflicts continued, activists of either generation recognized the merits of each other's position and their common past and future. Older-generation activist Ty Huynh commented favorably on the young leaders:

> You know our history, so much conflict. But to most of the refugee they are young and radical. What happens in the past does not mean what will happen in the future. We very open, we are willing to learn and we are willing to cooperate.

Young activist Vinh Hue described his reverence for older refugees:

Gold: You say that your organization is made up of the younger people. I have heard some of the younger generation say that the older ones' mentality was destroyed by corruption.

Vinh Hue: No, we are not thinking that way. The older was the good advisor. They provide us with their experiences and give us the best advice. We have our energy for doing things but the older know how to control it and know how to give out the best advice.

Finally, some refugees saw a division of labor among activists. The assimilated young generation provided "public" leaders, best for dealing with the American community. Older, Vietnam-oriented "private" leaders exerted influence within the refugee community itself. Personalities who commanded respect in both spheres were exceedingly rare (Finnan and Cooperstein 1983:63). Vu Tran, a refugee businessman who was not himself an activist, but knew the community intimately, expressed this position:

> I like that guy Huang Co Minh who gives up the easy life in this country to go fight the Communists in Vietnam. At least he does something. I contribute to him.

> But for Vietnamese association, there are so many and always fighting. It is our culture. So I don't join. When there is one or two organization, then I join. There are no leaders now, we cannot lead and the old people they cannot lead. We need to have a good leader that everyone will believe. John Nguyen [young activist director of Resettlement Center] is a

good leader for here, for American problems, but some people think he is Communist. But for a leader for us, we don't have yet.

Within both Soviet Jewish and Vietnamese populations, activists were involved in efforts to organize their respective communities. Although refugee activists were some of the most skillful and energetic members of either community, no one group or cause has been able unify significant numbers of refugees. Instead, both communities have remained factionalized.

Cultural and Religious Groups

In addition to economic and political cooperation, a third important basis of competitive community solidarity is found in the desire of refugees to maintain cultural and social patterns retained from the country of origin. A large body of research describes immigrant and ethnic groups that are unified by their desire to maintain religion, customs, language, social patterns, and other cultural features from the home country or region (Cohen 1969; Gorelick 1982; Thomas and Znaniecki 1920; Woldemikael 1987).

For example, several writers have noted how language, especially Spanish, is retained as an important source of cultural identity in the United States (Padilla 1987; Portes and Rumbaut 1990; Schaefer 1990). Ethnic-based religious congregations offer another set of key institutions among many immigrant groups (Breton 1964; Cohen 1969; Farber 1987; Glazer and Moynihan 1963; Padilla 1987; Wirth 1928). Ethnic churches maintain a variety of religious, welfare, and social activities that reinforce ethnic identity and solidarity among members.

During fieldwork, I observed or was informed of various culturally oriented ethnic organizations among Soviet Jewish and Vietnamese populations. The following discussion is based upon the two organizations with which I had the closest contact: the Chabad-Russian program and Vietnamese Buddhist practitioners. Each involved the preservation of traditional religions in the United States.

While many religious groups were active in Soviet Jewish and Vietnamese communities, only a fraction self-consciously organized refugees as an independent constituency. Instead, most worked for American religious institutions, ministering to new arrivals. However, traditional religious leaders intentionally used the culture and religion of the "old country" to build community among refugees in the United States.

In contrast to political activists, who were regarded with a high degree of suspicion, religious groups and leaders enjoyed a reputation of trustworthiness. Especially among the Vietnamese, who have been resettled by religious groups and agencies, such organizations are seen as both well intentioned and capable of delivering desired resources. Possessing credibility, their influence was considerable, especially among elderly and traditionalistic refugees.

The Chabad Russian Synagogue

The Chabad Russian program was able to unify émigrés by appealing to their unique religious needs. Despite the status of Soviet Jews as a religiously defined refugee group, their involvement in religious activities in the United States is limited because they had little religious training prior to migration. Many had assimilated into atheistic Russian society.

Even religiously inclined émigrés had difficulty in participating in American Jewish activities because much of what they know of the Jewish religion has been passed down from the pre-revolution era and, as such, is quite different from that practiced by California Jews today. Further, many American synagogues embody a liberal political outlook that the generally conservative Soviet Jews disliked. Finally, the most religious members of the Soviet Jewish population are aged and know little English or Hebrew, the languages spoken in American synagogues. As a consequence, Soviet émigrés have a religious orientation that is quite distinct from that of the native Jewish populations (Markowitz 1988).

In Los Angeles, the religious needs of Soviet Jews, especially those of the elderly men who speak little English, were met by the Russian outreach activities of the Chabad-Lubovitch movement. I made several visits to two of these congregations. Located in storefronts, each was led by a Russian-speaking rabbi, who was himself an immigrant.

These rabbis were part of *Chabad,* a centralized and well-organized international Jewish movement that supports their synagogues. In the following quote, a Russian-speaking rabbi and cantor described his organization's appeal to Jewish émigrés:

We never push people, but they feel much better, more comfortable with their own community, with their own tradition, with their own language.

They come to me after being to American services and they say "Which kind of synagogue is this? What is it? Instead of a cantor is a lady? She sings with a guitar? Cantor has to be with a beard and stand with his back to the people and praying and a nice voice and you start to cry when he singing. What is she standing like that with a guitar and she smile?"

We make a lot of *brisses* [circumcisions of adults who did not undergo the ritual as infants] many, many things. And we give them real *Yidishkayt,* real Judaism. We don't fake them.

We have a special program for working people, the way we do is, we talk to them. I speak very good Russian, also good English. They are impressed. I give them lectures. Very, very high knowledge. And they love it. They can have more interest to come here.

Last year for high holidays, we have over 700 people inside that hall and 300 more are outside. We have people 50-60 years old and also 17-18 years old.

The Chabad Russian rabbis utilized a great deal of humor and enthusiasm to make their activities attractive and enjoyable to Soviet émigrés. Services were always followed with Russian-style meals of bread, salad, herring, and free-flowing vodka and whiskey. The rabbis led prayers for sick relatives and those still in the Soviet Union. Lively songs and religious lectures, all in Russian, provided a social life for the elderly participants of these congregations. The Russian synagogues also offered such social services as English classes, health care, and job referrals.

The Chabad Russian rabbis planned to increase their community activities by building a "religious cultural center":

We want to make a place that will be much nicer than all the others in the city, and to make everything for sure kosher, without profit. With a swimming pool, a health club, with movies and a library. And when we get, this will unite the community.

The Chabad Russian program appeared to be influential among Soviet Jews. Its services were well attended on each of my visits. Further, the émigré community paid for the extensive remodeling of the program's West Hollywood *shul* (synagogue). However, since most of the participants were elderly, the long-term effect of Russian-language religious activities upon the émigré community is unclear.

The Chabad Russian synagogues had a well-developed ideology for mobilizing Russian Jews. Because the rabbis were themselves Russian, they were among a very small number of émigrés who commanded the respect of co-ethnics, both prior to and after migration. Further, while they are party to Russian Jewish culture, they are also connected to an international, multi-ethnic Jewish movement (Belcove-Shalin 1988).[3] Chabad self-consciously distinguishes itself from other styles of Jewish practice through clothing, ritual, life-style, and organization. Claiming "we love Jewish people, but we don't like reform Judaism," they intentionally seek to include all Jews in their program.

Although it is a broad-based movement, Chabad tolerated and even encouraged the maintenance of local culture and language among Jewish immigrant groups in the United States. Rabbi Zaltsman explained the movement's commitment to cultural diversity among Jews:

> Jewish people come from the entire world—from Persia, from Soviet Georgia. In Israel, they tried to bring all together, but they made some mistakes. The neighbors didn't work together. One can't take the gefilte fish smell, the other can't take the fried cheese. I cannot tell my Russian Jewish, you know, "come make some things to eat Persian style." There is no point.[4]

In sum, the Chabad synagogues emphasized Russian language and experience. In addition, they were openly critical of the outlook maintained by mainstream American Judaism. As a consequence, these synagogues provide a base for cultural assertion among Soviet Jews in the United States.

Vietnamese Religious Leaders

Like the Soviet Jewish community, the Vietnamese community also included religious leaders who built congregations on the basis of traditional spirituality, language, and culture. I interviewed two of these: a self-described "teacher of Oriental philosophy and meditation" and a Buddhist *bonze* (monk).

In contrast to assimilation-oriented Vietnamese Christian congregations, these spiritual leaders asserted that Vietnamese identity has its foundations in Eastern religion. In the words of the Buddhist monk:

> The fact is that Buddhism has existed in Vietnam for 2,000 years. It goes to the blood, it goes to the bone. So it becomes another flesh. So it becomes a kind of nature.

Spiritual leaders subscribed to a tradition of self-sacrificing charity toward other Vietnamese. While both spiritual leaders were college-educated and shared many characteristics with the 1975 cohort of elite refugees, including fear of hostility by the communists, they chose to remain in Vietnam after the communist takeover. It was only after living under communist domination and being subjected to political reeducation with anti-religious ideology that they escaped from Vietnam. As boat people, they experienced the same suffering as recent arrivals. Thus they could elude accusations of self-interest that detracted from the credibility of other refugee leaders.

Further, because of their immersion in Vietnamese religion and culture, they were able to develop rapport with traditionalistic refugees in a manner unavailable to assimilated Vietnamese-American activists. Like other refugee activists, the religious leaders found employment and visibility through involvement in the resettlement system. The Buddhist bonze was a bilingual instructor's aide for a Bay Area school district; the teacher of Oriental philosophy ran a housing office for a community agency. In carrying out official duties, they also developed contacts beneficial to their religious communities.

Vietnamese religious leaders offered a critique of American life to remind refugees why they should retain their traditional spiritual outlook. Ha Le, teacher of Oriental philosophy, contended that while the United States is a country of great technology and material wealth, it is sorely lacking in spirituality and links with the past:

American culture is to teach people to have ego. We call egotistic, ego-centric, something like that. But in Vietnam, we teach the student to be ego-less, to be humble.

The American look in the book okay, statistics, lots of proof and everything. But no. Because the world is composed of the known and the unknown, the visible and the invisible, the manifest and the unmanifest, the positive and the negative to have life.

So they only know the positive, the known, the visible. But they don't accept, they don't realize the potential of the reverse side: the unknown, the invisible, the unmanifest, because they cannot see it.

The Vietnamese Buddhist monk had a similar, although more moderate, critique of American life. While tolerating the assimilation of

American customs, he also asserted the need for the preservation of a
Vietnamese past:

> In general terms, you have to know what the culture is and then of course try
> to adapt yourself. Adapt yourself, that means not lose yourself. But remem-
> ber, two generations later, your children, your grandchildren, your great-
> grandchildren. They are still Vietnamese. They still have Vietnamese blood,
> their skin will be the same skin, so there is no way that we can change our
> eyes from black to the color of American eyes. So adapt yourself, but retain
> something. You are yourself only when you keep something.

Building upon their criticism of American life, these Buddhists predicted an expansion of Eastern religion and looked forward to a cultural synthesis between East and West.

> You see it is very interesting to me, because people in the West started
> looking to the East and Eastern people are starting to look to the West.
> You know, I read a book a long time ago: Kipling. "East is East and
> West is West." It's not true any more. The world is beginning to look to
> Japan because of its successfulness in economy, and they also retain the
> culture. It's our most perfect combination. A well developed country.
> But also they retain their traditional culture.

In summary, Vietnamese spiritualists organized their community in
order to maintain traditional religious activities in the United States.
They rejected both the elitism of old activists and the assimilationism
of the young. Despite their immersion in Vietnamese tradition, both
religious leaders worked within the refugee resettlement bureaucracy
and saw assimilation as ultimately necessary for the integration of
refugees in to the United States. Hence, they used their connections to
American society in order to further the cause of ethnic solidarity and
tradition.

In combining resettlement and traditional spiritualism, the religious
leaders were involved in a complex style of adaptation to American
society that included both cultural preservation and the acceptance of
dominant practices. (In Woldemikael's terminology, they synthesized
assertion and accommodation.) Both hoped to establish organizations
based upon, and intended to preserve, the "old way" of life. Yet, both
contacted their constituencies and supported their organizations
through employment in the American welfare system, something
which is neither Vietnamese nor spiritual.

CONCLUSIONS

The case of Soviet Jews and Vietnamese community organizations demonstrates the great deal of difficulty involved in creating viable and inclusive ethnic organizations among segmented refugee populations. Among these groups, organization and solidarity were strongest at the local level, uniting individuals who were already bonded by commonalties of origin, immigration experience, ideological orientation, religious outlook, and occupation. On the level of the entire ethnic population, various subgroups competed with each other, sometimes reinforcing local segmentation and, occasionally, with great effort, creating broader alliances to approach the larger society.

Soviet Jewish and Vietnamese efforts to organize their communities bear certain similarities to those of recent immigrant groups. For example, Kim (1981), Okamura (1983), and Herbstein (1983) note like patterns such as an abundance of small, unaffiliated associations, a general reluctance to organize, and generation-based community conflicts among Koreans, Filipinos, and Puerto Ricans. To a great extent, however, the community activities of Soviet Jews and Vietnamese were a product of their experience as refugees. Refugees appear to follow patterns of unification and mobilization often distinct from those associated with immigrant groups (Portes 1987:365).

State policy, in the form of eligibility for legal residency and resettlement benefits, played an important role in determining this behavior. Resettlement programs fund mutual assistance associations, subsidize activists, and may contribute to the creation of a refugee middle class. Further, through the resettlement system, refugees are put into a "patron/client" relationship with the institutions and individuals of the host society in a manner uncommon for immigrants (Chan and Indra 1987; de Voe 1981).

By their very existence, resettlement services offer a disincentive to group formation. To quote from Hechter's *Principles of Group Solidarity:* "If the state provides many such goods (education, unemployment benefits, health insurance and social security), then this also diminishes the motive to form many kinds of groups" (Hechter 1987:177). Consequently, the modern welfare state, while mobilizing refugee organizations through funding and legislation, also takes over some of their purposes for existence.

In giving Soviet Jews and Vietnamese a prized political status, economic benefits, and sponsors, the state attenuates their motivation for participating in solidarity-fostering conflict with the dominant society. This deflection of anti-host hostility sometimes intensifies the already segmented character of these populations. As a consequence, competition and conflict were more commonly expressed within refugee populations than directed at outsiders in a manner that would foster group-wide solidarity.

In addition to its legal implications, another way that the refugee experience affects Soviet Jewish and Vietnamese mobilization is by accentuating their concern with cultural preservation. Knowing that they are among the last bearers of Russian Judaism (secular or religious) or Vietnamese Buddhism, Soviet Jews and Vietnamese in California felt the need to maintain their traditions in a way that voluntary immigrants from nontotalitarian societies may not. As a consequence, activists and religious leaders of both refugee populations were often concerned with cultural assertion in a manner not suggested by the ethnic mobilization paradigm. This outlook was better understood in terms of Woldemikael's theory of cultural assertion.

In conclusion, a combination of structural and cultural factors surrounding the experience of Soviet Jewish and Vietnamese refugees yield distinct patterns of community development. Whereas ethnic mobilization theory suggests that immigrant and ethnic groups would organize on a group-wide basis in pursuit of political and economic interests, these refugees tend to mobilize within localized and segmented units, competing within the ethnic community over cultural as well as economic and political concerns. With time, amalgamation may occur, but thus far, relatively little movement in this direction has been apparent.

NOTES

1. This issue was most relevant in San Francisco and Los Angeles. In Orange County, liberal groups have little if any political power at the local level.

2. In 1975, 12,867 Vietnamese nationals registered under the alien address program (INS 1975:Table 34). This is about 2.3% of the approximately 570,000 Vietnamese in the United States as of the end of fiscal 1989 (ORR 1990:75).

3. While all Jews are considered members of a single ethnic group, in reality the world Jewish community contains great ethnic diversity, with members from North and South America, several European countries, the Soviet Union, the Middle East, Latin America, and South Africa.

4. Chabad offers a similar kind of program, complete with an immigrant rabbi, for Middle Eastern Jews in Los Angeles.

9

Refugee Adaptation:
Concluding Comments

As of this writing, Soviet Jews and Vietnamese have been in the United States for barely 15 years. Consequently, their communities are in the early stages of formation. Nevertheless, patterns of adjustment are observable. Eluding the polarities of community mobilization and rapid assimilation, the experience of Soviet and Vietnamese refugees in California involves a third pattern of adaptation in which distinct, localized networks play a central role.

Although neither population reveals inclusive organizations, both are involved in a variety of informal and local-level, self-help activities. Intimate collectivities based upon family, social network, regional origins, profession, religion, education, and common ethnicity reveal high levels of localized social solidarity. Relying on such small groups, refugees share information and economic resources, open businesses, aid co-ethnics, and build political movements. Further, although their formal unification is limited, each population does maintain identifiable geographical concentrations around residential and commercial areas and connects its members through native language print and broadcast media.

Despite the well-planned and sometimes subsidized efforts of activists, these populations are only beginning to witness the amalgamation of segmented communities. Because Soviet Jewish and Vietnamese immigrations are marked by both diversity and segmentation, multiple patterns of adaptation exist simultaneously in a way that few studies would predict. At present, ethnic solidarity remains most viable at the subgroup level.

This study contends that refugee adaptation is best understood by synthesizing three approaches to the behavior of immigrant and ethnic communities. First, I conditionally accept the thrust of the large body of recent research that states that collectivism is a major force in immigrant adaptation. Ethnic solidarity provides refugees with invaluable social, economic, and informational resources. Yet, while ethnic collectivism is a vital resource for these refugees, it remains most influential and effective at the local level. Broader community unification has yet to be achieved. Further, although beneficial, the various forms of immigrant collectivism that I observed (entrepreneurial, political, religious) lack the power and resources to solve many of the problems refugees find most pressing.

In discussing the limitations of collectivism, we come to the second major factor shaping Soviet Jewish and Vietnamese refugee adaptation—that of background. As I have emphasized throughout this book, Soviet Jewish and Vietnamese refugee populations are marked by diversity in terms of class, region, ideology, ethnic and national identity, religious outlook, experience with collectivism, and a variety of other factors. These differences are sometimes overcome, yielding organized communities. However, the refugee experience and effects of the resettlement system often heighten the effects of prior dissimilarity, yielding contentious, stratified, and segmented communities that resist unification. Refugees' consciousness is profoundly shaped by their personal histories. Preferences, loyalties, and antipathies of the past are often maintained, shaping patterns of adaptation in the United States and affecting the nature of mobilization.

Finally, the larger social structure—ranging from the world system to the availability of jobs and housing in communities of settlement—is a central factor in determining refugees' adaptation. The displacement of refugee populations from certain nations and their resettlement in others can only be understood in terms of the political and economic relations among the world's nations.

Similarly, refugees' patterns of economic incorporation are not only a product of their own skills, community networks, and resources, but also of the broader social and economic processes that shape urban America. These affect the availability of jobs and determine with whom refugees must compete for employment. Further, if refugees become self-employed because existing jobs do not satisfy their needs and expectations, then the larger social structure and economy establishes the entrepreneurial context—framing the nature of economic opportunity and the accessibility of capital, labor, and consumer markets.

Refugee status, as a product of Cold War politics and the modern welfare state, is another key structural aspect of the refugee experience; one that fixes benefits, residency status, and access to training. Through the resettlement system, refugees' relations with natives and co-ethnics are conditioned. Even the disproportionate settlement of refugees in California can be directly traced to the state's unique culture, economy, and entitlements.

Consequently, this study indicates that the findings of the various models of immigrant adaptation, each in their way, contribute to the understanding of Soviet Jewish and Vietnamese refugees' experience. Yet no single model adequately explains the greater process of their resettlement and community formation. Rather, an eclectic perspective best approaches this goal.

SOVIET JEWS AND VIETNAMESE COMPARED

Because Soviet Jewish and Vietnamese refugees are so recently arrived, there exists a paucity of literature on their experience, especially in such areas as resettlement systems, self-employment, and activism. Fortunately, however, the contrasts made available by the use of a comparative approach offered a valuable resource. By simultaneously evaluating the behavior and context of each group through that of the other, I was able to establish a basis for analysis.

This technique led me to several counterintuitive findings. Take, for example, the realm of community formation. Theories concerning middleman minorities and twice-migrant groups would predict Soviet Jews' rapid organization upon arrival in the United States, suggesting a similar pattern for the Chinese-Vietnamese. The ethnic Vietnamese, lacking a shared notion of ethnic identity prior to migration, might be less organized (Bhachu 1985; Bonacich 1973; Espiritu 1989). However, the real experience of these groups contrasts with predictions. As we have seen, while many Chinese-Vietnamese were highly organized, the Soviet Jews seldom developed formal collective activities, and the Vietnamese were active, but segmented.

The reason Soviet Jews stray from the twice-migrant model can be traced to their inability to act collectively prior to migration. Consciousness of kind is not sufficient to yield an organized community.

Group members (like the Chinese-Vietnamese who affirm the model) must also possess experience in ethnic collectivism to turn sentiments into self-help. Without comparison, I would have been unable to make this and other distinctions.

Despite the differences between Soviet Jews and Vietnamese, these groups revealed many similar patterns of adaptation. Corresponding subgroups operated in either community. Both populations featured sizable, relatively unorganized "grass roots" settlements that were socially distinct from the host society and heavily dependent on institutionally complete ethnic communities for goods, services, a social life, and, sometimes, employment.

Both refugee populations also revealed several organized subgroups that acted as brokers and service providers to the rank and file: politicized activist groups, government-subsidized health-care professionals, religious traditionalists, and ethnic entrepreneurs. Regionalism, differences in generation and religiosity, and variations in political ideology were other sources of segmentation common to both communities.

Although these forms of internal diversity were present among both groups, the Soviet Jewish population was ultimately more uniform. Its members shared a common religion, urban origins, a high educational level, and similar middle- to working-class standing. Additionally, Jews' commonalities were reinforced through their resettlement by a centralized, coordinated, and professionally staffed resettlement system. Their relatively rapid economic integration bears marked similarity to that of educated, nonrefugee, new immigrant groups like Indians or Filipinos (Mangiafico 1988).

In contrast to the Soviets' uniformities, the Vietnamese were segmented by religious and ethnic differences and a full range of class diversity, ranging from a Western-educated elite to rural peasants. While the 1975-era, first-wave Vietnamese have much in common with other new immigrant groups, many of the more recently arrived and disadvantaged Vietnamese have experienced blocked mobility, social isolation, and welfare dependency—a pattern distinct from that of more skilled and less traumatized migrant populations. Differences in background were sometimes enhanced through interactions with a locally based, "patchwork" resettlement program.

Finally, a major contrast between Soviet Jewish and Vietnamese populations was their age and gender composition. While the Soviet community included numerous retirees and was disproportionately female, the Vietnamese were young and predominantly male.

As Etzioni and Du Bow (1970) note, by providing a basis for understanding differences between groups, the comparative method emphasizes context and reduces ethnocentric interpretations of behavior. Through the application of this approach, we see that the high levels of collectivization observed among such immigrant groups as the Chinese, Japanese, Cubans, and Koreans is a unique product of context and background and not an inevitable product of ethnicity. As the case of Soviet Jewish and Vietnamese activists shows, the achievement of a broadly organized, mobilized ethnic community is a very difficult task, one that requires both country-of-origin links and unifying factors in the host context.

ETHNIC SOLIDARITY GROWS WITH TIME

While Soviet Jewish and Vietnamese refugees have not formed the broadly unified and mobilized communities depicted in many reports on the subject of immigrant collectivism, neither have they abandoned their ethnic attachments to rapidly merge into American society. In fact, ethnic consciousness appears to be growing as refugees experience greater contact with the dominant culture. Throughout the book, we saw illustrations of this trend, reflected among subgroups as diverse as assimilated activists, religious traditionalists, and doctors. In different ways, subgroups placed a strong value on co-ethnic interaction and traditional language and culture. For example, an émigré insurance man connected this outlook to his inability to have fulfilling interactions with the native born:

You can't mix yourself with Americans. A lot of our people try to do it but they can't.

I can spend an hour talking to Americans, but we don't meet because we are different people, you know. Not because they are bad people or I don't like them. We are just different.

You Americans have this expression "nice people." But I don't know if they are nice. I don't know what means nice or not. For me I'm not going

along with him. I don't trust him because I don't know where to find this
point to trust him or not to trust him.

With the passage of time, many Soviet Jewish and Vietnamese activists have become concerned with creating their own institutions
separate from those controlled by nonrefugees. Recognizing opportunities within the enclave, having experienced discrimination, or simply accepting their basic differences from Americans, assimilated
refugees have come to reemphasize the importance of their native language and world view.

This phenomenon was especially noticeable among Soviet Jews,
who have recently become more organized and culturally assertive.
With thousands of glasnost-era émigrés entering the country and
those still in Russia imperiled by growing anti-Semitism, the émigré
community has been enlarged and mobilized. These events, according
to Soviet Jewish activists, have initiated a process of glasnost and
perestroika within the émigré community itself, fostering cooperation
in ways previously unachievable.

In their reemphasis of ethnic attachments, Soviet Jewish and
Vietnamese refugees are reversing the trend toward assimilation generally posited as the fate of American immigrant groups. With time
and upward mobility, previous immigrant populations have often left
urban ethnic neighborhoods to participate in mainstream American
society (di Leonardo 1984; Sowell 1981). In contrast, among Southern California Soviet Jews and Vietnamese, regions of ethnic concentration (West Hollywood for Soviet Jews, Little Saigon and the San
Gabriel Valley for Vietnamese) are gaining, rather than losing, importance as ethnic centers. Because of the high cost of California real estate, home ownership in the ethnic neighborhood hás become a luxury
affordable only to affluent refugees. Soviet Jews and Vietnamese with
fewer resources must rent, or purchase homes in less costly areas outside the ethnic neighborhood, saving for the day they, too, can live
with co-ethnics.

Further, while localized solidarity predominates, a shared, Ameri-
can-based ethnic consciousness is developing among some refugees.
As communist regimes tumble and time away from the home country
passes, certain antipathies rooted there fade in the face of commonalities discovered in America. As this book has shown, a collective
identity takes time and effort to build among internally diverse refugee populations with little background in collective self-help—

especially when competing models of ethnicity are advanced by contentious leaders.

However, groups of refugees do demonstrate some movement toward broader unification. For example, ethnic-Chinese entrepreneurs and Vietnamese military officers would have been unlikely friends in Southeast Asia and may continue to eye each other with suspicion in the United States. But, as I have observed in my own classes, their children establish amiable relations and build student associations on the campuses of colleges in California.

In sum, the experience of Soviet Jewish and Vietnamese refugees in the United States reveals three interrelated patterns. First, a lack of community-wide organizations; second, a prevalence of local-level, often informal types of cooperation, rooted in commonalities based in the country of origin or produced through the experience of migration and resettlement. Third, underlying these patterns of community development is the large amount of diversity contained in contemporary refugee populations.

These findings suggest that we reconsider the recent body of research that demonstrates the benefits achieved by highly organized and cooperative ethnic communities, such as Koreans and Cubans in the present era or Chinese, Japanese, and Jews in the past (Cummings 1980; Light 1972; Min 1988; Portes and Bach 1985). Given the experience of Soviet Jews and the Vietnamese, we should regard these groups' ability to organize as all the more impressive, and pay special attention to the conditions—historical, cultural, and contextual—that have allowed such unification to take place. While we can hope that other groups might share in the benefits of ethnic solidarity, we should also realize that highly organized, mutually beneficial communities are by no means common. In fact, a careful second look demonstrates that even those groups noted for their highly organized communities contain a level of diversity and conflict that is often obscured in the rush to celebrate their collectivism (Fernandez 1987; Kim 1981; Light 1972; Lyman 1974; Wirth 1928).

REFUGEES AND INDEPENDENT RESEARCH

I close with a reflection on the state of refugee research. Community segmentation and diversity—central findings in this report—have received little emphasis in the literature on refugee groups. I believe this to be the case because nearly all such studies have been guided by the needs and funding of public and private social service agencies. These policy-making bodies seek answers to fiscal and bureaucratically framed questions, not sociological ones. The predetermined, closed-ended questions such studies often use to generate "objective" statistics for agencies' consumption offer respondents few opportunities to give their own interpretations of community formation, adaptation, and solidarity. Moreover, research conducted for policy-making purposes need not attend to the highly problematic distinction between "refugee" and "immigrant" since the central concern guiding such research is not migrants' behavior, but eligibility for funding.

In contrast, few studies of refugees have been directed by the tradition of the immigrant ethnography, one of the oldest and most productive approaches in American sociology. My point here is not to criticize the results of policy-oriented studies per se. Most are highly compatible with the findings of reports using other approaches. Rather, the perspectives of policy studies are often incomplete. If we are going to continue to develop broad-based knowledge about social issues—whether they be refugee adaptation or other concerns—then we should maintain the tradition of independent, holistic scholarship. Sociologists' knowledge must be applied not only to collecting and analyzing data for others' needs, but also to deciding research questions and determining appropriate methodologies in the ways that they, as sociologists, see fit. Otherwise, as Vidich, Lyman, and Goldfarb write:

> If present trends continue, the intellectual will be further separated from even the chance or opportunity to define an original problem, giving up both autonomy and the critical spirit and deferring to an external source for intellectual direction. (Vidich et al. 1982:360)

Policy studies are valuable sources of information for administrators. However, they tell only part of the story and certainly do not answer the kinds of questions suggested by the tradition of independent sociological inquiry.

References

Abrams, Israel. 1911. "Jews." Pp. 371-410 in *Encyclopaedia Britannica,* Eleventh Edition, Vol. XV.

Ahrari, Mohammed E., (ed). 1987. *Ethnic Groups and U.S. Foreign Policy.* New York: Greenwood Press.

Almirol, Edwin B. 1978. "Filipino Voluntary Associations: Balancing Social Pressures and Ethnic Images." *Ethnic Groups* 2:65-92.

Anderson, Jervis. 1975. "Haitians of New York." *New Yorker* (March 31):50-75.

Andreski, Stanislav. 1979. "Communism and the Jews in Eastern Europe." *International Journal of Comparative Sociology* 20(1-2):151-161.

Arax, Mark. 1987. "Refugees Called Victims and Perpetrators of Fraud." *Los Angeles Times,* Part I (February 9):1,3.

Aronowitz, Michael. 1984. "The Social and Emotional Adjustment of Immigrant Children: A Review of the Literature." *International Migration Review* (18)2:237-257.

Bach, Robert L. and R. Carroll-Seguin. 1987. "Labor Force Participation, Household Composition and Sponsorship Among Southeast Asian Refugees." *International Migration Review* 20(2):381-404.

Baker, Reginald P. and David S. North. 1984. *The 1975 Refugees: Their First Five Years in America.* Washington, DC: The New Transcentury Foundation.

Balvanz, Bill. 1988. "Determination of the Number of Southeast Asian Refugee Births and Pregnancies by California County." *Migration World* 16(3):7-16.

Belcove-Shalin, Janet S. 1988. "The Hasidim of North America: A Review of the Literature." Pp. 183-207 in *Persistence and Flexibility: Anthropological Perspectives on the American Jewish Experience,* edited by Walter P. Zenner. Albany, NY: SUNY Press.

Bellah, Robert, Richard Madsen, William M. Sullivan, Ann Swidler and Steven M. Tipton. 1985. *Habits of the Heart: Individualism and Commitment in American Life.* Berkeley: University of California Press.

Bernard, William S. 1977. "Immigrants and Refugees: Their Similarities, Differences and Needs." *International Migration* 14(4):267-281.

Bhachu, Parminder. 1985. *Twice Migrants: East African Sikh Settlers in Britain.* London: Tavistock.

237

Billiris, Irene. 1990. "Southern California Asian Population, June 30, 1985 Estimate."
    Los Angeles: KSCI TV 18.
Bonacich, Edna. 1972. "A Theory of Ethnic Antagonism: The Split Labor Market."
    American Sociological Review 37:547-559.
———. 1987. "Making It in America: A Social Evaluation of the Ethics of Immigrant
    Entrepreneurship." *Sociological Perspectives* 40(4):446-455.
———. 1990. "Asian & Latino Immigrants in the Los Angeles Garment Industry: An
    Exploration of the Relationship Between Capitalism and Racial Oppression."
    University of California, Los Angeles, *Institute for Social Science Research
    Working Papers in the Social Sciences 1989-1990,* 5(13).
Bonacich, Edna and John Modell. 1980. *The Economic Basis of Ethnic Solidarity:
    Small Business in the Japanese-American Community.* Berkeley: University of
    California Press.
Bossevain, Jeremy and Hanneke Grotenbreg. 1986. "Culture, Structure and Ethnic En-
    terprise: The Surinamese of Amsterdam." *Ethnic and Racial Studies* 9(1):1-23.
Boswell, Thomas and James R. Curtis. 1984. *The Cuban American Experience: Cul-
    ture, Images and Perspectives.* Totowa, NJ: Rowman and Allenheld.
Bozorgmehr, Mehdi and Georges Sabagh. 1991. "Exiles and Immigrants in Los Ange-
    les." Pp. 121-144 in *Iranian Refugees and Exiles Since Khomeni,* edited by As-
    ghar Fathi. Costa Mesa: Mazda.
Breton, Raymond. 1964. "Institutional Completeness of Ethnic Communities and the
    Personal Relations of Immigrants." *American Journal of Sociology* 84:293-318.
Brody, Jeffery. 1986. "Vietnamese: Statistics Belie the Image of the Superachiever."
    Orange County Register. (May 12): A 5-6.
Brower, Imogene. 1981. "Counseling Vietnamese." Pp. 224-240 in *Bridging Cultures:
    Southeast Asian Refugees in America.* Los Angeles: Asian American Community
    Mental Health Training Center.
Bryce-Laporte, Roy S. (ed.) 1980. *Source Book on New Immigration.* New Brunswick,
    NJ: Transaction Books.
Brym, Robert J. 1985. "The Changing Rate of Jewish Emigration from the USSR:
    Some Lessons from the 1970s." *Soviet Jewish Affairs* 15(2):23-44.
Buchanan, Susan Huelsebusch. 1979. "Language and Identity: Haitians in New York
    City." *International Migration Review* 13(2):298-312.
Bui, Diana, Le Xuan Khoa and Nguyen Van Hien. 1981. *The Indochinese Mutual Assis-
    tance Associations: Characteristics, Composition, Capacity Building Needs, and
    Future Directions.* Washington, DC: Indochinese Refugee Action Center.
Burawoy, Michael. 1976. "The Function and Reproduction of Migrant Labor: Compara-
    tive Materials from Southern Africa and the United States." *American Journal of
    Sociology* 81:1050-1087.
Burnam, M. Audrey, Richard L. Hough, Marvin Karno, Javier I. Escobar and Cynthia
    A. Telles. 1987. "Acculturation and Lifetime Prevalence of Psychiatric Disorders
    Among Mexican Americans in Los Angeles." *Journal of Health and Social Be-
    havior* 28(1):89-102.
Buttinger, Joseph. 1958. *The Smaller Dragon.* New York: Praeger.
———. 1972. *A Dragon Defiant: A Short History of Vietnam.* New York: Praeger.
Caplan, Nathan, John K. Whitmore and Quang L. Bui. 1985. *Southeast Asian Refugee
    Self-Sufficiency Study.* Report prepared for Office of Refugee Resettlement by
    The Institute for Social Research, University of Michigan.

Carp, Joel M. 1990. "Absorbing Jews Jewishly: Professional Responsibility for Jewishly Absorbing New Immigrants in Their New Communities." *Journal of Jewish Communal Service* 66(4):366-374.

Castells, Manuel. 1989. *The Informational City.* Oxford, England: Basil Blackwell.

Castles, Stephen and Godula Kosack. 1973. *Immigrant Workers and Class Structure in Western Europe.* New York: Oxford University Press.

Chan, Janet B.L. and Yuet-Wah Cheung. 1982. "Ethnic Resources and Business Enterprise: A Study of Chinese Businesses in Toronto." Paper presented at the annual meeting of the American Sociological Association, San Francisco, September 6-10.

Chan, Kowk B. and Doreen Indra, eds. 1987. *Uprooting, Loss and Adaptation: The Resettlement of Indochinese Refugees in Canada.* Ottawa: The Canadian Public Health Association.

Chen, King C. 1987. *China's War with Vietnam, 1979: Issues, Decisions and Implications.* Stanford, CA: Hoover Institution Press.

Chesler, Evan. 1974. *The Russian Jewry Reader.* New York: Behrman House Inc.

Cichon, Donald J., Elizabeta M. Gozdziak and Jane G. Grover. 1986. *The Economic and Social Adjustment of Non-Southeast Asian Refugees, Volume I: Analysis Across Cases.* Dover, NH: Research Management Corporation.

Cohen, Abner. 1969. *Custom and Politics in Urban Africa.* Berkeley: University of California Press.

Cohon, J. Donald, Jr. 1981. "Psychological Adaptation and Dysfunction Among Refugees." *International Migration Review* 15(1):255-275.

Collins, Beth, Melissa Glazer, Cara Kates, Jilla Lavian, Ellen Rabin, Dan Rathblatt and Robin Segal. 1986. *Family and Community Among Iranian Jews in Los Angeles.* Master's Thesis, Hebrew Union College and University of Southern California.

Coughlin, Maria and Regina Rosenberg. 1983. "Health Education and Beyond: A Soviet Women's Group Experience." *Journal of Jewish Communal Service* 60(1):65-69.

CSEARR (Center for Southeast Asian Refugee Resettlement). 1984. *If You Mean Business: 1984 Manual for Southeast Asian Refugees.* San Francisco: Author.

Cummings, Scott, ed. 1980. *Self-Help in Urban America: Patterns of Minority Business Enterprise.* Port Washington, NY: Kennikat Press.

Cunnigham, Marina and Nina Dorf. 1979. "Prenatal Group for Soviet Immigrants." *Journal of Jewish Communal Service* LVI (1):73-76.

DeFreitas, Gregory. 1988. "Economic Effect of Recent Immigration on American Workers." *Migration World* 16(1):7-15.

de Leonardo, Micaela. 1984. *Varieties of the Ethnic Experience: Kinship, Class and Gender Among California Italian-Americans.* Ithaca, NY: Cornell University Press.

Department of the Army. 1966. *Minority Groups in the Republic of Vietnam.* Washington, DC: Government Printing Office.

Desbarats, Jacqueline. 1985. "Indochinese Resettlement in the United States." *Annals of the American Association of Geographers* 75:522-538.

———. 1986a. "Policy Influences on Refugee Resettlement Patterns." *Kroeber Anthropological Society Papers* 65-66:49-63.

———. 1986b. "Ethnic Differences in Adaptation: Sino-Vietnamese Refugees in the United States." *International Migration Review* 20(2):405-427.

de Voe, Dorsh. 1981. "Framing Refugees as Clients." *International Migration Review* 15(1):88-94.

———. 1987. "Keeping Refugee Status: A Tebetan Perspective. Pp. 54-65 in *People in Upheaval,* edited by Scott Morgan and Elizabeth Colson. New York: Center for Migrations Studies.

Di Franceisco, Wayne and Zvi Gitelman. 1984. "Soviet Political Culture and Covert Participation in Policy Implementation." *American Political Science Review* 78(3):603-621.

Dorf, Nina and Fay Katlin. 1983. "The Soviet Jewish Immigrant Client: Beyond Resettlement." *Journal of Jewish Communal Service* 60(2):146-154.

Drake, St. Clair and Horice R. Cayton. 1945. *Black Metropolis.* New York: Harcourt Brace Jovanovich.

DSS (Department of Social Services, State of California). 1983. *State Plan for Refugee Assistance and Services, Federal Fiscal Year 1983.* Sacramento: Office of Refugee Services.

Dun and Bradstreet. 1983. *The 1981 Dun and Bradstreet Business Failure Record.* New York: Dun and Bradstreet.

Durkheim, Emile. 1951. *Suicide.* New York: The Free Press.

Eckles, Timothy J., Lawrence J. Lewin, David S. North and Dangole J. Spakevicius. 1982. "A Portrait in Diversity: Voluntary Agencies and The Office of Refugee Resettlement Matching Grant Program." Lewin and Associates.

Efron, Sonni. 1989. "Sweatshops Expanding Into Orange County." *Los Angeles Times.* (November 26):1, 38.

———. 1990. "Few Viet Exiles Find U.S. Riches." *Los Angeles Times.* (April 29):1, 34, 35.

Eisenstadt, S. N. 1956. *From Generation to Generation: Age Groups and Social Structure.* New York: The Free Press.

Emmons, S. and D. Reyes. 1989. "Gangs, Crime Top Fear of Vietnamese in Orange County." *Los Angeles Times* (Feb. 5).

Espiritu, Yen Le. 1989. "Beyond the Boat People: Ethnicization of American Life." *Amerasia* 15(2):49-67.

Etzioni, Amitai and Fredric L. Du Bow. 1970. "Introduction." Pp. 1-16 in *Comparative Perspectives: Theories and Methods,* edited by Amitai Etzioni and Fredic L. Du Bow. Boston: Little, Brown and Co.

Farber, Bernard, Charles H. Mindel and Bernard Lazerwitz. 1988. "The Jewish American Family." Pp. 400-437 in *Ethnic Families in America,* edited by Charles H. Mindel, Robert Habenstein and Roosevelt Wright, Jr., third edition. New York: Elsevier.

Farber, Don. 1987. *Seeking Refuge in the U.S.A.* Millerton, NY: Aperture.

Fernandez, Damian J. 1987. "From Little Havana to Washington, D.C.: Cuban-Americans and U.S. Foreign Policy." Pp. 115-134 in *Ethnic Groups and U.S. Foreign Policy,* edited by Mohammed E. Ahrari. New York: Greenwood Press.

Fernandez, John P. 1972. *Black Managers in White Corporations.* Washington, DC: The Urban Institute.

Finnan, Christine R. and Rhonda Cooperstein. 1983. *Southeast Asian Refugee Resettlement at the Local Level.* Menlo Park, CA: SRI International.

Frankel Paul, Ellen and Dan N. Jacobs. 1981. "The New Soviet Migration in Cincinnati." Pp. 77-144 in *Studies in the Third Wave: Recent Migrations of Soviet Jews* to the U.S., edited by Dan N. Jacobs and Ellen Frankel Paul. Boulder, CO: Westview Press.

Fratoe, Frank A. 1984. "Abstracts of the Sociological Literature on Minority Business Ownership (with additional references)." Research Division, Office of Advocacy, Research and Information, Minority Business Development Agency. Washington, DC: U.S. Department of Commerce. (Mimeo).

Fruchtbaum, Irene and Rodney Skager. 1989. "Influence of Parental Values on Dating Behavior of Young Russian Women: A Cross-Cultural Perspective." Los Angeles: UCLA Department of Education. (Mimeo).

Fuchs, Lawrence H. 1985. "The Search for a Sound Immigration Policy: A Personal View." Pp. 17-48 in *Clamor at the Gates,* edited by Nathan Glazer. San Francisco: Institute for Contemporary Studies.

Gardner, Robert W., Bryant Robey and Peter C. Smith. 1985. "Asian Americans: Growth, Change and Diversity." *Population Bulletin* 40(4):51.

Gelernter, Carey Quan. 1990. "Strictly Business: Southeast Asian Residents Overcome Harsh Realities in No-Holds-Barred Pursuit of an American Dream." *Seattle Times* (May 6):E1,6.

Gilson, Jerome M. 1981. "The Resettlement of Soviet Jewish Émigrés: Results of a Survey in Baltimore." Pp. 29-56 in *Studies in the Third Wave: Recent Migrations of Soviet Jews to the U.S.,* edited by Dan N. Jacobs and Ellen Frankel Paul. Boulder, CO: Westview Press.

Gitelman, Zvi. 1978. "Soviet Immigrants and American Absorption Efforts: A Case Study in Detroit." *Journal of Jewish Communal Service* 55(1):77-82.

Gitelman, Zvi, Henry Morton and Robert Stuart, eds. ND. *Working the Soviet System: Citizens and Urban Bureaucracies in the Contemporary Soviet City.* New York: M.E. Sharpe.

Glazer, Nathan and Daniel Patrick Moynihan. 1963. *Beyond the Melting Pot.* Cambridge, MA: MIT Press.

Goebetz, Giles Edward. 1980. *Adjustment and Assimilation of Slovenian Refugees.* New York: Arno Press.

Goffman, Irving. 1961. *Asylums.* New York: Anchor Books.

Gold, Steven J. 1985. "Refugee Communities: Soviet Jewish and Vietnamese Refugees in the San Francisco Bay Area." Doctoral Dissertation, University of California, Berkeley.

———. 1986. "Style of Activism Among Refugee Communities: The Case of Soviet Jews and Vietnamese." *Kroeber Anthropological Society Papers,* 65-66: 35-48.

———. 1987. "Dealing with Frustration: A Study of Interactions Between Resettlement Staff and Refugees." Pp. 108-128 in *People in Upheaval,* edited by Scott Morgan and Elizabeth Colson. New York: Center For Migration Studies.

———. 1988. "Refugees and Small Business: The Case of Soviet Jews and Vietnamese." *Ethnic and Racial Studies,* 11(4):411-438.

———. 1989. "Differential Adjustment Among New Immigrant Family Members." *Journal of Contemporary Ethnography* 17(4):408-434.

———. in press. "Nascent Mobilization in a New Immigrant Community: The Case of Soviet Jews in California." *Research in Community Sociology* (2).

Gold, Steve and Nazli Kibria. 1989. "Vietnamese Refugees and Mobility: Model Minority or New Underclass." Paper presented at the annual meeting of the American Sociological Association, San Francisco, August 10.

Goldberg, Simcha R. 1981. "Jewish Acculturation and the Soviet Immigrant." *Journal of Jewish Communal Service* 57(3):154-163.

Goodman, Jerry. 1984. "The Jews in the Soviet Union: Emigration and Its Difficulties." Pp. 17-28 in *Soviet Jewry in the Decisive Decade 1971-1980,* edited by Robert O. Freedman. Durham, NC: Duke University Press.

Gordon, Linda W. 1982. "New Data on the Fertility of Southeast Asian Refugees in the U.S." Paper presented at the annual meeting of the Population Association of America, San Diego, April 29-May 1.

————. 1987 "The Missing Children: Mortality and Fertility in a Southeast Asian Refugee Population." Paper presented at the annual meeting of the Population Association of America, Chicago, May 2.

Gorelick, Sherry. 1982. *City College and the Jewish Poor.* New York: Schocken Books.

Greeley, Andrew. 1974. *Ethnicity in the U.S.* New York: John Wiley.

Gusfield, Joe. 1967. "Tradition and Modernity: Misplaced Polarities in the Study of Social Change." *American Journal of Sociology* 72(4):351-362.

Haines, David. 1987. "Patterns in Southeast Asian Refugee Employment: A Reappraisal of the Existing Research." *Ethnic Groups* 7:39-63.

Haines, David, Dorothy Rutherford and Patrick Thomas. 1981. "Family and Community among Vietnamese Refugees." *International Migration Review* 15(1):310-319.

Harris, George L. Robert J. Catto, Frederic H. Chaffee, Frederica Muhlenberg, Frances Chadwick Rintz and Harvey H. Smith. 1962. *U.S. Army Handbook for Vietnam.* Washington, DC, Government Printing Office.

Hechter, Michael. 1987. *Principles of Group Solidarity.* Berkeley: University of California Press.

Hein, Jeremy. 1988. "State Incorporation of Migrants and the Reproduction of a Middleman Minority among Indochinese Refugees." *Sociological Quarterly* 29(3):463-478.

Henkin, Alan B. and Liem Thanh Nguyen. 1981. *Between Two Cultures: The Vietnamese in America.* Saratoga, CA: Century Twenty One Publishing.

Herberg, Edward N. 1989. *Ethnic Groups in Canada.* Scarborough, Ontario: Nelson.

Herbstein, Judith. 1983. "The Politicization of Puerto Rican Ethnicity in New York: 1955-1975." *Ethnic Groups* 5:31-54.

Hickey, Gerald Cannon. 1964. *Village in Vietnam.* New Haven, CT: Yale University Press.

Ho, David Yau-Fai. 1976. "On the Concept of Face." *American Journal of Sociology* 81(4):867-884.

Hoang Van Chi. 1964. *From Colonialism to Communism: A Case History of North Vietnam.* New York: Praeger.

Hong-Kingston, Maxine. 1979. *China Men.* New York: Vintage International.

Howe, Irving. 1976. *World of Our Fathers.* New York: Bantam Books.

Hulewat, Phillis. 1981. "Dynamics of the Soviet Jewish Family: Its Impact on Clinical Practice for the Jewish Family Agency." *Journal of Jewish Communal Service* 58(1):53-60.

Hutchinson, Edward P. 1966. "The New Immigration: An Introductory Comment." *The Annals* 367:1-3.

Immigration and Naturalization Service. *1975 Annual Report.* Washington, DC: Author.

Indochinese Community Center. 1983. "Entrepreneurship Among Southeast Asian Refugees." Office of Refugee Resettlement Report. Washington, DC: Author.

Indra, Doreen. 1987. "Bureaucratic Constraints, Middlemen and Community Organization: Aspects of the Political Incorporation of Southeast Asians in Canada." Pp. 147-170 in *Uprooting, Loss and Adaptation: The Resettlement of Indochinese Refugees in Canada,* edited by Kwok B. Chan and Doreen Indra. Ottawa: The Canadian Public Health Association.

———. 1989. "Ethnic Human Rights and Feminist Theory: Gender Implications for Refugee Studies and Practice." *Journal of Refugee Studies* 2(2):221-242.

IRAC (Indochinese Refugee Action Center). 1982. *Survey of Refugee Self-Help Initiatives.* Washington, DC: Author.

Isaacs, Harold R. 1975. "Basic Group Identity: The Idols of the Tribe." Pp. 24-52 in *Ethnicity: Theory and Experience,* edited by Nathan Glazer and Daniel Patrick Moynihan, 1963. Cambridge, MA: Harvard University Press.

ITAP (Indochinese Technical Assistance Project). 1981. *Indochinese Mutual Assistance Association and Resource Directory.* Washington, DC: Author.

Jackson, Bryan O. 1988. "Ethnic Cleavages and Voting Patterns in U.S. Cities: An Analysis of the Asian, Black and Hispanic Communities of Los Angeles." Conference on Comparative Ethnicity, UCLA, June 1-3.

Jacobs, Dan N. 1981. "Introduction." Pp. 1-10 in *Studies of the Third Wave: Recent Migrations of Soviet Jews to the United States,* edited by Dan N. Jacobs and Ellen Frankel Paul. Boulder, CO: Westview Press.

Johnson, Phyllis J. 1988. "The Impact of Ethnic Communities on the Employment of Southeast Asian Refugees." *Amerasia* 14(1):1-22.

Kanter, Rosabeth Moss. 1977. *Men and Women of the Corporation.* New York: Basic Books.

Karklins, Rasma. 1987. "Determinants of Ethnic Identification in the USSR: The Soviet Jewish Case." *Ethnic and Racial Studies* 10(1):27-47.

Katz, Jack. 1988. *Seductions of Crime.* New York: Basic Books.

Kelly, Gail Paradise. 1977. *From Vietnam to America: A Chronicle of the Vietnamese Immigration to the United States.* Boulder, CO: Westview Press.

———. 1986. "Coping With America: Refugees from Vietnam, Cambodia and Laos in the 1970s and 1980s." *The Annals* 487 (September):138-149.

Kibria, Nazli. 1989. "Patterns of Vietnamese Refugee Women's Wagework in the U.S." *Ethnic Groups* 7:297-323.

———. 1990. "Power, Patriarchy, and Gender Conflict in the Vietnamese Immigrant Community." *Gender and Society* 4(1):9-24.

Kim, E. Y. 1987. "Assimilation Patterns of Koreans in the United States." Pp. 144-158 in *People in Upheaval,* edited by Scott Morgan and Elizabeth Colson. New York: Center for Migrations Studies.

Kim, Illsoo. 1981. *New Urban Immigrants: The Korean Community in New York.* Princeton, NJ: Princeton University Press.

Kitano, Harry H. L. and Roger Daniels. 1988. *Asian Americans: Emerging Minorities.* Englewood Cliffs, NJ: Prentice-Hall.

Kliger, Hannah. 1989. "Ethnic Voluntary Associations in Israel." *The Jewish Journal of Sociology* 31(2):109-118.

Kochan, Lionel, ed. 1978. *The Jews in Soviet Russia Since 1917.* London: Oxford University Press.

Kosmin, Barry. (1990). *The Class of 1979: The 'Acculturation' of Jewish Immigrants from the Soviet Union.* New York: Council of Jewish Federations.

Kuznets, Simon. 1975. "Immigration of Russian Jews to the United States: Background and Structure." *Perspectives in American History* 9:35-124.

Lane, A. T. 1987. *Solidarity or Survival? American Labor and European Immigrants 1830-1924.* New York: Greenwood Press.

Lappin, Jay and Sam Scott. 1982. "Intervention in a Vietnamese Refugee Family." Pp. 483-491 in *Ethnicity and Family Therapy,* edited by Monica McGoldrick, John K. Pearce and Joseph Giordano. New York: Guilford Press.

Leba, John K. 1985. *The Vietnamese Entrepreneurs in the U.S.A.* Houston: Zielecks.

Levkov, Ilya I. 1984. "Adaptation and Acculturation of Soviet Jews in the United States: A Preliminary Analysis." Pp. 109-143 in *Soviet Jewry in the Decisive Decade 1971-1980,* edited by Robert O. Freedman. Durham, NC: Duke University Press.

Lewin and Associates. 1986. *Assessment of the MAA Incentive Grant Initiative.* Washington DC: ORR Report.

Lieberson, Stanley. 1981. *A Piece of the Pie.* Berkeley: University of California Press.

Light, Ivan. 1972. *Ethnic Enterprise in America: Business and Welfare among Chinese, Japanese and Blacks.* Berkeley: University of California Press.

⸻. 1979. "Disadvantaged Minorities in Self-Employment." *International Journal of Comparative Sociology* 20(1-2):31-45.

⸻. 1980. "Asian Entrepreneurs in America." Pp. 33-57 in *Self Help in Urban America: Patterns of Minority Business Enterprise,* edited by Scott Cummings. Port Washington, NY: Kennikat Press.

⸻. 1984. "Immigrant and Ethnic Enterprise in North America." *Ethnic and Racial Studies* 17(2):195-216.

⸻. 1985. "Immigrant Entrepreneurs in America: Koreans in Los Angeles." Pp. 161-178 in *Clamor at the Gates: The New American Immigration,* edited by Nathan Glazer. San Francisco: Institute for Contemporary Studies.

Light, Ivan and Parminder Bhachu. 1990. "Immigrant Networks and Immigrant Entrepreneurship." UCLA: *ISSR Working Papers in the Social Sciences 1989-90.* Vol. 5, No. 1.

Light, Ivan and Edna Bonacich. 1988. *Immigrant Entrepreneurs.* Berkeley: University of California Press.

Liu, William T., Maryanne Lamanna and Alice Mirata. 1979. *Transition to Nowhere: Vietnamese Refugees in America.* Nashville, TN: Charter House.

Long, Nguyen and Harry Kendall. 1981. *After Saigon Fell.* Berkeley: Institute of East Asian Studies, Research Papers and Policy Studies #4.

Lubin, Nancy. 1985. "Small Business Owners." Pp. 151-164 in *New Lives: The Adjustment of Soviet Jewish Immigrants in the United States and Israel,* edited by Rita J. Simon. Lexington, MA: Lexington Books.

Lyman, Stanford. 1974. *Chinese Americans.* New York: Random House.

⸻. 1977. *The Asian in North America.* Santa Barbara, CA: ABC Clio.

Mangiafico, Luciano. 1988. *Contemporary American Immigrants: Patterns of Filipino, Korean, and Chinese Settlement in the United States.* New York: Praeger.

Markowitz, Fran. 1988. "Jewish in the USSR, Russian in the USA." Pp. 79-95 in *Persistence and Flexibility: Anthropological Perspectives on the American Jewish Experience,* edited by Walter P. Zenner. Albany, NY: SUNY Press.

Marr, David G. 1971. *Vietnamese Anticolonialism 1885-1925.* Berkeley: University of California Press.

————. 1981. *Vietnamese Tradition on Trial, 1920-1945.* Berkeley: University of California Press.

Massey, Douglas S. 1989. "Social Structure, Household Strategies, and the Cumulative Causation of Migration." Paper presented at the annual meeting of the American Sociological Association, San Francisco, August 13.

Massey, Douglas S., Rafael Alarcon, Jorge Durand and Humberto Gonzalez. 1987. *Return to Aztlan.* Berkeley: University of California Press.

Mayhew, Leon. 1968. "Ascription in Modern Societies." *Sociological Inquiry* 38 (Spring): 105-120.

Merton, Robert. 1949. *Social Theory and Social Structure.* Glencoe, IL: Free Press of Glencoe.

Min, Pyong Gap. 1985. "Some Significant Differences Between the New Asian Immigrants and the Earlier Immigrants and the Theoretical Implications." Paper Presented at the annual meeting of the American Sociological Association, Washington, DC, August 28.

————. 1986. "Korean Entrepreneurs in Los Angeles." Paper presented at UCLA Department of Asian American Studies, November 12.

————. 1987. "Filipino and Korean Immigrants in Small Business: A Comparative Analysis." *Amerasia* 13(1):53-71.

————. 1988. *Ethnic Business Enterprise: Korean Small Business in Atlanta.* Staten Island, NY: Center for Migration Studies.

Montero, Darrel. 1979. *Vietnamese Americans: Patterns of Resettlement and Socioeconomic Adaptation in the United States.* Boulder, CO: Westview Press.

Murray, Michael and Associates. 1981. *A Report on Refugee Services in San Francisco.* San Francisco: Center for Southeast Asian Refugee Resettlement.

Nagel, Joane. 1986. "The Political Construction of Ethnicity." Pp. 93-112 in *Competitive Ethnic Relations,* edited by Susan Olzak and Joane Nagel. Orlando, FL: Academic Press.

Nagel, Joane and Susan Olzak. 1982. "Ethnic Mobilization in New and Old States: An Extension of the Competition Model." *Social Problems* 30(2):127-143.

Ngan, Nguyen Ngoc. 1982. *The Will of Heaven: The Story of One Vietnamese and the End of His World.* Toronto: Van Lang.

Nguoi Viet, English Edition 1989, December 24.

Nguyen, Liem T. and Alan B. Henkin. 1984. "Vietnamese Refugees in the United States: Adaptation and Transition Status." *Journal of Ethnic Studies* 9(4):110-116.

Nguyen Van Hien, Diana Bui and Le Xuan Khoa. 1983. "Ethnic Self-Help Organizations." Office of Refugee Resettlement Report. Washington, DC: U.S. Department of Health and Human Services.

Nguyen Van Vinh. 1949. *Savings and Mutual Lending Societies (Ho).* New Haven, CT: Yale University, Southeast Asian Studies.

Nielsen, Francois. 1985. "Towards a Theory of Ethnic Solidarity in Modern Societies." *American Sociological Review* 50(2):133-149.

Noonan, Leo. 1988. "Russians Go Republican." *The Jewish Journal,* November 18-24:31.

North, David. 1988. "Aliens and the Regular and Irregular Labor Markets." Paper presented at the U.S. Department of Labor Conference on Immigration, Washington, DC, September 15-16.

North of Market Planning Coalition. 1979. "Tenderloin Action Plan on Southeast Asian Refugees."

Novak, Michael. 1971. *The Rise of the unmeltable Ethnics.* New York: MacMillan.

Okamura, Jonathan Y. 1983. "Filipino Hometown Associations in Honolulu." *Ethnology* 22:341-353.

Okely, Judith. 1979. "Trading Stereotypes: The Case of The English Gypsies." Pp. 17-36 in *Ethnicity at Work,* edited by Sandra Wallman. London: MacMillan.

Olzak, Susan. 1983. "Contemporary Ethnic Mobilization." *Annual Review of Sociology* 9:355-374.

Olzak, Susan and Joane Nagel, eds. 1986. *Competitive Ethnic Relations.* Orlando, FL: Academic Press.

Orbach, Alexander. 1980. "The Jewish of Soviet-Jewish Culture: Historical Considerations." *Journal of Jewish Communal Service* 57(3):145-153.

Orleck, Annalise. 1987. "The Soviet Jews: Life in Brighton Beach, Brooklyn." Pp. 273-304 in *New Immigrants in New York,* edited by Nancy Foner. New York: Columbia University Press.

ORR (Office of Refugee Resettlement). 1982. "Report to Congress: Refugee Resettlement Program." Washington, DC: U.S. Department of Health and Human Services.

———. 1982a. "Report to Congress: Refugee Resettlement Program: Employment Service." Washington, DC: U.S. Department of health and Human Services.

———. 1983. "Report to Congress: Refugee Resettlement Program." Washington, DC: U. S. Department of Health and Human Services.

———. 1984. "Report to Congress: Refugee Resettlement Program." Washington, DC: U.S. Department of Health and Human Services.

———. 1986. "Report to Congress: Refugee Resettlement Program." Washington, DC: U.S. Department of Health and Human Services.

———. 1987. "Report to Congress: Refugee Resettlement Program." Washington, DC: U.S. Department of Health and Human Services.

———. 1988. "Report to Congress: Refugee Resettlement Program." Washington, DC: U.S. Department of Health and Human Services.

———. 1989. "Report to Congress: Refugee Resettlement Program." Washington, DC: U.S. Department of Health and Human Services.

———. 1990. "Report to Congress: Refugee Resettlement Program." Washington, DC: U.S. Department of Health and Human Services.

Owan, Tom Choken. 1985. "Southeast Asian Mental Health: Transition from Treatment Services to Prevention—A New Direction." Pp. 141-167 in *Southeast Asian Mental Health: Treatment, Prevention, Services, Training and Research,* edited by Tom Choken Owan. Washington, DC: U.S. Department of Health and Human Services.

Padilla, Felix M. 1987. *Puerto Rican Chicago.* Notre Dame, IN: Notre Dame Press.

———. 1986. "Latino Ethnicity in the City of Chicago." Pp. 153-172 in *Competitive Ethnic Relations,* edited by Susan Olzak and Joane Nagel. Orlando, FL: Academic Press.

Panish, Paul. 1981. *Exit Visa.* New York: McCann and Geoghegan.

Parlin, Bradley. 1976. *Immigrant Professional in the United States.* New York: Praeger.

Patterson, Orlando. 1975. "Context and Choice in Ethnic Allegiance A Theoretical Framework and Caribbean Case Study." Pp. 305-349 in *Ethnicity: Theory and*

Experience, edited by Nathan Glazer and Daniel Patrick Moynihan. Cambridge, MA: Harvard University Press.

Peters, Heather A. 1988. "A Study of Southeast Asian Youth in Philadelphia: A Final Report." Philadelphia: Institute for the Study of Human Issues.

Peters, Heather, Bambi Schieffelin, Lorraine Sexton and David Feingold. 1983. "Who Are the Sino-Vietnamese? Culture, Ethnicity and Social Categories." Philadelphia: Institute for the Study of Human Issues.

Pfefferman, Naomi. 1989. "The Viennese Connection." *The Jewish Journal.* (February 10-16):18.

Pinkus, Benjamin. 1985. "National Identity and Emigration Patterns Among Soviet Jewry." *Soviet Jewish Affairs* 15(3):3-27.

Piore, Michael J. 1979. *Birds of Passage.* New York: Cambridge University Press.

———. 1986. "The Shifting Grounds for Immigration." *The Annals* 485 (May):23-33.

Portes, Alejandro. 1984. "The Rise of Ethnicity: Determinants of Ethnic Perceptions Among Cuban Exiles in Miami." *American Sociological Review* 49:383-397.

———. 1987. "The Social Origins of the Cuban Enclave Economy of Miami." *Sociological Perspectives* 30(4):340-372.

Portes, Alejandro and Robert Bach. 1985. *Latin Journey: Cuban and Mexican Immigrants in the United States.* Berkeley: University of California Press.

Portes, Alejandro and Jozsef Borocz. 1989. "Contemporary Immigration: Theoretical Perspectives on Its Determinants and Modes of Incorporation." *International Migration Review* 23(87):606-630.

Portes, Alejandro and Robert D. Manning. 1986. "The Immigrant Enclave: Theory and Empirical Examples." Pp. 47-68 in *Competitive Ethnic Relations,* edited by Susan Olzak and Joane Nagel. Orlando, FL: Academic Press.

Portes, Alejandro and Ruben Rumbaut. 1990. *Immigrant America: A Portrait.* Berkeley: University of California Press.

Purcell, Victor. 1965. *The Chinese in Southeast Asia.* London: Oxford University Press.

Refugee Reports. 1987. "Elderly Southeast Asian Refugees: Still Strangers in a Strange Land," 8 (5) May 15. pp. 1-7.

Reider, Jonathan. 1985. *Canarsie: The Jews and Italians of Brooklyn Against Liberalism.* Cambridge, MA: Harvard University Press.

Reimers, David M. 1985. *Still the Golden Door: The Third World Comes to America.* New York: Columbia University Press.

RIIES (Research Institute on Immigration and Ethnic Studies). 1976. "Occasional Papers No. 1: Caribbean Immigration to the United States." Washington, DC: The Smithsonian Institution.

Rischin, Moses. 1962. *The Promised City.* Cambridge, MA: Harvard University Press.

Rose, Peter. 1982a. "Links in a Chain: Observations of the American Refugee Program in Southeast Asia." *Catholic Mind* (March):2-25.

———. 1982b. "Southeast Asia to America: Links in a Chain, Part II." *Catholic Mind* (April):11-25.

———. 1985. "Asian Americans: From Pariahs to Paragons." Pp. 181-212 in *Clamor at the Gates: The New American Immigration,* edited by Nathan Glazer. San Francisco: Institute for Contemporary Studies.

Rosner, Lydia. 1986. *The Soviet Way of Crime: Beating the System in the Soviet Union and the U.S.A.* South Hadley, MA: Bergin and Garvey.

Rubin, Lillian. 1976. *Worlds of Pain.* New York: Basic Books.

Rueschemeyer, Marilyn, Igor Golomshtok and Janet Kennedy. 1985. *Soviet Émigré Artists: Life and Work in the USSR and the United States.* Armonk, NY: M. E. Sharpe.

Rumbaut, Ruben. 1986. "The Structure of Refuge and Southeast Asian Refugee Resettlement: A Portrait of a Decade of Migration and Resettlement 1975-1985." Paper presented at annual meeting of the American Sociological Association, New York, August 30-September 3.

———. 1989a. "Portraits, Patterns and Predictions of the Refugee Adaptation Process: Results and Reflections from the IHARP Panel Study." Pp. 138-182 in *Refugees as Immigrants: Cambodians, Laotians and Vietnamese in America,* edited by David W. Haines. Totowa, NJ: Rowman and Littlefield.

———. 1989b. "The Structure of Refuge: Southeast Asian Refugees in the United States, 1975-1985." *International Review of Comparative Public Policy* 1:97-129.

Russell, Raymond. 1985. *Sharing Ownership in the Workplace.* Albany, NY: SUNY Press.

Samora, Julian. 1971. *Los Mojados: The Wetback Story.* Notre Dame, IN: Notre Dame University Press.

Sanders, Jimmy and Victor Nee. 1987. "Limits of Ethnic Solidarity in the Ethnic Enclave Economy." *American Sociological Review* 52:745-767.

Sassan, Saskia. 1988. "New York City's Informal Economy." Pp. 60-77 in *The Informal Economy,* edited by Alejandro Portes, Manuel Castells and Lauren A. Benton. Baltimore, MD: Johns Hopkins.

Schaefer, Richard T. 1990. *Racial and Ethnic Groups.* Glenview, IL: Scott Foresman.

Schiff, Alvin I. 1980. "Language, Culture and the Jewish Acculturation of Soviet Jewish Émigrés." *Journal of Jewish Communal Service* 57:(1):44-49.

Schuck, Peter H. 1985. "Immigration Law and the Problem of Community." Pp. 285-307 in *Clamor at the Gates,* edited by Nathan Glazer. San Francisco: Institute for Contemporary Studies.

Schuetz, Alfred. 1944. "The Stranger: An Essay in Social Psychology." *American Journal of Sociology* 49(6):499-507.

Schwartz, Larry R. 1980. "Soviet Jewish Resettlement: Operationalizing Jewish Consciousness Raising." *Journal of Jewish Communal Service* 57(1):50-55.

Silverman, Myrna. 1988. "Family, Kinship and Ethnicity: Strategies for Social Mobility." Pp. 165-182 in *Persistence and Flexibility: Anthropological Perspectives on the American Jewish Experience,* edited by Walter P. Zenner. Albany, NY: SUNY Press.

Simon, Julian L. 1986. "Basic Data Concerning Immigration to the United States." *The Annals* 487:12-56.

———. 1984. "Don't Close Our Border." *Newsweek,* Feb. 27.

Simon, Rita J. (ed.) 1983. "Refugee Families' Adjustment and Aspirations: A Comparison of Soviet Jewish and Vietnamese Immigrants." *Ethnic and Racial Studies* 6(4):492-504.

———. 1985. *New Lives: The Adjustment of Soviet Jewish Immigrants in the United States and Israel.* Lexington, MA: Lexington Books.

Simon, Rita J. and Melanie Brooks. 1983. "Soviet Jewish Immigrants' Adjustment in Four United States Cities." *Journal of Jewish Communal Service* 60(1):56-64.

Simon, Rita J. and Julian Simon. 1985. "Social and Economic Adjustment." Pp. 13-45 in *New Lives: The Adjustment of Soviet Jewish Immigrants in the United States and Israel,* edited by Rita J. Simon. Lexington, MA: Lexington Books.

Simon, Rita J., Julian Simon and Jim Schwartz. 1982. "The Soviet Jews' Adjustment to the United States." *Council of Jewish Federations.* New York. (Mimeo).

Skinner, Kenneth. 1980. "Vietnamese in America: Diversity in Adaptation." *California Sociologist* 3(2):103-124.

Slote, Walter H. 1972. "Psychodynamic Structures in Vietnamese Personality." Pp. 114-133 in *Transcultural Research in Mental Health,* edited by William P. Lebra. Hawaii: University Press of Hawaii.

Sluzki, Carlos E. 1979. "Migration and Family Conflict." *Family Process* 18(4):381-394.

Sowell, Thomas P. 1981. *Ethnic America.* New York: Basic Books.

Statistical Abstract of the United States. 1984. Washington, DC: U.S. Department of Commerce, Bureau of the Census.

Statistical Abstract of the United States. 1989. Washington, DC: U.S. Department of Commerce, Bureau of the Census.

Stinchcombe, Arthur. 1984. "The Origins of Sociology as a Discipline." *Acta Sociologica* 27(1):51-61.

Swanson, Guy E. 1971. "Frameworks for Comparative Research: Structural Anthropology and the Theory of Action." Pp. 141-202 in *Comparative Methods in Sociology: Essays on Trends and Applications,* edited by Ivan Vallier. Berkeley: University of California Press.

Takaki, Ronald. 1989. *Strangers from a Different Shore: A History of Asian Americans.* Boston: Little, Brown and Co.

Thomas, W. I. and Florian Znaniecki. 1920. *The Polish Peasant in Europe and America.* New York: Richard Badger.

Teitelbaum, Michael S. 1985. "Forced Migration: The Tragedy of Mass Expulsion." Pp. 261-283 in *Clamor at the Gates: The New American Immigration,* edited by Nathan Glazer. San Francisco: Institute for Contemporary Studies.

Tran, Anh K. 1986. "Economic Base of the Vietnamese Community in the Los Angeles and Orange County Area." Los Angeles: UCLA Department of Asian-American Studies.

Trankiem, Luu. 1986. "Economic Development Opportunities for Indochinese Refugees in Orange County." California Community Foundation.

Trullinger, James Walker, Jr. 1980. *Village at War: An Account of Revolution in Vietnam.* New York: Longman.

Underwood, Kelsey Clark. 1986. "Image and Identity: Tamil Migration to the United States." *Kroeber Anthropological Society Papers* 65-66:65-72.

Ungar, Sanford J. 1989. "Freedom's Door Shut in Face of Soviet Jews." *Los Angeles Times.* (November 12): M2, M8.

U.S. Bureau of the Census. 1983. 1980 Census of Population, Detailed Population Characteristics, Part 6, California Section 1.

Vidich, Arthur, Stanford Lyman and Jeffrey Goldfarb. 1981. "Sociology and Society: Disciplinary Tensions and Professional Compromises." *Social Research,* Summer 1981, 48(2):322-361.

Vietnam Courier. 1979. "Those Who Leave: The Problem of Vietnamese Refugees." Hanoi.

Vigil, James Diego and Steve Chong Yun. 1990. "Vietnamese Youth Gangs in Southern California." In *Gangs in America,* edited by R. Huff. Newbury Park, CA: Sage.

Wain, Barry. 1981. *The Refused: The Agony of the Indochina Refugees.* New York: Simon and Schuster.

Waldinger, Roger. 1986. *Through The Eye of the Needle.* New York: NYU Press.
———. 1987. "Changing Ladders and Musical Chairs: Ethnicity and Opportunity in Post-Industrial New York." *Politics and Society* 15(4):369-401.
Waldinger, Roger, Howard Aldrich and Robin Ward and Associates. 1990. *Ethnic Entrepreneurs: Immigrant Business in Industrial Societies.* Newbury Park, CA: Sage.
Wallman, Sandra. 1986. "Ethnicity and The Boundary Process in Context." Pp. 226-245 in *Theories of Race and Ethnic Relations,* edited by John Rex and David Mason. Cambridge, England: Cambridge University Press.
Ward, Robin H. 1986. "Orientation and Opportunity: An Interpretation of Asian Enterprise in Western Society." Paper presented at annual meeting of the American Sociological Association. New York, August 30-September 3.
Ware, Caroline F. 1931. "Ethnic Communities," Vol. 5, Pp. 607-613; "Immigration," Vol. 7, Pp. 587-595. In the *Encyclopedia of the Social Sciences.* New York: Macmillan.
Weber, Max. 1927. *General Economic History.* London: George Allen & Unwin.
———. 1958. *The Protestant Ethic and the Spirit of Capitalism.* New York: Scribners.
Werbner, Pnina. 1984. "Business on Trust: Pakistani Entrepreneurship in the Manchester Garment Trade." Pp. 166-168 in *Ethnic Communities in Business: Strategies for Economic Survival,* edited by Robin Ward and Richard Jenkins. Cambridge: Cambridge University Press.
Wellman, David. 1977. *Portraits of White Racism.* Cambridge: Cambridge University Press.
Whitmore, John K. 1985. "Chinese from Southeast Asia." Pp. 59-76 in *Refugees in the United States: A Reference Handbook,* edited by David Haynes. Westport, CT: Greenwood Press.
Whyte, William F. 1955. *Street Corner Society.* Chicago: University of Chicago Press.
Wichmann, Henry, Jr. 1983. "Management Ability: The Key to Survival in Small Business." *Colorado Business Review* 16(3):2-4.
Wilensky, Harold L. and Anne T. Lawrence. 1979. "Job Assignment in Modern Societies: A Re-examination of the Ascription-Achievement Hypothesis." Pp. 202-248 in *Societal Growth: Processes and Implications,* edited by Amos Hawley. New York: The Free Press-Macmillan.
Willette, Joanne L., Marion F. Shaycroft and Carl V. Haub. 1985. *The Sociology of Minority Business Enterprise: An Overview.* Arlington, MD: Development Associates.
———. 1987. *The Truly Disadvantaged.* Chicago: University of Chicago Press.
Willie, Charles Vert. 1988. *A New Look at Black Families,* third edition. Dix Hills, NY: General Hall.
Wilson, Kenneth L. and W. Allen Martin. 1982. "Ethnic Enclaves: A Comparison of the Cuban and Black Economies in Miami." *American Journal of Sociology* 88(1):135-160.
Wilson, Wendell L. and Michael A. Garrick. 1983. "Refugee Assistance Termination Study." Washington State Department of Social and Health Services.
Wilson, William J. 1978. *The Declining Significance of Race.* Chicago: University of Chicago Press.
Wirth, Louis. 1928. *The Ghetto.* Chicago: University of Chicago Press.

Woldemikael, Tekle M. 1987. "Assertion Versus Accommodation: A Comparative Approach to Intergroup Relations." *American Behavioral Scientist* 30(4):411-428.

Woo, Elaine. 1989. "Anticipated Reunion Turns Into a Nightmare for Soviet Émigré." *Los Angeles Times.* (November 24): B1, B12.

Zahler, Gayle. 1989. Jewish Identity and the Soviet Émigré Newcomer. Paper presented at the National Conference of Jewish Communal Workers, Boca Raton, Florida, September.

Zenner, Walter P. 1983. "The Jewish Diaspora and the Middleman Adaptation." Pp. 142-155 in *Diaspora: Exile and the Jewish Condition,* edited by E. Levine. New York: Jason Aronson.

Zhou, Min and John R. Logan. 1989. "Returns on Human Capital in Ethnic Enclaves." *American Sociological Review* 54(5):809-820.

Zucker, Norman L. and Naomi Flink Zucker. 1987. *The Guarded Gate: The Reality of American Refugee Policy.* New York: Harcourt Brace Jovanovich.

Index

Abrams, Israel, 26
Activists, 206-221
  Soviet Jewish, 206-212
  Vietnamese, 213-221
Aged refugees, 77
Ahrari, Mohammed, 206
Andreski, Stanislav, 26-27
Anti-Semitism, 26, 29-35, 79, 234
  institutional, 32-34, 45n
Arax, Mark, 114
Armenians, 193
Assertion and accommodation, 199-200

Bach, Robert, 6, 10, 118
Bellah, Robert, 6
Bernard, William, ix
Bhachu, Parminder, 231
Birobidzhan (USSR), 27
"Boat people." See under Vietnamese
  refugees
Bonacich, Edna, 7-8, 10, 197
Bozorgmehr, Mehdi, ix
Breton, Raymond, 67
Brighton Beach (NY), 189
Bryce-Laporte, Roy S., x, 7
Brym, Robert, 12, 89n
Buddhism, 50, 52-53
Burawoy, Michael, 9-11
Buttinger, Joseph, 48-50

California, refugee population of, 65. *See
  also* Chinatown; Little Saigon;
  Monterey Park; Oakland; Orange
  County; San Francisco; Tenderloin;
  West Hollywood
Caplan, Nathan, 149
Castells, Manuel, 9-11
Cayton, Horace, 1
Chabad-Russian program, 98-99(photos),
  163, 222-224
China, 47-49
Chinatown (Los Angeles), 188-189, 192
Chinese-Vietnamese, 62-63, 104-106,
  188-189, 192, 202, 205, 231-232
  associations, 161-162
  entrepreneurs, 182-183
Community, 228
  factors discouraging formation, 18-22
  segmentation, 196, 229
Confucianism, 52-56
Cooperstein, Rhonda, 55
Cubans, 169, 191
Cultural conflict, 143, 146, 152-153
  Soviet vs. American, 84
Cummings, Scott, 167, 205

de Voe, Dorsh, x, 18
Dependent elderly, 86-87
Dependent youth, 84-86

Desbarats, Jacqueline, 66n
di Leonardo, Micaela, 6, 234
Diem, Ngo Dinh, 50-51
Discrimination, 19
    against American ethnic groups, 73
    against Chinese-Vietnamese, 63
    and scapegoating, 12
Doctors, refugee, 158-159, 189-190
Drake, St. Clair, 1
Dual labor market, 10
Durkheim, Emile, 16

Economic integration, 170
Entrepreneurship. *See* Ethnic entrepre-
    neurship
Espiritu, Yen Le, 25, 52, 231
Ethnic Chinese. *See* Chinese-Vietnamese
Ethnic collectivism, 6, 8
Ethnic communities, 6, 76. *See also* Eth-
    nic enclaves
Ethnic conflict, 109-110
Ethnic enclaves, 5
    definition, 89
    theory of, 168-171, 187-188
Ethnic entrepreneurship, 167-197, 201-
    206
    capital, 74, 179-183
    and community, 197
    consumer markets, 188-191
    culture theory of, 171-173
    disadvantage theory of, 172-174
    ethnic networks, 180-183
    family factors, 177-178
    independence, 175-179
    and labor, 183-188
    motives for, 171-179
    as a reaction to discrimination, 173-
    174
    refugees *vs.* immigrants, 175-176
    and resettlement systems, 193-194
    resources for, 179-191
    supplier networks, 191-193
    Soviet Jewish *vs.* Vietnamese, 194-195
    Vietnamese refugees, 111
Ethnic groups, as interest groups, 198-200

Ethnic identification, 7
Ethnic mobilization, 15-16, 20-21
Ethnic networks, 19, 191, 150-151, 230-
    231
    and businesses, 202-206
    conflict in, 204
    and resettlement agencies, 164-165
    Vietnamese, 115-116
Ethnic organizations, 21, 80
    disadvantage and, 16-18
    Soviet Jewish, 67
Ethnic solidarity, 6, 15-24, 230, 233-235
    and competition, 198-200
    and entrepreneurship, 170
Ethnic succession, 189
Ethnicity, situational determination of, 6-
    7
Etzioni, Amitai, 233

Family patterns, 54-57, 83-87
Family-based resources, 107-108
Farber, Bernard, 212
Finnan, Christine, 55, 64, 201
Fruchtbaum, Irene, 84

Garment industry, 187-188
Generational conflict, 77, 87, 212-221
    among Soviet Jews, 35-37, 45
    among Vietnamese, 125-126
Gitelman, Zvi, 19, 31
Glasnost, 26, 29, 234
Glazer, Nathan, 6, 166n
Goffman, Erving, 31
Goldfarb, Jeffrey, 236
Gorelick, Sherry, 184

Hebrew Free Loan Association, 193
Hebrew Immigrant Aid Society (HIAS),
    44, 144
Hechter, Michael, 227
Henkin, Alan, 52-54
Hickey, Gerald, 52, 54
Ho, David Yai-Fai, 215

Housing, 123
Hutchinson, Edward P., 7

Immigrant communities, sociological per-
    spectives on, 4-24
Immigrants, new, x, 7, 123
Institutional completeness, 67
Israel, 27, 29-30, 42, 74

Jacobs, Dan, 36
Jewish organizations (U.S.), 210-212
Jews. *See* Soviet Jews
Job finding, 17, 165n
    professional, 69, 72
Job placement, 146-149
Journal of Jewish Communal Service,
    155-156

Katz, Jack, 168
Kibria, Nazli, 55, 112, 177, 201
Kim, Illsoo, 7, 21, 173
Kosmin, Barry, 156-157

Labor
    ethnic, 127n
    family, 75
    immigrant, 9-15
    Latino, 186-188
Leba, John K., 128
Light, Ivan, 6-7, 10, 168, 171, 205
Little Saigon (CA), 187, 188, 190, 192,
    234
Localism in adaptation, 23
Lyman, Stanford, 6, 123, 168, 236

Mangiafico, Luciano, 7
Manning, Robert, 22, 185
Markowitz, Fran, 156, 209
Martin, W. Allen, 170
Media, ethnic, 103, 190, 203, 210
Methodology, 1-4
Middleman minorities, 172
Min, Pyong Gap, 6, 170

Monterey Park (CA), 188-189, 192, 234
Moynihan, Daniel Patrick, 6
Mutual Assistance Associations (MAAs),
    153-157, 164

Nagel, Joane, 16
Nee, Victor, 8
Nguyen, Liem Thanh, 52-54
Nguyen, Van Vinh, 177
Nielsen, Francois, 20
North, David, 113

Oakland (CA), 102
Olzak, Susan, 15-16, 198
Orange County (CA), 228n. *See also* Lit-
    tle Saigon
Organizations, cultural and religious,
    221-226
Orleck, Annalise, 27, 32
Owan, Tom Choken, 122

Padilla, Felix, 1, 199
"Pale of settlement," 26
Panish, Paul, 45n
Parlin, Bradley, 11
Patterson, Orland, 198
Pilau Bidong (refugee camp), 61
Portes, Alejandro, 6-7, 9-10, 16, 22, 118,
    185
Pseudofamilies, 122
Psychological therapy, 151-153

Racial prejudice, and Vietnamese refu-
    gees, 118
Reactive solidarity, 16, 207, 209
Refugee Act of 1980, 144
Refugee Cash Assistance (RCA), 144,
    185-186
Refugees
    vs. immigrants, ix, 17-22, 142, 195-
        197, 227-228, 236
    research on, 235-236
Reimers, David, ix-x, 5, 7, 12, 153
Remittances, 103, 188

Resettlement system, 23, 149-151
   client socialization in, 146-157
   and community segmentation, 159-160
   employment in, 157-158
   and ethnic networks, 149-151
   international efforts, 61
   and reactive solidarity, 160-164
   refugees' reactions to, 142-143
   Soviet Jews, 44, 80, 144-145
   Vietnamese, 120-121, 145
Resource mobilization, 199-200
Role reversals, 124-126
Rose, Peter, 61
Rotating credit associations (RCAs), 180-181, 205
Rumbaut, Ruben, 19, 64, 113
Russell, Raymond, 167

Sabagh, Georges, ix
San Francisco (CA), 67, 127n
San Gabriel Valley. *See* Monterey Park
Secondary migration, 65
Self-employment, and community building, 167-169. *See also* Ethnic entrepreneurs
Simon, Julian, 13
Simon, Rita, 33, 43
Skager, Rodney, 84
Social structure and immigrant adaptation, 8-15
Solidarity. *See* Ethnic solidarity; Reactive solidarity
Soviet Jews, 25-46, 67-89, 90-101(photos)
   ambivalence about social membership, 79
   case studies of, 68-76
   community leaders, 83
   compared to Vietnamese, 231-232
   conflicts with U.S. Jewish agencies, 162-163
   dislike of American culture, 79
   diversity of, 81
   family patterns, 83-87
   identity, 208-212
   interaction patterns, 76-89

   motives for emigration, 37-40, 80
   organizations, 81-83
   process of immigration, 40-43
   and regionalism, 81
   relations with sponsors, 78, 207-212
   religious identification, 26, 30, 32, 35-37
Sowell, Thomas, 234
Stalin era, 27

Taxi cooperatives, 202-203
Tenderloin (San Francisco neighborhood), 2, 127n
Thomas, W. I., 4
Traditions, ethnic, 18, 52-57, 216
Trankiem, Luu, 180, 183
"Twice minorities," 25, 83, 231-232

Ukraine, 28
Underground economy, 113, 150, 177
USCC (United States Catholic Conference), 144

Vidich, Arthur, 236
Vietnam Business Directory, 190, 200, 205
Vietnam War, 50-52
Vietnam
   history of, 47-52
   relations with China, 48-49
Vietnamese family, 54-57, 122-127
Vietnamese refugees, 47-66, 102-128, 129-141(photos)
   and assimilation, 117-118
   and blocked mobility, 64, 118
   "boat people," 59-63, 102-113
   Buddhist groups, 224-226
   case studies of, 102-112
   community subgroups, 100, 119-122, 127
   ethnic identity of, 116-127
   1975 cohort, 57
   perspectives on community, 114-122
   religious identification, 52-57
   spiritual outlook, 225-227

Voluntary Agencies (VOLAGs), 144

Waldinger, Roger, 14, 169, 184, 196
Ware, Caroline, 5
Weber, Max, 172
Welfare dependency, 113
Wellman, David, 45n
West Hollywood (CA), 189, 234
Wilson, Kenneth, 170
Wilson, William J., 15
Wirth, Louis, 26

Woldemikael, Tekle, 18, 199-200, 226
Women
    Soviet Jewish, 43
    Vietnamese, 55, 61, 66n, 122, 124-125
Woo, Elaine, 30
World system, 9-14, 230

Yiddish, 26, 77, 89n

Znaniecki, Florian, 4

About the Author

Steven J. Gold, whose grandparents were immigrant entrepreneurs, attended Brandeis University, University of California–Santa Cruz, and University of California–Berkeley. He has published articles in *Ethnic and Racial Studies, Journal of Contemporary Ethnography, Contemporary Jewry, Research in Community Sociology, Qualitative Sociology,* and *Society* as well as in several edited volumes.

Associate Professor of Sociology at Whittier College in California, his research interests include medical sociology and research ethics, as well as immigrant adaptation. The former president of the International Visual Sociology Association, he regularly publishes and exhibits photographs that explore social issues.